South Indian Brāhmins in Sri Lankan Culture

Assimilation in Sath Korale & Kandyan Regions

Bandara Bandaranayake, PhD

ISBN: 978-0-6452133-0-0

Bandaranayake Consulting Services Pty Ltd
Melbourne, Australia

Dedication

In loving memory of
my dear brother,
Punchi Banda Basnayake

What is this book all about?

———— ❧ ————

This book offers a fresh and provocative perspective on the migration of South Indians to Sri Lanka, challenging the conventional historical narratives.

Its central focus revolves around a group of South Indian Brāhmins who arrived in Sath Korale, within the Kurunegala District of Sri Lanka, during the 16th century, coinciding with the Mundukondapola regional kingdom. This group's enduring historical legacy is explored up to the present day. Furthermore, the book provides a concise account of these Brāhmin settlements in Sath Korale, with a comprehensive examination of Kambuwatawana Brāhmi village, where one particular Brāhmin contingent thrived.

The analysis draws from a range of sources, including historical palm-leaf manuscripts (Puskola Poth), sociological accounts, and recent genealogical records.

Notably, these South Indian Brāhmi immigrants were Hindus and Dravidian language speakers, ultimately assimilating into the Sinhala Buddhist society within Sath Korale and the wider Kandyan regions.

Additionally, the book briefly delves into the records of other South Indian migrants such as the Malala Bandaras (from Kerala) and Hettis, who arrived alongside or during the same period as the Brāhmin contingent. It also captures the historical facts of South Indian migrants who settled in various regions of Sri Lanka from the medieval times and became integrated into the local Sri Lankan society.

Remarkably, it becomes evident that none of the present-day descendants of these diverse migrant groups possess a comprehensive awareness of their South Indian origins, as these roots have faded from memory over the course of several centuries. This newfound information sheds considerable light on contemporary Sri Lankan racial and religious consciousness.

Contents

Acknowledgements

I would like to express my sincere gratitude to the individuals who have played instrumental roles in the completion of this publication.

First and foremost, I extend my heartfelt thanks to my friend, Udula Bandara Oushadhahamy, a renowned architect in Sri Lanka, for his unwavering support and encouragement throughout this journey. His valuable insights and suggestions upon reading the first draft were invaluable. Udula also generously provided palm-leaf manuscripts and designed the cover for this publication.

I am indebted to EM Sunil Bandara, for his continuous support from the inception to the culmination of this project. I extend my appreciation to YM Dharmasena Bandara for sharing palm-leaf manuscripts collected for his own book. RSWM Kumara Bandara deserves my gratitude for his feedback after reviewing the English version of this book and for contributing valuable manuscripts.

EM Bandumathie Ekanayake, who initially collected genealogical information of Kambuwatawana in 2003, and BM Senarathna Bandara, who updated that information, have my sincere thanks.

I would also like to express my gratitude to Hasitha Chamikara Gunasinghe and Ven Udagaladeniye Dhammawimala Thero from Kelaniya University for their assistance in providing information related to the historical Buddhist heritage of Niyadawane and

Pethiyagala temples, as well as texts about Ven Kambuwatawana Piyadassi Thero.

I am grateful to the following individuals who also contributed to this project: Late RM Karunarathna, Sirinaga Wimaladharma Nawarathna, Chandana Wanninayake, Rangana Kuruwita, Udaya Galagoda, late RMWM Bandara Manika (Monnakulama), Ven Danture Vipassi Thero (Kandulawa temple), Nuwan Bandara Basnayake, Lal Molagoda, Ajith Kiribamuna, HM Gunasiri (Kandulawa), BM Bandara Manika, Chamara Wanninayake, KMS Rakogama, Premarathna Eriyawa, WM Ratnayake (Atharagalla), AM Herath Banda (Pohorawaththa), Anura Gopallawa, Pradeep Ganepola, and R Maheswaran (Librarian of the Peradeniya University Library).

Last but not least, I extend my deepest appreciation to my wife, Chandra, for her patience and understanding during the countless hours I spent in front of a computer, often neglecting household duties.

I apologize if I inadvertently omitted anyone who contributed in various ways to this project.

I believe that many people who helped me were potentially unaware how this publication will pan out.

Bandara Bandaranayake,

Melbourne, Australia.

2023

Chapter One

Preface

This book provides a historical and sociological examination of a distinct group of South Indian Brāhmins[1], specifically the seven Brāhmin families, who established roots in Sath Korale[2]. The early history of these families is meticulously traced through the use of palm-leaf[3] manuscripts known as "puskola poth[4]."

This book unveils the process through which these families seamlessly integrated into the local Sri Lankan community. It delves into the historical accounts of the villages where they made their homes, shedding light on the intricate tapestry of their presence. Furthermore, the book offers a comprehensive exploration of the detailed genealogical records that document the enduring legacy of these families within the village of Kambuwatawana.

---

[1] According to the Indian tradition, Brāhmins are a varna (social class) accommodated in Hinduism.

[2] Kurunegala District.

[3] Also known as Ola-leaf manuscripts.

[4] Sinhalese word for palm-leaf manuscripts.

My Interest.

In the early 1970s, I had the opportunity to read an palm-leaf manuscript titled "Nikawa Gampaha Korale Vitti saha Mayim Wattoru[5]," which left a lasting impression on me due to its historical content and socio-anthropological significance. The manuscript contained previously unknown information about a group of seven Brahmin families who migrated from South India during the Sithawaka-Kotte kingdoms' era and settled in villages like Borawewa, Kambuwatawana, Rakwana, and Dembatogama in Sath Korale. It also provided their original Indian names and the honorary names bestowed upon them by the regional king of Mundukondapola, a kingdom in Sath Korale, upon their arrival. These villages, the honorary names, and their descendants were real and verifiable, yet their historical background was largely unknown to the local villagers.

Upon discovering this intriguing historical account, I became determined to delve deeper into the enigmatic past and share the underlying narrative of the South Indian connection with a broader audience. It became evident that these villages were not unique in this historical phenomenon, as many villages in Sath Korale and other parts of Sri Lanka had experienced similar South Indian migrations. I realized that the stories of these peaceful migrants and their enduring legacy, which includes assimilation into local communities, had not received the recognition they deserved in Sri Lanka's celebrated history.

My mission is to shed light on these overlooked chapters of history and provide the historical recognition of this migrant group of Brahmins and their descendants. The focus of my detailed study

---

5   "Events and boundary details of Nikawagampaha Korale Division" also known as "Nikawagampaha Brahmanavaliya".

was on Kambuwatawana Brahmi village, situated in the Polpithigama Divisional Secretariat Division of Kurunegala District, within the North-Western Province of Sri Lanka (approximately 7.937990 degrees North latitude and 80.392371 degrees East longitude). Other Brahmin villages where this migrant group settled, such as Dembatogama, Kandulawa, Kiribamuna, Borawewa, Rakwana, and Mataluwawa, are near Kambuwatawana.

During the reign of the Sithawaka and Kotte Kingdoms (1412-1597 AD), the arrival of South Indian Brahmi immigrants brought about a transformation in many villages in Sath Korale, and Kambuwatawana was fortunate to be among them. Prior to their arrival, Kambuwatawana was a modest and potentially sparsely populated village. However, with the settlement of South Indian Brahmins in the 16th century, the dynamics of the village changed dramatically.

The local population warmly welcomed these newcomers, recognising their superiority, higher social status, and the benefits they brought. The immigrants were seen as novel, powerful, and irresistible figures in the community. Their rapid integration and acceptance into the local society allowed them to quickly ascend to prominent positions as local chieftains, without encountering any social and political barriers. As a result, the village of Kambuwatawana became an integral part of the regional political structure, exerting influence on both social and political aspects of the region for several centuries.

However, as time passed and the societal roles and dynamics evolved, the prominence of the Brahmin community began to decline. Over the course of approximately four centuries, Kambuwatawana gradually faded from the limelight, and its significance diminished as the role of Brahmins in Sri Lankan society changed. Today, Kambuwatawana stands as a humble village in the dry zone, facing economic challenges that have become prevalent in the area.

Despite its transformation over the centuries, remnants of the Brahminic origin persist in Kambuwatawana. What is particularly striking is that the current generation of inhabitants is largely unaware of the historical events that transpired in their village, as well as the South Indian legacy that once played a significant role in shaping their community.

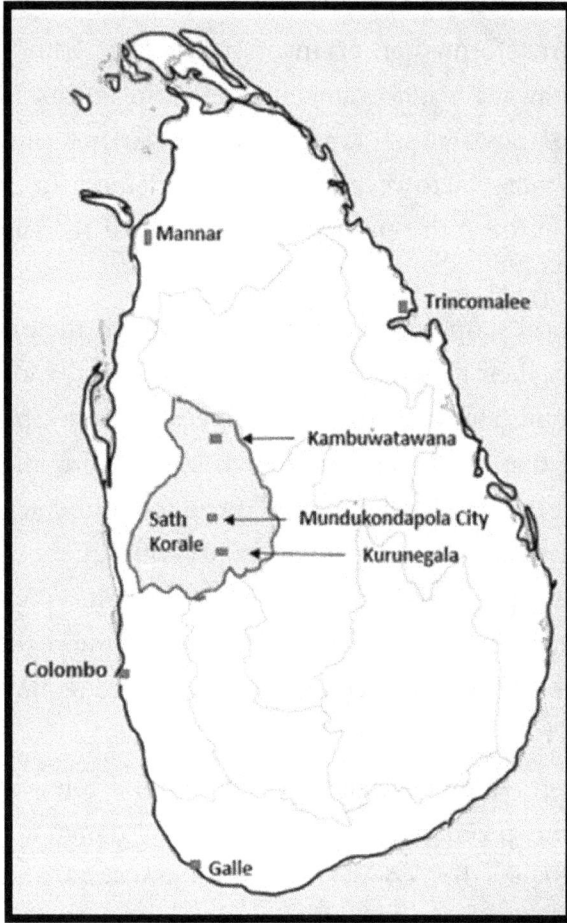

Map 1: Sath Korale & Kambuwatawana Village

Truth About Indian Migration.

Sri Lanka's geographical location, situated at the southern tip of India and separated from the Indian mainland by a mere thirty-five kilometres across the Palk Strait, has made it a natural destination for South Indian migration. Throughout history, this proximity has facilitated various interactions and migrations between the two regions.

Sri Lanka has witnessed several well-documented South Indian invasions, particularly during periods when powerful empires emerged in South and North India. Additionally, Sri Lankan kings often sought military assistance from Indian allies during times of internal disputes. As a result, thousands of Indian soldiers were brought to Sri Lanka, and over time, many of them chose to make the island their permanent home.

Trade, work, and fishing opportunities in Sri Lanka attracted Indians, leading to a steady influx of immigrants. The absence of stringent visa requirements or immigration policies in historical times allowed them to settle in the country with ease. India also served as a source for marriage alliances among Sri Lankan royals and political elites throughout history.

Furthermore, some Indians sought political asylum in Sri Lanka during periods of violent internal political conflicts and devastating famines. The island nation provided refuge to those in need.

In addition to these factors, small groups of skilled South Indian migrants occasionally ventured to Sri Lanka, often with the patronage of Sri Lankan rulers. This book specifically focuses on a series of such "silent migrations" and delves into the study of one particular group and its enduring legacy within Sri Lanka's history.

Forgotten Past.

Traditional Sri Lankan historical accounts often overlook the presence of peaceful colonists and immigrants from South India. One of the reasons for this omission may be the relatively small size of these immigrant groups. However, it's essential to shed light on their history, particularly since some of these immigrants were openly sponsored and welcomed by local kings. This publication also provides a brief account of the lesser-known Mundukondapola kingdom in Sath Korale, which actively supported and sponsored new immigrants during medieval times.

The contemporary immigrant groups that settled in Sath Korale included South Indian Brāhmins, Malala princes from Kerala, Hettis, and various skilled professionals. These immigrants primarily spoke Dravidian languages such as Tamil, Malayalam, or Telugu, and they were predominantly Hindus. However, there is some evidence to suggest that a few South Indian Buddhists may have been among the immigrants.

Local rulers played a significant role in welcoming these migrants and allowing them to integrate into the local culture. They encouraged and facilitated the immigrants to learn local languages and even embrace the local religion, Buddhism. The support of local rulers went beyond mere hospitality; they also granted land, recruited immigrants into security forces, bestowed titles, and provided them with local Sinhala authoritative names. This royal sponsorship facilitated the smooth assimilation of these immigrant groups into the new land and culture.

Conceptual Framework.

It's important to clarify certain concepts[6] at the outset to help explain the adaptation process of new migrants into a new country. Here are three key concepts:

- **Integration:** Integration is a form of adaptation where individuals adopt the cultural norms of the dominant or host culture while still maintaining elements of their original culture. It's synonymous with multiculturalism, indicating a coexistence of different cultural backgrounds within a society.

- **Assimilation:** Assimilation occurs when individuals adopt the cultural norms of the dominant or host culture to a significant degree, including values, behaviours, and beliefs, often to the extent that their original culture becomes less prominent or even disappears. Assimilation can happen relatively quickly, sometimes within three generations.

- **Acculturation:** Acculturation is a more comprehensive process in which individuals adopt not only the social, psychological, and cultural elements of the host nation but also incorporate the memories, sentiments, and attitudes of that culture. This gradual process can take centuries to fully manifest. It may occur more rapidly when there are similarities in the physical appearance (biological factors) between the two communities.

With these concepts in mind, the examination in this publication seeks to determine whether the South Indian Brāhmins and other immigrants who arrived in the 16th century in Sri Lanka were integrated, assimilated, or primarily acculturated into the Sri Lankan community.

---

6   Alba, R. & Victor Nee, 1997; Park and Burgess, 1969, p 735; Crul, Maurice. & Jens Schneider. 2010; Brown and Bean, 2006; Yinger, 2010.

Ethnic and Cultural Identity.

This publication deals with the complex and contentious issue of Sri Lankan ethnic identity, which has been further complicated by the ethnic conflict, particularly between the Tamil and Sinhalese communities, and shifting political ideologies, especially in the 20th century. The recognition and celebration of various forms of ethnic and cultural assimilation, mixed identities, and ongoing patterns of assimilation have been somewhat overlooked within Sri Lanka.

In the introduction to the palm-leaf manuscripts, "Malala Vittiya and Malala Kathawa," Gananath Obeyesekere (2005) acknowledges the historical process of South Indian colonisation in Sri Lanka. These manuscripts reveal how Sri Lankan kings in medieval times welcomed and sponsored South Indian immigrants to settle in sparsely populated regions of the country. This phenomenon represents one of the intriguing patterns of South Indian colonisation in Sri Lanka.

Obeyesekere (Introduction to Bandarawaliya manuscript, 2005) suggests that vitti books, or event books, can provide a more balanced view of Sinhala society from a sociological perspective rather than presenting a singular Sri Lankan history.

The focus of this book is on seven Brāhmin families that originated from either Kerala or a region near Madurai in South India. They were Hindus and spoke Dravidian languages. Several palm-leaf manuscripts refer to these Brāhmin immigrants, including "Madurapuren Avittiya"[7] (the aristocrats who came from Madurapura[8]) and "Vanni Vittiya[9]," both of which contain

---

[7] Index number 277674, Peradeniya University Main Library.

[8] Presently known as Madurai

[9] This means "events occurred in Vanni region."

information about other immigrant groups like the Malala Princes and Hettis.

Challenges arose during the research process, including resistance from some locals who were ideologically reluctant to acknowledge the potential South Indian Dravidian connection, often suggesting alternative origins such as North India or Burma. Burma was more appealing to Sinhala consciousness as a Buddhist country. While it is true that some immigrants came from North India and other Southeast Asian countries like Burma[10], this book focuses on establishing a clear South Indian Dravidian connection, particularly regarding the Brāhmin group.

The book's aim is to uncover a potential historical process and model that could explain the formation and evolution of the current Sri Lankan ethnic composition. It is essential to emphasize that this recognition of Indian roots and influence does not discount the unique Sri Lankan cultural identity[11]. Sri Lanka, as an island nation, has developed, preserved, and nurtured distinct cultural elements, including the Sinhala language, Theravada Buddhism, a locally evolved hydraulic civilization, unique architecture, arts and crafts, and a multicultural and multireligious heritage.

The 16th-century Indian migrants naturally assimilated into the local culture, religion, and language under the influence of these superior cultural elements. The role of local rulers was instrumental in orienting the newcomers to the local culture and establishing a social and political infrastructure for their adaptation.

In the context of migration, it's often the privileged, powerful, wealthy, skilled, and adventurous individuals who have the

---

[10] It is also possible some Burmese, Thai and other south Asian migrants settled in Sri Lanka

[11] Ananda Coomaraswamy. (2011). Mediaeval Sinhalese Art.

advantage of crossing borders and adapting to new countries. The Brāhmin migrants discussed in this publication belonged to a socially privileged and wealthy class, making them well-suited to navigate the events and processes of medieval times. These processes occurred within a feudalistic context, characterized by royalty, aristocracy, warna, and caste, which are different from modern ideologies and values. However, these elements are integral to the historical evolution of Sri Lankan society.

In essence, this publication uncovers a unique Sri Lankan experience and process that unfolded within a distinctive political and cultural context, shedding light on the multifaceted nature of Sri Lankan identity.

Cautions.

The palm-leaf manuscripts used in this publication serve as valuable historical records, shedding light on the past and providing insights into the lives and experiences of the people who lived in these villages. While it's true that some palm-leaf manuscripts may contain symbolic or inflated information, they are not devoid of historical accuracy. These manuscripts were maintained by literate and intellectual individuals within the villages, preserving their traditions and history for future generations. As such, they offer a glimpse into the genuine experiences and events of these communities.

The types of palm-leaf manuscripts utilized in this study, including vitti books, kadayim books, bandaravaliyas, and sannas, provide a diverse range of historical information spanning the 16th to 18th centuries. These records not only reveal the early events and expansion of the new migrants but also offer insights into their social structures, kinship patterns, and the interconnections between different Brāhmin villages.

It's important to acknowledge that palm-leaf manuscripts, like any historical source, have their limitations. Some gaps in the medieval history of the migrant villages in Sath Korale, including Kambuwatawana, may exist within these manuscripts. However, this publication strives to overcome these gaps by supplementing the information with data from other reliable historical sources, genealogical records and interview accounts. The result is a comprehensive exploration of the Brāhmin legacy, genealogy, and cultural assimilation within the context of Sri Lankan history.

My Approach.

My research methods are rooted in qualitative, ethnographic, and cultural anthropological approaches. Despite the historical materials being close to the region where I was born and brought up, I believe that I maintained objectivity throughout the research process.

I deeply acknowledge the inhabitants of Kambuwatawana village and other vintage Brāhmin villages, both past and present. I respectfully recognize their roots, identity, and the enduring connection they have to their land. Their adaptability in an ever-evolving environment is a testament to their resilience.

Furthermore, I extend my recognition to scholars like Gananath Obeyesekere, who have emphasized the value of palm-leaf manuscripts and the importance of these historical events. I also acknowledge that I have extensively used his materials in this research.

Further Work

A Sinhalese version of this book is published separately (දකුණු ඉන්දියානු බ්‍රාහ්මීන්ගේ ශ්‍රී ලාංකීකරණය: සත් කෝරළේ සහ කන්ද උඩරට සංක්‍රමණය)

Further, there is a separate book on palm-leaf manuscripts collected for this publication. "Immigrants from Madurapura: A

Collection of Palm-leaf Manuscripts in Sri Lanka" (මදුරාපුර සංක්‍රමණ: සත් කෝරලේ විත්ති පොත් එකතුවක්). This is a bilingual book (Sinhala and English). Most of those manuscripts contained in this book are rare and have not published elsewhere.

Chapter Two

Authenticating the Palm-leaf Records of Seven Brāhmin Families

This publication precisely traces the historical migration of seven contingents of Brāhmaṇa Rālas (Brāhmi gentlemen) from South India to Sath Korale. This migration occurred during the Sithawaka or Kotte kingdoms' reign (1412-1597 AD). These seven Brāhmins[12] initially settled in seven villages and an area referred to as "rata" (country), subsequently expanding their presence to several other villages.

The following is a soft translation of pertinent sections from three vitti (or events) books that shed light on the seven Brāhmaṇa Rālas, thereby substantiating the Brāhmi connection.

1. **Nikawa Gampaha Korale Vitti and Kadayim Wattoru** (abbreviated as **N1**): claimed to be written by Dembatogama Rajakaruna Mohottala Lekam (registrar). The Sinhalese full version of the vitti book is provided in my publication

---

[12] Each person had been joined by their extended families and other entourage later. It was not a single person settling in a village.

"Immigrants from Madurapura: A Collection of Palm-leaf Manuscripts in Sri Lanka".

[Translation] During the illustrious reign of King Sri Wikrama Sinha[13] Buvanekkadhi, ruler of the mighty Sithawaka kingdom, seven cousins hailing from the distant land of Rakkandu Desha[14] in India arrived in Sri Lanka, accompanied by a servant bearing a precious "thowilpotha[15]."

Upon their arrival at the grand royal palace in Mundukondapola, each of them respectfully presented offering[16]s, including a pair of exquisitely gold-plated shoes and a sacred "tis ryan[17] mundasana[18]," to the benevolent king. They humbly requested permission to settle in the lands of Sath Korale[19].

The gracious king agreed to grant them land in any region where no prior royal decree had allocated land to others. Consequently, the following choices were made: "Kiri" Brāhmaṇa Rāla chose Kiri Bamuna village, "Kandulassa" Brāhmaṇa Rāla selected Kandulawa village, "Rakkandu Bandi" Brāhmaṇa Rāla settled on Rakwana village, "Mahipala" Brāhmaṇa Rāla made Borawewa village his home, "Jothipala" Brāhmaṇa Rāla found residence in Mataluwawa village, another Brāhmaṇa Rāla embraced Matale Dunuwila Village, and the eldest Purohit[20] Brāhmaṇa Rāla was bestowed with Dembatogama Village.

To honour the esteemed position of Purohit Brāhmaṇa Rāla, the king presented him with the entire Dembatogama

---

[14] Rakkandu country.

[15] A traditional sunshade/fan to symbolise the social status of the group.

[16] "Dakum" in Sinhala

[17] Approximately 15 meters long.

[18] Head wrapping bandana

[19] Seven Korale division/district.

[20] Priest/royal advisor.

14

region, along with a magnificent elephant named Hiththara, a beautifully adorned "hunupoth gediya[21]", a valuable ran panhinda[22], and an exquisite "rathram boththam hatte[23]".

2. **"Madurapuren Avittiya" (or Vanni Vittiya)** *(Abbreviated as N2)*: a copy kept by Balagolle Ranhamy and Weebadde Rala (obtained from "Vanni Upatha", published by Gananath Obeyesekere, 2005, pg. 31-32).

"[Translation] Seven Bamini Brāhmaṇa Rālas, bedecked in traditional rankadu attire and adorned with seven sacred garlands around their necks, arrived at the Karaduwa port following a maritime journey from India, accompanied by a precious thowilpath. Their destination was the royal court of the Sithawaka Mundukondapola Palace.

Individually, each Brāhmaṇa Rāla presented dakum[24] as a mark of reverence and humbly requested parcels of land to establish their homes. The benevolent king graciously granted them the freedom to choose the villages they desired to settle in.

Among their selections were: Kandulassa, who chose Kandulawa; Kiri Brāhmaṇa Rāla, who settled upon Kiri Bamuna; Mapa Brāhmaṇa Rāla, who opted for Parawagama; the Brāhmaṇa Rāla bedecked in rankadu attire, who laid claim to Rakwana; another Brāhmaṇa Rāla, who made Borawewa their new abode; and the youngest among them, who selected Nambadewa.

In a gracious gesture, the Purohit Brāhmaṇa Rāla, the eldest among them, presented the king with a resplendent thisriyan blue silk dress. In return, he was granted the privilege of choosing the Dembatogama country, which had previously been at the centre of a boundary dispute with a land granted to a Malala Bandara.

---

21 Potentially a betel lime box.

22 A golden pen

23 A golden button attached on an upper jacket, a Sinhala aristocratic dress.

24 Offering gifts

To mark this occasion, the great Edirisuriya King of the Mundukondapola Palace bestowed upon the Dembatogama Purohit Brāhmaṇa Rāla the honorific title of Rajakaruna Mudiyanse, along with valuable gifts, including a golden pen, a jacket embellished with golden threads, and a majestic elephant known as Hiththara".

3. **Malala Vittiya and Malla Kathawa saha Rajasingha Rajuge Pruthugesi Satan Pilibandawa Sandahan Vitti Book,** Gananath Obeyesekere, 2005, pg. 81:

"[Translation] A group of Bamunu Brāhmins arrived in Chilaw and journeyed through Apaladeniya and Bamunugama to reach Bamunakotuwa. They received sannas, formal land grants, and brought sacred charms infused with the divine power of God Vishnu, using them in a milk-spreading yaga ceremony to invoke blessings. Kiri Brāhmaṇa was allocated Kiri Bamuna village, and he also became steward of five neighbouring villages—Bamunugedara Mahe, Rambewa, Herathgama, Nikawewa, and Borawewa—previously granted through a Sannasa to Diwakara Unnehe in Demangama. In Galluwa, other Brāhmins settled, naming a village Balagolla due to the presence of Bala trees, tracing its roots to the Yapahu kingdom. Balagollagama housed Brāhmins like Imihami of Rangaswewa, Imihami, and Hitihamy of Balalla, boasting a rich, continuous historical heritage. Kirimatiyawa thrived with Kiri Brāhmins, enriching the region's Brāhmin settlements."

The first two records are thorough about the arrival of the seven Brāhmins. The last record was written later and only acknowledges the event symbolically and mixes it up with another group of Brāhmi immigrants.[25]

The above quotes acknowledge that the king at the Mundukondapola[26] regional kingdom in Sath Korale welcomed the

---

[25] Discussed later in the book, in chapter, "Brāhmi Identity and Brāhmi Migration".

[26] This book contains chapter 6 about this kingdom.

group and awarded them villages (or *Nindagam*) and titles. Mundukondapola was a little-known regional kingdom that existed in Sath Korale during the Sithawaka and Kotte kingdoms. Etymologically speaking, Mundukondapola is the rounded topknot worn by male yogi or Brāhmi and hence Mundukondapola means "a place in the shape of a top-knot". This name suggests its location on a hill that rises from low land. I have allocated a chapter to Mundukondapola regional kingdom.

The vitti books provide information about various other South Indian migrant communities, including the "Malala Bandaras" and the "Hettis," who arrived in Sri Lanka. These communities are briefly introduced in a separate chapter to illuminate the fact that Sri Lanka welcomed a diverse range of South Indian independent migrants during that historical period.

Vintage Settlement

Since all three historical records acknowledge the arrival of seven Brāhmins, it is logical to assume that it was a significant event in Sath Korale at the time.

The authors of these records have different recollections about two of the Brāhmins among the group. The five Brāhmins who settled at Kandulawa, Kiribamuna, Rakwana, Borawewa and Dembatogama are undisputed. One manuscript notes Mataluwawa and Matale Dunuwila as the other places where the other two Brāhmins settled while the other manuscript refers to Parawagama and Nambdewa as the other two places. Mataluwawa and Nambadewa are in the proximity to other Brāhmin villages, but Parawagama and Dunuwila are outside Sath Korale.

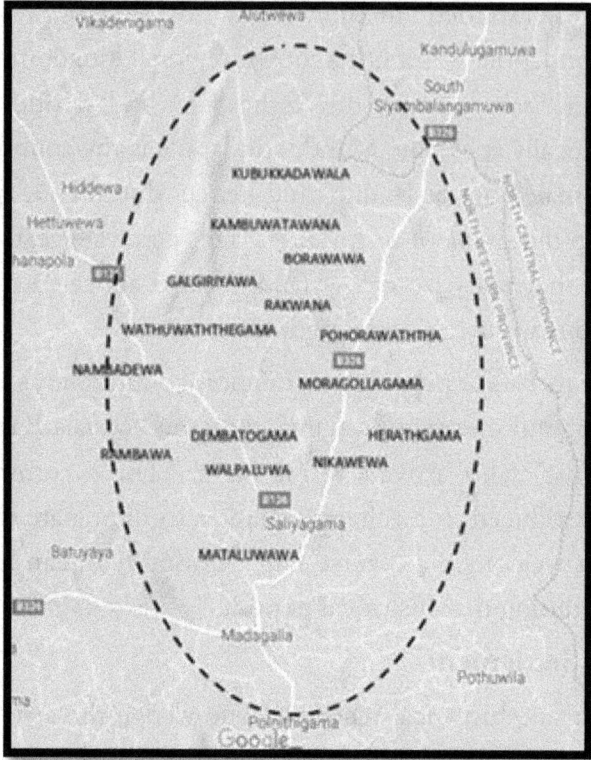

Map 2: Nikawagampaha Korale and Brahmi Villages

It also appears that each record had been written a few decades apart and updated several times giving slightly different versions.

The three Brāhmaṇa Rālas of Rakwana, Borawewa and Dembatogama have been recorded as brothers. They resided close to each other. The other four Brāhmaṇa Rālas were cousins of these three. Potentially, Brāhmaṇa Rālas of Kiri Bamuna and Kandulawa were also brothers, as they settled in villages next to each other, but approximately thirty kilometres away from the rest of the group.

The Dembatogama Rala was the eldest, and potentially the most influential and educated. He was a Hindu Priest and a king's advisor (*Purohit*). Fittingly, he was given the control of Dembatogama *rata* (country) which also included five subdivisions that were granted to five Brāhmaṇa Rālas of the group.

As already noted, a few palm-leaf manuscripts[27] refer to the arrival of these seven Brāhmins, probably because of their high social status. They were different from the locals in their appearance, dress, ornaments, and language.

The group was led by a purohit, which was a significant inclusion. Ariyapala (1969, p.97) states that the purohit wields great influence in the king's court, and he was a king's advisor on all matters – spiritual, temporal, official, or private, hence a trusted companion. The tradition of Purohit was maintained up to the last phase of the Sinhala kingdom. The appointment of a Brāhmin to this office in Sri Lanka was to maintain the Indian tradition at the royal court. It is to be noted that the purohit position was not always held by a Brāhmin.

In India, he had a powerful influence because of his religious knowledge, mastery in various sciences, astrology, omens etc. He advised the king on what to do and when, thus wielding great influence on him.[28] It is uncertain if the Dembatogama purohit advised the local king or not. At the least, he played an important role and was readily available for royal services.

According to N1, Mahipala Maha Brāhmaṇa Rāla had been given twelve villages, including Kambuwatawana village and the main Borawewa village. The other villages were: Kubukkadawala, Kaduruwewa, Nipunagama, Elipichchegama, Indipitiya, Watthegala, Kadahatuwewa, Archirigama, Dikkweheragama and Karagaswewa. Mahipala Brahman Rala had been given the honorary name of "Chandrasekara Maha Basnayake Mudiyanse" by the

---

27 N1, N2, Vanni Vitti, Vanni Upatha.

28 Ariyapala, pg. 98.

regional king. Later, according to N1, Kambuwatawana village was granted to his eldest son, who joined him later from India, with the title of "Maha Basnayake Mudiyanse". As illustrated in preceding sections of this book, several of his grandchildren also resided at Kambuwatawana.

The close observations of the vitti book reveals that there were marriages among Brāhmin families of Borawewa, Kambuwatawana, Rakwana, Kandulawa, and Dembatogama and were among a few other historical villages in Sath (Seven) Korale and Sathara (Four) Korale.

Over a period of a few centuries, Kambuwatawana became more prominent and influential. The vitti books and other historical records provide evidence that Kambuwatawana descendants held positions like Korala (division/rata/country administrator), Rate Mahaththaya (chief of a hathpattu) and it produced a *"Disawa"* (district administrator reporting to the Kandyan king/the British Governor). The disawa position was the highest reward for the descendants of these seven Brāhmana Rālas.

Kambuwatawana Flag

Kambuwatawana village keeps a historical flag that is believed to have belonged to a Disawa of Sath Korale who hailed from this village. This seems to be a specimen that portrays the recognition of the Kambuwatawana Brāhmin clan in the old system of things.

Tropical Agriculturalist (1904) edited by the Hon. John Ferguson, C.M.G, states on page 135:

> "During the time of the Kandyan Kings, the Seven Korale had always a Disawa, having been one of eleven principal divisions or disawanies, into which the ancient Kingdom was divided. The first Disawa, after the British occupation, was Kambuwatawana, the elder. Both he and his brother were Ratemahatmayas. After their death, the name is extinct."

The actual name of this disawa is not available (some close sources suggest it was potentially "Kambuwatawana Banda"). The flag could have been a symbolic gift awarded to the person when he was appointed to the disawa position. There are two writings on the flag to read *"Kambuwatawana Mahadisawage"* (belongs to Kambuwatawana *Maha Disawa (Great Disawa)* and *"Kambuwatawana Walawwe Disawa"* (Disawa from Kambuwatawana aristocratic mansion).

The flag features a prominent Kinduru (Kinnara) figure, displaying distinct characteristics reminiscent of Brāhminic style. This intriguing imagery raises questions about its potential historical or mythical significance.

Kambuwatawana Flag

In both Buddhist and Hindu mythology, the Kinnara is portrayed as a celestial musician, embodying a unique blend of human and animal attributes. In Vaishnavism, Kinnara is recognized as a demigod renowned for playing musical instruments and singing alongside the Gandharvas (Musicians). Gandharvas themselves are heavenly beings acknowledged in Hinduism, Buddhism, and Jainism. According to the Puranic Encyclopedia, Kinnaras are a sect of Devas, often depicted holding Veenas (musical instruments) in their hands. In Sanskrit literature, Kinnaras are categorized as mythical beings, characterized by their half-human, half-animal form, and they are said to reside in the Himalayas. These mythical creatures also find mention in certain Buddhist texts, such as the Lotus Sutra.

The Kinduru figure depicted on the flag is portrayed holding a musical instrument resembling a harp, Indian Thampura, or Saraswati veena. The unique size and shape of this instrument stand out, as it is not commonly used in Sri Lankan musical traditions but is featured in artistic designs.

The intricate border design (liyavel) on the Kambuwatawana flag does not align with popular Sri Lankan artistic traditions. Additionally, the Hastha (hands) mudra of the Kinnara figure showcases a significant yoga mudra known as "Prana," which is renowned for activating dormant energy within the human body. Such mudras are not commonly found in other Kinnara depictions in Sri Lanka.

This flag has been preserved in the village for over two and a half centuries, if not longer, and has been displayed during various ceremonies to celebrate the village's legacy. It is said to have adorned wedding ceremonies as a decoration for head tables or used to cover stools placed in front of newlywed couples. Over time, it has acquired stains and, at some point, had writings added to it to emphasize its historical importance and honour the village clan and their heritage. While these inscriptions may have compromised its original elegance, they serve as reminders of its significance and the need to protect it.

Upon initial examination, the flag appears to represent a blend of Hindu and Buddhist mythology. However, the connection between the flag and the Maha Disawa from Kambuwatawana remains unestablished. The flag's exact age remains unknown, yet it exhibits distinct features suggestive of Indian origins and hints at elements of Puranic Hinduism. Further exploration is needed to determine whether the flag symbolizes an Indian mythical past of the Brāhmin generation in Kambuwatawana.

This chapter was dedicated to establishing historical facts surrounding the arrival of the South Indian Brahmin contingent, drawing records from multiple palm-leaf manuscripts. Furthermore, an investigation was conducted to determine whether the symbolic representation of the Kambuwatawana flag alluded to any Hindu-Buddhist mythology, thereby hinting at a potential Indian connection to the village's historical artifacts. The subsequent chapter will give an introduction to the Brahmin community and identify the places of origin of the Brahmin groups that migrated to Sri Lanka.

Chapter Three

Introduction to Brāhmins and their Place of Origin

Who are Brāhmins?

According to Indian tradition, Brāhmins belong to a varna (class) system within Hinduism.

In the early periods of the Aryan community in North India, society was divided into four primary varnas: Brāhmins, Kshatriyas, Vaishyas, and Shudras. The Brāhmins traditionally held the role of priests in Hindu temples and performed important duties at socio-religious ceremonies. In theory, Brāhmins occupied the highest rank among the four social classes and played a central role in Hindu society. Their responsibilities included studying, teaching, conducting sacrifices, and officiating at religious services. Brāhmins were the spiritual and intellectual leaders of society. It's worth noting that Indian texts indicate that Brāhmins also engaged in various occupations, including agriculture, warfare, trade, and other roles throughout history.

Kshatriyas were primarily rulers and warriors responsible for protecting and governing society. They held positions of nobility and were tasked with safeguarding and promoting the material well-being of the community. Vaishyas were engaged in agriculture and trade, contributing significantly to the economic prosperity of society. Shudras, on the other hand, were workers or servants who provided manual labour and services required by the other three varnas.

In mythology, it's often said that Brāhmins originated from the head, Kshatriyas from the shoulders, Vaishyas from the loins, and Shudras from the feet of the supreme deity.

While this classification system is well-documented in Indian tradition, it's important to note that it was primarily theoretical. References to a more complex social structure can be found in ancient texts, indicating that the varna system was not as rigid as it might appear. Nonetheless, analysing these four primary social classes helps describe the caste system, which was based on birth and justified by moral and religious concepts. For instance, an individual's birth into a particular varna was believed to be determined by their past karma (actions and deeds).

> "Those whose conduct here [on earth] has been good will quickly attain some good birth – birth as a Brāhmin, birth as a kshatriya, or birth as a vaisya. But those whose conduct here has been evil will quickly attain some evil birth – birth as a dog, birth as a pig, or birth as a chandala" (Chandogya Upanishad, 10(7)).

In South India, the Aryans were predominantly classified as the Brāhmin class. However, over the course of history, there were instances where non-Aryan traders and certain communities, like the Chettis of Southern India, were granted the title of Vaishya.

Additionally, a few individual families with fair complexions were sometimes considered to be of Aryan descent (Singh, 2008).

It is widely recognized that Brāhminism played a significant role in modernizing the South Indian states. Historically, the powerful South Indian kingdoms included the Chera, Chola, and Pandya dynasties. In the region north of Travancore on the Malabar coast, part of the country underwent early Brāhminisation, leading to the transformation of the word "Chera" into "Kerala." This term was used in Sanskrit to refer to all Chera peoples and regions. The Chola dynasty, in particular, greatly benefited from Brāhminical civilization, and its influence extended to the Pandyan kingdom, South Travancore, and Northern Sri Lanka, contributing to cultural and civilizational developments in these regions[29].

Brāhmin Legacy in India.

Brahmins are found across India, and influential Brahmin communities exist within various major language groups. In South India, particularly in Tamil Nadu, language played a significant role in creating a division between Aryans and Dravidians (Laxman, 2016). Aryans were associated with Sanskrit, while Dravidians primarily identified with Tamil and other South Indian languages. This linguistic distinction led to social mobilization against caste hegemony and discrimination, with Brahmin identity closely linked to Aryan identity to uphold traditional caste superiority. In response, non-Brahmins identified with Dravidian identity to challenge caste-based hierarchies, eventually giving rise to distinct political movements and agendas associated with these identities.

While Brahmins are more concentrated in North Indian language groups, there are smaller Brahmin populations in the southern Indian states of Tamil Nadu, Karnataka, and Kerala. Brahmins have

---

[29] Singh, 2008, 574

migrated to Sri Lanka throughout history from both North India, particularly Madhya Pradesh, and the southern Indian states mentioned earlier.

During the eighth and ninth centuries, the emergence of powerful dynasties in India led to interregional conflicts. The establishment of large armies, including mercenaries and allied troops, may have contributed to the overall weakening of Indian powers during this period. Brahmins began to assume essential roles not only in religious affairs but also in economic and political domains. They served as administrators, members of royal councils, and compilers of royal genealogies. Brahmins, known for their education, actively participated in state and temple administration. With the rise of numerous kingdoms, Brahmins migrated to different regions, including Maharashtra, Bengal, Orissa, and South India, where they played influential roles (Singh 2008: 574).

Place of Origin.

The place of origin of these seven Brāhmin contingents in India are not clearly identified. The vitti book, N1, records the migrants came from Rakkandu Desha of Dambadiva (India), yet there this area has not been found. Vanni Upatha (N2) explains that the group came from "Rankadu Desha" and landed at Karaduwa, which is most likely Kalpitiya port at Puttalam.

The Nikawewa vitti book[30] states that, "Dembatogama Purohit Brāhmaṇa Rāla came from Malala Desha[31]" and, before coming to Sri Lanka, he was honoured in that country. He landed at Dasthota, a port in Sri Lanka, and from there, he passed through Mabole and Bonale.

---

[30] Dharmasena Bandara, 2011.
[31] Potentially Kerala

The N1 manuscript at one occasion states that these Brahmins came from "Malayala Desha" which refers to Kerala State where the majority speak Malayali, a Dravidian language. Potentially the area of Rankadu or Rakkandu Desha could be in Kerala State (Malala or Malayala country) or an area close to Madurai (Madura Pura) in Tamil Nadu.

Kandure Bandarawaliya (Obeyesekere, 2005, pg. 45) states a group of seven *"Kallu"* princes came from *Kalu Desha* in India and landed at Karaduwa. It is difficult to identify who the Kalu desha or Kallu kings were. These terms could have been Sinhalised[32] over time.

The Matale vitti book[33] presents another group of Brāhmins who came from India and settled in Matale. They apparently came from Madda-desa. This is the area where the Buddha's dispensation took place. Obeyesekere says, "Madda-desa in Indian topography of the period mostly refers to the area of the present-day Buddha Gaya in Bihar and not the contemporary Madya Pradesh".[34] Matale vitti book also refers to a group of Brāhmins who came from Srīdanta Desa region. Matale vitti books appeared to stand together the origin of Brāhmin roots with Buddhist legendary roots.

Vanni palm-leaf manuscripts[35] primarily focused on a group known as the Malalas or Mallas. They appeared to be a Kshatriya warna (or "varna", the term for a traditional Hindu social class). In India, a war between the Malla king and Marawara kings led to the Malla king being defeated. The seven princes of the Malla king fled the kingdom and hid in the Bodimalu temple. Two of those princes

---

32 Sinhalese meaning of "Kalu" is black or dark. So, these people were dark complexioned when compared to the locals.

33 G Obeyesekere, 2013, The coming of Brāhmi Migrants.

34 G Obeyesekere, 2013.

35 Vanni Vitti, Vanni Vittiya, Malala Vittiya etc.

entered the Buddhist Order and became monks. They, together with a group of followers, decided to seek refuge in Sri Lanka.

They claimed their ancestors had migrated to Sri Lanka many centuries ago, before this incident took place, with the arrival of the Bodhi Tree[36]. So, they left Bodhimalu and reached Madura Pura, then travelled to Mayila Pura, and then to Ayoththi Pattalama, where they had joined with a group of Hettis and Brāhmins. Obeyesekere (2013) believes that they were pushed out of the place known as Malakkava by the Maravars, the latter, of course, are well-known as warrior groups inhabiting the Ramnad district. Malala origin myths say that they came from a place associated with the bōdhi mandala.

Obeyesekere (2013) explains that these people wanted to be known as Buddhists in South India and that they had replicated the Bōdhi Maṇḍala there just as the Sinhala kings did when the branch of the Bōdhi tree was planted in Anuradhapura. Or it is more likely that the idea of the Bōdhi Maṇḍala was to legitimize the Malalas as Buddhist, albeit living in a Hindu country. Obeyesekere provocatively claims these stories are probably fictions but powerful ones providing symbolic validation and legitimacy for many distinguished migrants originating mostly from South India and speaking Demala ("Tamil"), namely South Indian languages.[37]

Vanni Upatha (pg. 32) also gives details about the route the Malala princes (the Kerala Kshatriya group) used when they voyaged to Sri Lanka. Their place of origin appeared to be Kerala, they first came to Madurapura (Madura or Madurei city), then they

---

[36] The Bodhi Tree ("tree of awakening"), also called the Bodhi Tree or Bo Tree, was a large and ancient sacred fig tree, the spiritual teacher who became known as the Buddha, is said to have attained enlightenment or Bodhi circa 500 BCE under it. A sapling of this sacred tree was brought by Sangamittā (the eldest daughter of Emperor Ashoka 304 BC – 232 BC) together with her brother Mahinda to Sri Lanka and planted in Anuradhapura.

[37] Obeyesekere, 2013, The comings of Brāhmins.

had travelled to Mailapura, and then to Ayoththi Pattalama and finally they reached the Thoothukudi port (formerly Tuticorin) from where they sailed to Pomparippu port (Puttalam – Mannar coast) in Sri Lanka.

Pomparippu was a popular port in the past, where trade in the Indian Ocean was accommodated. There is an archaeological site at Pomparippu that dates to ancient times.[38] This is part of ancient Sri Lanka that falls into the Thambapanni region. This was a popular trade route between India and Sri Lanka, and possibly to other parts of the world. It is most likely that the seven Brāhmins also took a similar route to Sri Lanka. Indrapala (2009) explains that Madurai and Thambapanni regions belonged to the same cultural area.

Devaraja (1972, pgs. 46-49) suggests that the "Bandaras" who came to Sri Lanka during the medieval times were Kerala people. The word *bandara* derives from the Tamil word *Pantharam*. They belonged to the Vellala caste in South India. Raghavan (1964) specifically states that Ceylon colonists mostly were from Kerala and the districts of Ramnad, Tinnevelly and Madura. He points out that Vaiya Padal poem gives a cross section of innumerable groups from these regions swarmed into Northern Ceylon.

The seven Brāhmaṇa Rālas could have also followed this trend and route to migrate to a new country.

The next chapter presents the South Indian context in medieval times that influenced the seven Brāhmin families' (and Malala Bandara and Hetti groups) migration and the Sri Lankan local context that facilitated the immigrants.

---

[38] http://amazinglanka.com/wp/pomparippu/.

Chapter Four

Reasons for Brāhmi Group Migration to Sri Lanka

This chapter is organised to examine the Indian context that influenced the migration of seven Brāhmin groups and the Sri Lankan context that facilitated the migration.

Indian Context.

As a country situated thirty-five kilometres below southern India in the Indian Ocean, Sri Lanka always attracted different types and waves of Indian migrants throughout history. However, there had been political changes in South India since the decline of the Vijayanagar Empire in the 15th century, which contributed to a new influx of migrants to Sri Lanka.

Rasanayagam (1926) says that since the 14th century, the Chola and Pandya kingdoms suffered from disintegration. Vijayanagar kings had been hard-pressed. Naik kings planted Telugu Polygars, a class of territorial administrative and military governors, which was an unfamiliar development for local nobles. Further, the Nayaka rulers of South India (notably the Vijayanagara Empire, Madurai Nayakas) oversaw small regions of Madura and Tanjore districts. According to Obeyesekere (2017, pg. 29) Nayakas were governors of administrative districts of Vijayanagar Empire. They administered all parts of Tamil Nadu except Ramand (Ramanathapuram).

This new regional administrative structure was not linked to the traditional subjects of Vijayanagar. There had been regular conflicts between regional chieftains. Vanni Upatha states that during the reign of Buwanekabahu in Sri Lanka, King Marawara who ruled in Dambadiva raged a war against Malala country which had caused the migration of some Malala princes (Malala Vittiya, Obeyesekere, 2005).

During the 14th and 15th centuries, the North Indian Muslim rulers started invading South India. Vijayanagar empire held Mohammadians in check for two centuries. In 1479, the Vijayanagar dynasty came to an end. By the close of the 15th century, the power of Vijayanagar was acknowledged as paramount for the entire peninsula.

On top of that, Malik Kafur and Muhammadians (Muslims), invaded several times and ravaged southern India. In such times, many respectable Tamil Vellalar families migrated to Sri Lanka. According to Rasanayagam (1920), Vellalar is a generic Tamil term used primarily by various castes who traditionally pursued agriculture as a profession in the Indian states of Tamil Nadu, Kerala, and the north-eastern parts of Sri Lanka. Some of them settled in Jaffna, and others sought refuge under the Sinhalese kings. They accepted positions of honour and trust, and they then became the forebearers of some of most respectable Vellalar families of the south.

These Vellala families could be related to royal families of Nayakas. The Brāhmin groups possibly were the advisers for the Nayaka rulers as expected of Indian scheme of things.

Local Conditions

Palm-leaf manuscripts recorded the migrations of South Indians and creation of settlements in Vanni regions, especially in the Puttalam and Kurunegala districts. Obeyesekere[39] believes that new kingdoms of Kotte and Kandy opened large, forested areas for agricultural production, but what they lacked was workers. Therefore, new migrants were a rapid Sri Lankan version of the Southeast Asian spectacle, not just for territorial expansion, but for the subjugation of working people.

The Sri Lankan plan was to encourage migrants to develop less populated and forested areas suitable for rural agriculture, so that they could be incorporated into the dry zone. The Vanni region was opened for this colonisation. The region where the seven Brāhmins settled was rural and had less rainfall, which made for a shrinking population.

Obeyesekere believes that the Batticaloa district was free from this historic plan[40]. This is because the Batticaloa people came from the ancestral pantheons of Kerala long before the kingdoms of Kotte, Kandy, Dedigama, and Gampola i.e. before the 14th century. They tolerated the linguistic and cultural content of later kingdoms, such as Jaffna, Kotte, and Kandy.

The Kotte and Sithawaka periods were full of conflict and constant territorial battles. Many lost their lives, and the security forces were also becoming thin. It was difficult to seek military assistance from Indian kings at the time. The South Indian political context was also volatile, and there was an added stress of the potential European threat that was also gradually increasing. Under these conditions, local kings wanted a new class of local leaders.

---

[39] Obesekara, (2004) The Matrilineal East Coast Circa.
[40] Ibid

They wanted to strengthen their forces against any potential threats – local or international – and new migrants were the most feasible strategy.

The attraction of people to Sath Korale to increase agricultural production and to strengthen local forces continued during the Kandyan Kingdom too. Sath Korale Kadayim and Vitti manuscript illustrates how the Kandyan monarch Kirthi Sri Rajasinghe encouraged people from coasted areas (Colombo, Negombo and Puttalam etc.) to shift to Sath Korale and Kandyan regions giving rewards and land grants. He also had a motive to weaken the Dutch power in the coastal regions for his military advantage.

The South Indian migration, subsequent colonisation and internal migration discussed herein, which took place in medieval periods, increased the population, but also filled the region with necessary leaders.

Migrants and Buddhist Connection.

Buddhism was declining in South India after the 10th century CE.[41] Brahminical supremacy was inapplicable with Buddhist temples, and in larger segments, it had been passed back into Hindu temples.[42] Religious competition with Hinduism, and later Islam, also resulted in the decline. Islamic invaders destroyed many Buddhist temples and Buddhist universities in South India.[43]

There have been Buddhist migrants from India since the medieval times. For example, all Alagakkonaras (Alakeshwaras) and Mehenawaras families who came from Kerala and settled in Gampola, Raigama and Kotte were Buddhists, even in their original settlement, Vansi which was under the influence of the Vaithulist

---

[41] Wikipedia.
[42] Wikipedia.
[43] Sarao, 2012, Decline of Buddhism in India.

religions in India.[44] However, it is difficult to recognise all the Malala and Hetti who migrated to Sri Lanka, as described in vitti books, were Buddhists.

It is to be noted here that a traditional conversion to Buddhism is not applicable since the philosophy of Buddhism is totally contrasting with the other accepted religions of India (e.g., Hindu, Islam, Jain). For instance, a Hindu or any other peoples can observe Buddhism without getting converted.

Malala Vithiya (pgs. 17-18) and the Vanni Vitti (pg. 67) explains the reasons for a group of Malala princes to migrate to Sri Lanka. As previously mentioned, after a defeat from a war, seven princes of the Malala king fled the kingdom and hid in the Bodimalu temple. Two princes entered the Buddhist order and became monks. They, together with a group of followers, decided to seek refuge in Sri Lanka, claiming their ancestors also migrated to Sri Lanka many centuries before with the arrival of the Bodhi Tree. Vanni Vitti (pg. 65) states about the two Buddhist monks, namely, Budhdhamithra and Saranankara who were granted villages/lands of Mahathota, Widagama, and Thotagamuwa. It is possible that the scholastic Thotagamuwa Buddhist school was founded by these elite migrant monks.[45]

In addition, there is a record about offering a large country including Maruppu Korale village and other sixty-four villages to the monk named Prince Malala Pandiya Thera (Vanni Vitti, pg. 66) indicating more Malala princes had become Buddhist monks. Some Malala migrants who decided to migrate to Sri Lanka knew that Sri Lanka was a safe Buddhist country for them. Their beliefs of origin states that they came from a place associated with the Bodhi

---

[44] Obeyesekere, 2004. Balachandran, PK. (2006).
[45] Obesekara, 2018. Speech at Open University, Sri Lanka.

Mandala. Or it is more likely that the idea of the Bodhi Mandala was to legitimize the Malala as Buddhist, albeit living in a Hindu country.[46]

Even Vanni Vitti (pg. 63, Poem 69) reveals that Malala's princes had claimed that their seventh great, great grandparents came to Sri Lanka with the sacred Bo Tree and given countries in Sri Lanka. They wished they wanted to reclaim those countries to settle in. As stated elsewhere, Matale Kadayim book (M2) also reveals a claim by Brāhmin migrants about their vintage connection to those who brought the Bo Tree during the time of King Devanampiyathissa.

N1 also records the allocation of *Galgiriyawa* village to Bogoda Thero by the Mundukondapola Palace with the acknowledgement of Dembatogama Purohit Brāhmaṇa Rāla. Galgiriyawa later became a stronghold for Malwathu Buddhist order (Chapter) starting from the time of the Kandyan kingdom.

It is impractical to imagine that the seven Brāhmaṇa Rālas were Hindus, but they embraced Buddhism after their arrival and continued their Hindu practices and rituals as usual.

This chapter presents the Indian context that influenced the Brāhmins and other South Indian migrants to leave India, as well as the Sri Lankan local conditions that facilitated the migration. The next chapter goes into detail of their settlement in Sri Lanka as explained in palm-leaf manuscripts.

---

[46] Obeyesekere, 2013, The comings of Brāhmi migrants.

Chapter Five

Brāhmi Settlements as in Palm-leaf Manuscripts

In this chapter, the details of the Brāhmi migration and their settlement, as described in the palm-leaf manuscript, are further explored.

The Nature and Tradition of Vitti Books

In the medieval times, and even up into the recent past, palm leaves were methodically prepared, conditioned, and used by the local intellectuals and scholarly monks.[47]

There are at least four types of palm leaf manuscripts for historical records in Sri Lanka: a) *Vitti poth*, books on past events; b) *Kadaim poth*, books of boundaries, written for the purpose of describing boundaries of the main divisions of the island; c) *Bandaravaliya*, these manuscripts contain histories of aristocratic families that are simply a Sri Lankan version of family genealogies that are found in many cultures; and d) *Sannas*. these are royal deeds for land grants etc.

---

[47] Ola-leaf manuscripts are mostly kept by rural villagers and in temples. Some collections are available at London Museum (Hugh Nevil Collection), National Archives, Sri Lanka Museum and universities like Peradeniya University.

Obeyesekere (2005 and 2013) found that, "all historical chronicles pose problems of interpretation, and the vitti poth are no exception. Thus, they deal with stories or narratives of migration, and these are in the form of myths. But myths can and do express historical realities that invite interpretation."

According to him, one methodological problem that emerges in these texts (and indeed in all historical chronicles), is that distinction between the time period in which a particular text was written and the period to which it refers. The texts deal with stories or narratives of migration, and these are in the form of myths. But myths can, and do, reveal historical facts.

Sources of Palm-leaf Manuscripts.

For the analysis of the seven Brāhmin group migration, in terms of their arrival, settlement, and expansion, I have used the following primary sources of palm-leaf manuscripts. I have also indicated the information contained in each which was useful for the analysis in this publication:

1. Nikawa Gampaha Korale Vitti Saha Mayim Wattoru (N1).

The manuscript contains historical information about the Division or Korale called Nikawagampaha Korale in Sath Korale. It contains historical events, and mayim (or kadayim) which means clarifications of boundaries of the Korale (division). This manuscript is not published anywhere else. This book is referred to as N1 for convenience. This vitti book not only presents boundaries of villages at that time, but also the prominent historical event of Brāhmi families and their expansion. This briefly contains information about:

- ✧ Seven Brāhmi migrants who came from South India,
- ✧ The villages they settled in,
- ✧ Villages allocated for these migrants to oversee,

✧ Adjacent villages and village holders,

✧ Boundaries of Dembatogama country,

✧ Honorary names awarded to those new migrants,

✧ Early and prominent marriages,

✧ Names of three generations,

✧ Village boundaries,

✧ Village title holders, and

✧ Boundary disputes.

However, I observed that this manuscript has at least two different versions adding new leaves or copying to different set of leaves. This must be because of the records were updated at different times[48].

According to the text, this book claimed to be written by Dembatogama Rajakaruna Mohottala in 1007 Shaka year.[49] He had been appointed to a "Lekam" position (Registrar) by the Sithawaka king. The Sinhalese full version of the vitti book is provided in my publication "Immigrants from Madurapura: A Collection of Palm-leaf Manuscripts in Sri Lanka".

2. Mahasammatha Vitti Book (N3)

This is also an original and unpublished manuscript.[50] The first part of this manuscript contains similar information to "Kurunegala Vistaraya", but the second part gives information about another Brāhmi chieftain, Sri Chandrasekara Purohitha Brāhmaṇa Rankadu Bandi Wijesingha Senewirathna Mudiyanse, who settled at

---

[48] I copied it from a handwritten copy by a gentleman from Wathuwaththegama (RM Tikiri Banda). He apparently had copied it from an original ola-leaf manuscript (puskola potha) belonging to a Nikawewa Buddhist temple. I copied this manuscript in 1970's but this original could not traced at this stage.

[49] That is 1085AD (1007+78). This timeframe is not reliable. It could be 1685 AD (1607+78).

[50] Some parts of this manuscript are included in the book by YM Dharmasena (2011).

Pohorawaththa village of the Dembatogama country and his legacy. This manuscript has information related to:

- ✧ Previous residents of Dembatogama country,
- ✧ Where the skilled professionals who came with the chief (his army) settled,
- ✧ The wars in which the chieftain was involved,
- ✧ Disputes with contemporary migrants, and
- ✧ Boundaries of villages and countries.

The Sinhalese full version of the vitti book is provided in my publication "Immigrants from Madurapura: A Collection of Palm-leaf Manuscripts from Sath Korale".

3. Vanni Vitti and Kadayim Books.

I have also extensively used the following publications, palm-leaf manuscripts compiled by Gananath Obeyesekere in 2005:

- a) ***Vanni Upatha, Vanni Vitthiya[51] saha Kadayim potha.*** This publication contains a collection of manuscripts named after Vanni Upatha, Vanni Vittiya, Vanni Vitti, and Vanni Kadayim potha.

- b) ***Vanni Rajawaliya.*** Even though this book titled as Vanni Rajawaliya it contains information similar to the famous Rajawaliya but it got this name because this version was written in Vanni.

- c) ***Bandaravaliya saha Kadayim potha.*** This publication contains the vitti books of Hemamala Bandarawaliya, Kandure Bandarawaliya, Malala Bandarawaliya, Sirilak Kada Ayuru Potha, Rajawaliya, and Laggala Kadayim potha.

- d) ***Malala Vittiya, Malala Kathawa and Rajasinghe Rajuge Portuguese satan pilibanda sandahan Vitti potha.*** This is a collection of three vitti books as titled in this publication.

---

[51] Vanni Vittiya is the segment that also refers as "Madurapuren Avittiya".

These publications helped me to find information about South Indian immigrants, including seven Brāhmins group and compatriots.

4. Sath Korale Kadayim Saha Vitti.

This is also an original and unpublished palm-leaf manuscript potentially written towards the end of Kandyan Kingdom. The first part of the manuscript provides details about the early history of Sri Lanka including the boundary information of three Sinhala grand territories (Ruhunu rata, Maya rata and Pihiti rata) and the kings of Kandyan Kingdom. The second part of the manuscript is all about the endeavors of the king Kirthi Sri Rajasinghe including his battles against the Dutch in coastal fronts. It explains how the king lured costal people who were supporting the Dutch to settle in Sath Korale and Kandyan regions weakening the manpower in Dutch territories. The manuscript also discloses strategies used by the king to rally troops to conquer the Dutch stronghold of Puttalam after overcoming the disloyalty issues of Sath Korale chieftains (Bandaras).

5. Three Sinhale Kadayim Saha Vitti.

This has been compiled by A J W Marambe in 1926 and contains a collection of palm-leaf manuscripts. Some segments include: Matale kadayim books, Vanni Vittiya, Panduwasnuwara, Wararaja Gothraya and Sri Lanka, Manu Raja wanshaya, Kuweni Wilapaya, Galaboda Korale Idakadam, Satara Korale Nayyakkar Vittiya, Madurapuren Avittiya, and Kurunegala Vistharaya. Some of these segments are included in the above publications by Obeyesekere.

6. Nikawewa Vitti Book.

A book titled *A brief history of Nikawagampaha*[52] written by YM Dharmasena Bandara in 2011, provides information obtained from two other Vitti books held at Nikawewa and Herathgama villages.

---

[52] Dharmasena Bandara, YM. (2011). *"Nikawagampaha Aththathayen Bindak"*.

The original and complete copies of these vitti books are not available for reference. However, Dharmasena Bandara had copied these vitti books to include in his book which are reliable.

7. Madurapura Rajaparampara Rajawaliya.

This manuscript is stored at Peradeniya University (Index Number 277456). It contains information about marriage relationships that were established by Kandyan kings with the Nayakas royal family in Madurapura (Madurai). In addition, the extended family of these princesses who came to Sri Lanka, where they settled, the positions they held at the royal palace, and intimate details of the affairs of the royal family are contained in this manuscript. The Sinhalese full version of the vitti book is provided in my publication "Immigrants from Madurapura: A Collection of Palm-leaf Manuscripts in Sri Lanka".

Analysis of Palm-leaf Manuscripts Related to the Seven Brāhmins Arrival and Settlement.

N1 provides intimate details about the seven Brāhmins. The key information related to the interaction with the royal palace and subsequent proceedings as follow:

- ✧ The King in Sri Lanka at that time – "Sri Wickrama Buvanekkadhi"
- ✧ Kingdom – Kotte
- ✧ The country where the migrants came from – Dambadiva (India)
- ✧ The area where they came from in India – Rakkandu Desha.
- ✧ The composition of the group – seven Rakkandu Bandi Brāhmaṇa Rālas (seven Brāhmi gentlemen who were wearing golden bangles[53]).

---

[53] This description suggests that the costume could have been strange to the locals.

✧ Relationship to each other – "Mal Bayans" (cousins from an extended family).

✧ Dress of migrants – seven threads of yellow scarfs around the shoulder (*sath kapata puna nool karata gena*).

✧ Attendants who accompanied the group – a Thoilpath man (*thoilpath holder*). Also mentioned as "Sinhala *Viriduwa*" or Tamil *Nakathiya*. This person could be a service person but nakathiya means a drummer or tom-tom beater and who conducts devil service.[54]

✧ Voyage to Sri Lanka – in a ship.

✧ Where they attended to see the King – at "Mundukondapola Maha Wasala". (Mundukondapola Great Palace), also mentions at a few other places as *Devamadde Maha Wasala* (Devamadde Larger Aristocratic Palace).

✧ Appearance gifts they offered to the king – Miriwadi Sangala (gold embedded shoes), a turban made from thirty Riyans[55] length, golden scarf (*thhis riyan ranpata mundasanaya*).

✧ The request from the migrants – "*Viemasthi*" to settle in Sath Korale.

✧ Items awarded by the king to the senior, the Purohit Brāhmin – an elephant named Hithtara, punupoth (puhupoth) gediya,[56] ran panhinda (golden inscription pen) and "*rathran bothtam hatte*" (upper dress-jacket – studded with gold buttons).

The original names and the seven Brāhmaṇa Rālas and the villages they were offered by the king:

✧ *Kiri* Brāhmaṇa Rāla – Kiribamuna village,

---

[54] Raghavan, 1968, pg. 17, *Karawa of Ceylon*.

[55] "Riyana" is a cubit, a traditional Sri Lankan measurement of length from the elbow to middle finger.

[56] Potentially a betel lime box, "killota".

✧ *Kandulassa* Brāhmaṇa Rāla – Kandulawa Village,

✧ *Rakkandu Bandi* Brāhmaṇa Rāla – Rakwana Village,

✧ *Mahipala* Brāhmaṇa Rāla – Borawewa Village,

✧ *Jothipala* Brāhmaṇa Rāla – Mataluwawa Village,

✧ (another) Brāhmaṇa Rāla – Matale Dunuwila Village (in Sathara Korale) and

✧ Purohit Brāhmaṇa Rāla (Kings spiritual adviser) – Dembatogama village and the Dembatogama country.

As previously stated, there is conflicting information about two Brāhmaṇa Rālas in N1 and N2. However, Rakwane Rala, Dembatogama Rala and Borawewa Ralas were brothers. The Brāhmaṇa Rāla who settled in Dunuwila Matale introduced as Borawewa Mahipala Brāhmaṇa Rāla's *"massinā"* (brother-in-law).

As previously stated, the Mahipala Brāhmaṇa Rāla was given the honorary name of *"Chandrasekara Maha Basnayake Mudiyanse"* by the king at Mundukondapola Palace. As mentioned previously he was given the custody of Kambuwatawana, Kubukkadawala, Kaduruwewa, Nipunagama, Elipichchegama, Indipitiya, Watthegala, Kadahatha Wewa, Archirigama, Dikweheragama and Karagaswewa villages. Vanni Vitthiya manuscript (pg. 45) states that Borawewa Brāhmaṇa Rāla was given Borawewa village and *"bija daha ata amuna saha olagam hathai"* (approximately forty acres of paddy land and seven villages that either had no settlers or was sparsely populated).

Potentially, his wife (and children) joined him later. Some female family members were recorded as having joined the Brāhmaṇa Rālas later. For example, Mahipala's sister who was married to Ekanayake Mudiyanse of Parakumbura in Sathara Korale, had come to Sri Lanka at a later time.

N1 also provides updated information about Borawewa Mahipala Maha Brāhmaṇa Rāla and his family. His eldest son (official tenants) was awarded the surname of Maha Basnayake Mudiyanse and was settled at Kambuwatawana. After the death of Mahipala Maha Brāhmaṇa Rāla, the headmanship must have been passed on to his son, who potentially continued to live at Kambuwatawana or shifted to Borawewa.

The N1 manuscript provides the boundaries of the area that were given to the migrants. But it appears that the boundaries mentioned therein are the boundaries of a group of villages that appeared to fall into the *Nikawe Gampaha Korale* (the division of five greater villages) or Dembatogama rata:

- ✧ Eastern boundary – Kiriwalheena: a range of small hill,
- ✧ Northern Boundary – below kaduru galen oye gal wakkada, gal katiya wala, galtambe, below kangollawala: natural boundaries of streams and hillocks,
- ✧ Western boundary – Galgiriya kanda, paliha ketu gala and above athdath watuna wala of Mee Oya: natural streams and hillocks with marks created, and
- ✧ Southern boundary – Naipena alla, koragaha wala, galapita gala and below pothuwila kadawala: natural water holes and hillocks.

According to the Vitti Potha (N1), the original main five village cluster (*gam paha*) that represented the Nikawa Gampaha Korale were: Nikawewa, Dembatogama, Rakwana, Borawewa, and Herathgama. Walpaluwa village had been awarded to the Tamil Nakathiya who came with the group of Brāhmaṇa Rāla.

Gama Versus Rata.

According to Abayawardana (1978), *"gama"* is a Sinhala term derived from Sanskrit term *"grama"* and Pali *"gama"* and signifies a collective entity. Gama was the smallest unit of human settlements, including lands for cultivation, water retention and harvesting, as well as an area for the wildlife to be sustained. We must be mindful that in some contexts, *"gama"* also denotes land. Rata (*Ratta*) is known as country (part of country) which includes many villages and greater villages or divisions. It can also be a small regional kingdom.

N2 states that the migrants requested *"viee madithi"* for them to settle in. It might have meant a plot of paddy (rice) lands, which means several paddy plots that come under several village tanks. The king permitted them to settle in "grama" or villages. That perhaps meant that those villages had already existed and were inhabited by some early residents. N1 does not refer to any *"olagams"* but the Vanni books refer to them.

The land granted to the purohit by the king was termed "gama" (a village) as well as *"rata"* (a larger collective of villages). All seven Brāhmaṇa Rālas had selected villages but as an acknowledgement of the social status, and perhaps the seniority, the Purohit Brāhmaṇa Rāla was granted the Dembatogama country (a large region in Dembatogama).

The nature and the composition of these villages and the country can be further examined. It is clear that gam or villages granted to Brāhmaṇa Rālas were simply not a single village. For example, Mahipala was given Borawewa village, but it included eleven other villages: Kambuwatawana, Kubukkadawala, Kaduruwewa, Nipunagama, Ellipihchegama, Indipitiya, Wattegala, Kadahathawewa, Archirigama, Dikweheragama, and Karagaswewa. That means Mahipala was granted a group of villages or a division to represent the governing regime. Even though it is not clearly defined in the vitti books, Purohit had the responsibility for a large locality, a country, which encompassed the areas given to a few other Brāhmaṇa Rālas. If they were all included, the Dembatogama country could have been expanded from Kala Oya (the river Kala drains down towards the west relative to this region) from the north to Ibbagamuwa from the south.[57] It is doubtful whether Dembatogama country included Kandulawa and Kiri Bamuna, where the other two Brāhmins resided. They appeared to be outside the Dembatogama country. When we examine the specific boundaries provided in N1 and N2, this Dembatogama country approximately expands from Kala Oya from the north to Thiththawella village near Kubukkgate to the south.

Were the Immigrants Total Strangers?

The vitti books (N1 and N2) provide hints that the seven Brāhmins were not total strangers to the new country. There have been similar migrations that took place around that time. This group of immigrants appeared to have some familiarity with the local environment. Tamil speaking Vanniyars (i.e., Eriyawe Pannikki Vaddha) helped them with the language barriers. They appeared to be confident as they belonged to an educated class and came from a peaceful Brāhmaṇa wansa. They had the prior confidence from being accepted by the rulers in the new country. It also shows that they knew about local protocols at the palace and were familiar with the prevailed political system. They could be identified not only as land seeking immigrants but intelligent elite migrants.

They followed certain protocols on arrival at the royal palace. They understood the traditions, conventions, attractiveness of valuable gifts, royal protocols, and the legal framework of the new country. They could have known about the local ruler, ruling class

---

[57] This area was the Ibbagamuwa Assistant Government Agent Division previously. Currently, it has been divided into two Divisional Secretariats – Ibbagamuwa and Polpithigama.

hierarchy, dynasty, the royal palace, where the palace was situated, and the distance to travel from the port to get there.

They offered gifts (*dakum*) to the king, and they received gifts in return. The offering of gifts back to the group and, particularly to the purohit by the king, is indicative about the prestige social and cultural status that the group had vested with. So, several palm-leaf manuscripts did not miss the opportunity to refer to their ceremonial arrival.

The safety for this group wasn't an issue. The group had come with only one companion who was a drummer and a person trained to assist the purohit in religious rituals. The group must have had some versatility of connections to the new country, knew compatriot migrants or from the class they belonged to. They probably had the advantage of being Brāhmins and belonging to a certain dynasty. As Indian Brāhmins, they could have had a similar respect and recognition in the Sri Lankan society.

Palm-leaf manuscripts suggest that the local king was curious of, and welcoming to, the Kshatriyas (Malala Bandaras) as they were battle - hardened warriors. Vanni Upatha (pg. 33) indicates that the king welcomed the Malala Princes, but he used intelligence to find out if they were enemies or friends ("hathuroda mithuroda"; whether they were friends or foes).

The Malala princes had to travel to the Sitawaka main palace, not to the regional Mundukondapola Palace, because they were war hardened warriors and the great king's attention was required. That suspicion would not warrant for a group of peaceful and educated Brāhmins who were led by a priest.

It is difficult for foreigners to settle in a brand-new country with different cultural, linguistic, and religious background. It is a possibility that this group had a close familiarity of the local culture, language, and religion. These aspects are further explored in later chapters. Overall, the royal patronage helped them not only to settle in effortlessly but also to extend their authority over the local inhabitants.

There are no records to indicate that the Brāhmins were accompanied by their wives from India at the first visit. That is probably because they were Brāhmins (Obeyesekere, 2013).

The seven Brāhmin migrant families had close relationships with each other. As indicated in Chapter 13, the villages that the migrants settled in still exist and the surnames mentioned in the book are still intact in these villages with minor and inevitable logical variations. Kambuwatawana genealogical information (basic), which is in Chapter 19, confirms the ongoing marriage relationships with these families and associated villages.

An Examination of the Information in N1.

The information provided by the vitti book N1 requires further analysis. As previously stated, this vitti manuscript also has not been published and acknowledged anywhere else to date.

The vitti book states that the seven Brāhmins came during the reign of "Sri Wikrama Buvanekadhi" of Kotte Kingdom (this kingdom existed from 1412 to 1597). Another section of the book (probably an updated version or later addition) states that they came during Sithawaka Kingdom (which lasted from 1521-1597). The time periods of both kingdoms and the political events overlap to some extent. However, Sri Lankan historical records do not provide a name of a king called Sri Wikrama Buvanekadhi. The closest name is King Buvanekabahu. Two kings with the name of Buvanekabahu reigned during the Kotte Kingdom: Buvanekabahu VI from 1472 – 1480, and Buvanekabahu VII from 1521 to 1551. It is possible that the vitti book refers to the reign of Buvanekabahu VII who ruled for thirty years and, therefore, becomes a good candidate for this historical record. Sri Wikrama could have been an honorary name used by the vitti books to glorify the king with the highest level of appreciation for his sponsorship. But this is just my speculation.

The palace that the seven Brāhmins attended the king was called Mundukondapola Maha Wasala (great palace) of the Kotte kingdom. This kingdom has been stated in ancient chronicles of Pujavaliya and Rajavaliya. A description is also included in the Kurunegala Vistharaya and in the records of PE Pieris.

This chapter introduced the nature of palm-leaf manuscripts, the names of the manuscripts that was referenced in this research, and the issues associated with their content. Further, the specific information about the arrival of the Brāhmin group, the areas where they settled in and the process that took place in the settlements were analysed.

The next chapter examines the Mundukondapola kingdom, the kings who reigned there, and the location of the palace, to provide the political context that facilitated the seven Brāhmins group settlement.

Chapter Six

Mundukondapola Regional Kingdom in Sath Korale

This chapter presents an introduction to a lesser-known regional kingdom, Mundukondapola in Sath Korale under the greater kingdom of Sithawaka-Kotte. The seven Brāhmins arrived here and paid respect to the king at the Mundukondapola Palace.

Composition of Kotte and Sithawaka Kingdoms

Kotte had been the major power in western Sri Lanka since its foundation in the early 15th century, under Parakramabahu VI (1412-1467). He was the last monarch to unite the entire island under one crown. By 1467, however, the Jaffna Kingdom to the north had claimed its independence. To the east, the kingdom of Kandy was operating with a considerable degree of independence. In 1505, the Portuguese arrived in Sri Lanka, and the political landscape became even more dynamic.

Vijayabahu VII of Kotte (1509–1521) was deposed in a palace coup known as the Spoiling of Vijayabahu (Vijayaba Kollaya) in 1521. The eldest son of Vijayabahu succeeded as Buvanekabahu VII, whilst the other two claimed parts of Kotte for themselves. Mayadunne established the kingdom of Sitawaka and Pararajasinha establishing the kingdom of Raigama. The kingdom of Kandy was outside of the control of these three states.

The kingdom of Sitawaka initially covered a relatively small area. The terrain was hilly, bordered to the east by Kandy and with no access to the sea. The capital city was the present Avissawella. Soon after his ascent to the throne, Buvanekabahu began to strengthen his ties with the Portuguese to secure his throne from any potential challenge from his brother Mayadunne at Sitawaka. Mayadunne attempted to seize Kotte in 1537 but failed, as the Portuguese provided military assistance to the king of Kotte. A truce was negotiated between Sitawaka and Kotte. Subsequently, Mayadunne turned his attention south, to the kingdom of Raigama. He eventually annexed it following the death of Raigam Bandara (Pararajasinha), his brother, in 1538.

Later, Mayadunne attempted a few more invasions to Kotte but failed due to Portuguese military assistance. The Portuguese involvement in the internal politics of Kotte increased by 1550 with an attack on Sitawaka later that year. Mayadunne had adopted a policy of simply evacuating his capital and retreating into the surrounding terrain when invaded. In 1551, Buvanekabahu was assassinated and succeeded by Dharmapala, who relied heavily on his European allies. Dharmapala ruled from 1541 – 1597 and was the last king of the Kingdom of Kotte. He ruled from the capital city of Kotte under the Portuguese military occupation.

The Mundukondapola Palace was an autonomous kingdom under the Kotte Kingdom and the seven Brāhmins appeared to have settled there before King Buvanekabahu was assassinated in 1551.

The historical records give hints that Sri Lanka was always governed by regional kings or rulers who pledged allegiance to a great king.

The oldest kadayim (boundaries) book, the Sri Lamkadvipaye Kadayim denotes the entire island was divided into three principalities or kingdoms (Abeywardena, 1978), namely Maya, Pihiti, and Ruhunu, consisting of one-hundred-fourteen "rata" s or countries. Maya had twenty-eight ratas, Pihiti had forty-three ratas and Ruhunu had forty-three ratas. The boundary pillars mark off the limits of ratas. Abeywardena (1978), examining all historical kadayim books, lists twenty-eight Maya rata compositions, twenty-seven Pihiti rata compositions and twenty-five Ruhunu rata compositions, including the boundaries of each composition. They were specific compositions, suggesting that each had a subordinate ruler owing allegiance to a great king.

It was logical to have regional rulers, due to geographical distance and accessibility issues for the entire kingdom. No well-constructed road network existed, which created difficulties for regular communication. Some countries were separated by mountains and rugged territories.

K M de Silva[58] notes the existence of co-rulers in Sri Lanka, particularly during medieval times, confirming the existence of semi-autonomous regions/ratas and kingdoms.

Mundukondapola

Gananath Obeyesekere[59] opened new research into this regional kingdom and the Brāhmin immigration. He observes that several group of migrants, "showed themselves before the Sitavaka Palace

---

[58] De Silva, KM, (2008), *A History of Sri Lanka.*

[59] Obeyesekere, G. (2019). On Mundukondapola: Resurrecting the History of a Defunct Kingdom.

at Muṇḍukoṇḍapola". The local king of Muṇḍukoṇḍapola is grandiosely identified as "the divine great king Edirisuriya residing in his great palace of Muṇḍukoṇḍapola in Dēvamādda".[60] Vanni vitti books also identify the regional king as Edirimannasuriya. It seems that seven Brāhmins came directly to Muṇḍukoṇḍapola, but Malala princes were sent to Buvanekabahu in his capital at Sitavaka-Kotte. The reasoning for this could have been that the seven Brāhmins were peaceful migrants, and Malala princes had more royal associations. Also, there could have been some limits of the regional king's authority in the Mundukondapola kingdom.

Obeyesekere notes that Mundukondapola was potentially a travel residence of Sithawaka kings (referred as "Sitavaka Palace of Muṇḍukoṇḍapola"). King Buvanekabahu of Sitavaka resided there when he visited Muṇḍukoṇḍapola, which was an important small kingdom within his domain. Mundukondapola potentially started as a regional kingdom during Kurunegala Kingdom (1287 to 1335), and it lasted until the palace was looted and demolished by the Portuguese in 1596 or 1597 (Obeyesekere, 2019).

Palm-leaf manuscripts use both terms of "Mundukondapola Palace" and "Devamadda Palace". Abayawardana (1978) implies that Devamadda means "De-o-mada" or the kingdom "Between Two Streams". These streams are Daduru Oya and Ma Oya. Mundukondapola Palace is also called Devamada Palace, as it was also situated in "Deva Mädi Hatpattuva", or "the seven districts encircled by gods or devas". There are many Devala or gods' shrines in this kingdom. For example, there are Maha-Devalas in Tissa village, and many Devalas in Mundakondapola Nuwara (city).

Sirilak Kada Ayuru Potha (Bandarawaliya, 2005, pg. 68) provides boundaries of this kingdom, which are Daduru Oya and Maha Guru

---

[60] Ibid

Oya. According to this manuscript, there is a village in the middle of the kingdom with the name of Thissa which has a god's shrine. Also, there is a sanctuary called Mudakoduki Sanctuary, where "Muda mahanun", or yogis, conducted retreats. This Sanctuary also inherits a city called Mudakondapola City. This area was also known as "Deomadirata" because it has been circled by a godly sanctuary and godly shrines.

Sirilak Kada Ayuru manuscript introduces that the people who lived there as "maha mani", which means they were fanatically proud and arrogant about themselves. They were also manipulative, rude, and scandalous (sondin mayan danna, sorasith saha sora Mayan aththo).[61] The women who were born there were regarded as morally loose and sensual. This description suggests that the city was lively and exciting, but the character was non-traditional. The four boundaries of the city were marked with twelve stone pillars engraved with parrot symbols.

Abayawardana (1978) also provides information about the number of villages in the kingdom to give an estimation of its size. There were ten thousand Patunugam, ten thousand Bamunugam (villages of Brāhmins), one hundred welanda gam (merchant villages) and one hundred mudali gams (chieftain villages). According to the book Sri Lankadipa Kadayim, the key settlements of the kingdom were Kadiyaya (present day Kadiyawa in Vanni-hat-pattu), Kolabumgama (perhaps Kolmbagama in Devamadi-hat-pattu), and Pandavava (to the south of Devamadi-rata identified as Panduwasnuwara).

We can suspect that the administration of Munḍukonḍapola had been decentralised further into small principalities. N1 provides a regional kingdom with the name of "Kalungu Nuwara". When there

---

[61] Bandarawaliya, 2005, pgs. 68-69.

was a land dispute between the Rakwana chiefs and Pohorawaththa chiefs, the matter was settled by this regional king, but not by the Sithawaka or Mundukondapola kings. We have also indicated in a preceding section about another potential principality centred around Galgiriyawa and Madagalla of Nikawagampaha Korale, overseen by King Marasinghe.

Dynasty of the Mundukondapola Kings.

In mythology, Mundukondapola had an illustrious history and influential kings. The royal dynasty of Mundukondapola relates to a specific lineage that might link to a stream of historical migrants from India.

The famous ruler of Mundukondapola was Prince Irugal Bandara who belonged to the Solar dynasty.[62] A well-known myth recorded in the Kurunegala Vistharaya[63] and elsewhere, says that Irugal Bandara's father was the sun, and his mother, Biso Bandara, was born of long leaved dunuke flower,[64] outside of normal bodily processes. The myth also says that the prince obtained milk from a stone. Because of Irugal's connection with the sun, his descendants were given the title of Suriya or sun.

The Surya clan could have been a clan that migrated from India many centuries ago, and who lived in the area and held local leaderships. Palm-leaf manuscripts often refer to migrants who belong to the Surya dynasty. The King Wimaladharmasuriya of Kandy also belonged to the same Surya dynasty. There are a few deities in Seven Korale with the name of Bandara, giving hints that this was an aristocratic clan (potential Indian migrants in early ages)

---

[62] Descends from the god sun, Irugal literally meaning "sunstone".

[63] Modder, F (1893), Kurunegala Vistharaya.

[64] Pandanus foetodus.

which produced notable chieftains but was gradually became extinct or assimilated.

Does the Sri Lankan Irugal race originate from India? Traditional Indian puranic literature discloses information about a Solar dynasty that blossomed in North India. Strangely, the sunflower was the symbol used to represent these people. The Indian Solar dynasty[65] was founded by the legendary King Ikshvaku in North India.[66] They lived in harmony with the Lunar dynasty, which comprises one of the other main lineages of the Kshatriya (kings) Varna. This information suggests that the Solar dynasty and the Lunar dynasty enjoyed similar high social status.

Vanni Vitti books and Bandaravaliyas refers to the stories of Brāhmi (Hirugot) and Kshatriya (Sandagot) dynasties that migrated to Sri Lanka in the medieval times. It is doubtful if all elite migrants who came to Sri Lanka belonged to either Hirugot or Sandagot, or it is possible some just claimed these dynasties for their advantage. It is also difficult to conclude that Irugal Bandara had any connection to the Indian Solar dynasty. Nevertheless, his lineage presents mythical stories about his origin, which are like Hindu legends.

Downfall of Mundukondapola.

According to Kurunegala vistharaya,[67] Irugal Bandara lived on Naathagena Kanda (Hillock or hill of Naathagane) while the Prince Idirimana (prince in Sinhalese is Kumaraya), his brother, resided at Bogoda. Prince Palanay Kumaraya, potentially another brother, lived at Kelimuna, a village next to Bogoda.

---

[65] Suryawansa, or Hirugot or Hiru gothra or the Ikshvaku dynasty.

[66] Zimmer, Heinrich (1952).

[67] Modder, F (1893), Kurunegala Vistharaya.

Irugal Bandara was a powerful and independent prince. And the tradition records that the prince was powerful and proud of himself and was terribly greedy. His enemies employed a band of hooligans to assassinate him. Nawagathe Rala was the person who assassinated Irugal Bandara. This incident took place at the Bandarakoswatta[68] tank while the prince was preparing to bathe. The legend says that the head, after being severed, had fallen on the rock, which formed part of the bund, and the rock was split apart. Owing to the circumstance, the rock was called Pattaragala (split rock).

Further, owing to the circumstances of this high crime, the people of Devamadda region were considered disloyal. To commemorate the incident, a stone pillar was erected, which served as a sign to prohibit recruitment of men of this district or for the service of the court. The leader of the coup, a man of Navagathte, was tried and hanged at Rukattana for this high crime. Of his accomplices, the man of Dikvehera was impaled, and the man of Rankaravuwa was tied to two high posts brought near to each other and released to be torn into two parts.[69]

Malala Vittiya (pg. 80) also records a story about the assassination of one of Irugal Malala Bandara at Bandarakoswaththa. There is no mention about a Mundakondapola ruler. However, according to the Malala Vittiya manuscript, this Bandara became a deity and was worshiped as Uduweriya Bandara. The proper connection between the deity Uduweriya Bandara and the ruler Irugal Bandara is not revealed.

Following the assassination of Irugal Bandara, the Prince Edirimanna (potentially Irugal Bandara's brother) became the king

---

[68] Bandarakoswatta means the king's jack tree grove (this was the place where Robert Knox and his father lived until the latter died.); Modder, F (1893), *Kurunegala Vistharaya.*

[69] Modder, F (1893), Kurunegala Vistharaya.

at Mundukondapola. This is the king that has been identified by vanni vitti books as "the divine Great King Edirisuriya residing in his great palace of Muṇḍukoṇḍapola in Dēvamädda".[70]

Rajavaliya refers to Mundukondapola when Vidiye Bandara had hostilities with Mayadunne at Sithawaka. Vidiye Bandara fled Kotte and presented himself before the king Edirimanna Surya of the Irugal race at that time, who ruled Mundukondapola. Both Rajavaliya[71] and Kurunegala vistharaya identify the Irugal race. There seems to be several Edirisuriyas or Edirimannasuriyas at Devamadda Palace at Mundukondapola. All belonged to the lineage of Irugal Bandara. Irugal Bandara was one of the many Bandara gods, most of them are worshiped by the ancestors in Sath Korale.

Historical records identify Edirimannasuriya as a cousin of Vidiye Bandara. Having no other place to retreat to, because of the hostilities existing in Sitawaka, Vidiye Bandara went there and presented himself before King Edirimanna Surya. This king gave him the village Bogoda where the king himself was living. Vidiye Bandara had earlier agreed to offer his son, Vijayapala, to a sister of Edirimanna Surya.

However, Vidiye Bandara staged a coup to kill Edirimanna Surya and to establish himself as the ruler of the Seven Korale, which was a large dominion. After his betrayal was revealed, he had to flee to the Jaffna kingdom with his son Vijayapala. Soon after, both were killed during a skirmish with a Jaffna chief (Modder, 1893, pgs. 176-177).

After Edirimanna Surya's death, a skilful Sinhalese army commander with the name of Domingo was conferred the title of

---

[70] Obeyesekere, 2019. Mundukondapola.

[71] Rajavaliya mentions a city names Mundukondapola in Devamadda and a king of Sola-lineage (Irugal) called Edirimanna who ruled from the city.

the king of Mundukondapola. It is believed that Domingo was also from Surya Dynasty, but he had been baptised by the Portuguese. He became the next king of Mundukondapola with the name of Edirimannasuriya Bandara.

The fame and good fortune of Domingo Edirimannasuriya was short-lived. His enemy was Dom Fernando, alias Samarakon Rala, a highly able and disciplined another Sinhala officer, loyal to Dharmapala and the Portuguese. In 1596, when Samarakon Rala was in Udunuvara, Domingo Edirimannasuriya attacked him with a large army, but he was beaten. He asked a pardon for his sin but in the European style of the time, he suffered the fate of those guilty of treason. He was killed on the 14th of July, in 1596.

Queyros, the famous Portuguese historian, writes about the slaying, "Forthwith his hands were cut off, and afterwards his head, and his body quartered and placed in public places …where it remained for some days till the boys played their games with his skull".[72]

The Portuguese looted and destroyed Mundukondapola Palace in 1597 with the assistance of Samarakon Rala. After that event, Samarakon Rala oversaw Seven Korale. Finally, Kuruvita Rala who enjoyed the support of the Portuguese as well as that of King Senerath of Kandy, oversaw Sath Korale. He was killed in 1620.

It is difficult to assume if Samarakon Rala or Kuruwita Rala were reigning from Mundukondapola. It can be assumed that the last trace of the glory and wealth of Mundukondapola ceased after 1597, when the palace was looted by the Portuguese.[73]

---

[72] De Queyroz, F. (1982). The Temporal and Spiritual Conquest of Ceylon.

[73] Obeyesekere, G. (2019). Mundukondapola.

Mundukondapola Palace – Where is it Located?

As previously mentioned Mundukondapola means "a place in the shape of a top-knot".[74] This name suggests its location on a hill that rises from low land.

Paul E Pieris gives us insight into the location of Mundukondapola Palace. He describes it as a sheltered hollow of a few acres, but apparently secured from enemies:

> "A majestic ring of stone encircles the great hollow; here and there rising thirty or forty feet from the surface, large caves afford a dry and secure retreat in times of peril. Artificial piles of stone helped to strengthen the natural depression in this majestic rampart, while the approach from the village of Kirimune lies over rugged ground hemmed in by enormous boulders. The entrance is through a tunnel formed by a rock, rising near a hundred feet in height, and resting against the great mass by its side". (Pieris, 1992, pg. 340)

Pieris refers to a Brāhmi inscription carved over a thousand years earlier, which states that one of the caves belonged to the monks of the four quarters, but in later times used as a guard post:

> "The top of the main rock, which can also be approached by means of some steps hollowed out in the surface of the stone, is a position of extraordinary strength, every approach being carefully protected by artificial works; and a handful of men posted here could hold a much stronger force at bay for an indefinite time. Even if the entrance were forced, the enemy would have to proceed through a passage a few feet broad between the main rock and the perpendicular side of an immense cube of stone." (Pieris, 1992, p. 340)

Though the source of Pieris' information is not clear, it seems that he had visited the spot. Rajavaliya refers to the Vidiye Bandara seeking refuge at Mundukondapola without a geographical

---

[74] Obeyesekere, G (2019). Mundukondapola.

reference to the location. Vidiye Bandara lived at Bogoda village. Gananath Obeyesekere (2019) states that his research could not identify the ruins of this city.

The location of the palace should be in the area between Wariyapola and Kurunegala cities, and in the vicinity of Nathagane and Bogoda villages. Any ruins of this palace and any fortresses apparently have not been yet clearly identified. Kurunegala vistharaya provides the principal villages surrounding the city of Mundukondapola were: Bogoda, Pallewahala, Natagena, Kudapathwehera, Kandegedara Rukaththana, Udakatura, Yatikatura, Navagatta, Sivalogedara, and Himukumbura.

Manawadu (2017) presents a different theory about the location of the Muṇḍukoṇḍapola Palace complex. Recent discoveries under the project Central Cultural Fund and named Wayamba Cultural Quadrangle, unearthed remnants of a building complex from Kande Medagama Raja Maha Viharaya (Nikasala Nuwara) site. According to Manawadu, these ruins did not belong to monastic architecture, and could be guessed as from the lost city of Muṇḍukoṇḍapola.

Halfway up the slope of a mountain, there is a cave temple with Kandyan paintings of the 17th century or afterwards and is believed to have been built by King Wimaladharmasuriya (1592-1604). Manawadu believes that it could have been built when the locality was flourishing as the capital city of Edirimannasuriya, or when it was transferred to a monastery at the destruction of the city in 1597. Manawadu emphasises that the historic layer unearthed from the Nikasala Nuwara Raja Maha Vihare site is not compatible with a conventional monastic establishment of Sri Lanka. It has closer resemblance with a regal complex of bygone days. There is another view that Nikasala Nuwara belongs to the era of Prince Wijaya, or he was buried there and built a tomb.[75]

This chapter presented an introduction to this regional kingdom of Mundukondapola, its kings and the political environment under which it operated when it welcomed and supported the seven Brāhmin families. The Palace of Mundukondapola, which held vivid significance with a diverse history, is still waiting to be discovered.

The forthcoming chapter will explore the broader historical context of Indian migration to Sri Lanka. Subsequently, three consecutive chapters will be dedicated to documenting and analysing the significant waves of Indian migrations to Sri Lanka, with a specific emphasis on the medieval period. These chapters will provide essential contextual information to facilitate a deeper understanding of the migration of the Brahmin contingents to Sri Lanka.

---

[75] Information provided by K M S Rakogama.

Chapter Seven

Historical Patterns of Indian Migration into Sri Lanka

In this chapter, I would like to spare a brief account of the South Indian migrations in a broader context to identify emerging historical patterns of Indian migration to Sri Lanka.

Evidence for the earliest human occupation of the island can be traced to approximately forty thousand years ago, when hunter-gatherer Mesolithic peoples occupied inland caves of the dry zone (S.U. Deraniyagala, 1992; Kennedy and S.U. Deraniyagala, 1989). However, until 900 BCE, there is little archaeological evidence of human settlement. That is, until the Iron Age brought permanent settlements, rice cultivation, cattle, and horse domestication.

As an island nation located at the southern tip of India, the civilisation in Sri Lanka grew amid the influence of India. The Indian ingredients (demographical, social, and cultural etc.) in Sri Lankan history go back a several millennia.

Indian Factor.

The biocultural landscape of Sri Lanka is the result of successive waves of immigrants from India. The latecomers interacted with the early inhabitants of the island. These interactions contributed to creating a range of cultural and biological composition among its people. There was a similar process taking place in India.

The modern humans from Central Africa crossed India to populate Southeast Asia and Australasia approximately 75,000 years ago.[76] Subsequently, several human migrations to India occurred at various stages and, by about 9,000 BC to 4,000 BC, these migrants represented Mesolithic people (middle stone age) in India and Sri Lanka.

Apparently, the recent South Indian history was formed by an intimate mixture of Northern Indian (Aryan) and Southern Indian (Dravidian) systems. Overall, three stages[77] of historical knowledge are recognisable. First, an aboriginal period prior to the Dravidian, a second Dravidian period, and third, a period of Aryan influence, particularly through religion and customs. However, the aboriginal and Dravidian features are still strongly continuing.[78]

Sagayadoss (2015)[79] supports an Aryan and Dravidian synthesis. Over many centuries, a fusion of Aryan and Dravidian occurred, and this is a complex process that historians have labelled as the "Indo-Aryan synthesis."

Lockard (2007, pg. 50) states that, "The encounters that resulted from Aryan migration brought together several very different peoples and cultures, reconfiguring Indian society. Over many centuries a fusion of Indo-Aryan peoples and Dravidian occurred, a complex process that historians have labelled the Indo-Aryan synthesis." Lockard suggests that "Hinduism can be seen

---

[76] Cunliffe, B (ed). (2001). Cassel's Atlas of World History.

[77] Manual of the administration of the Madrass Presidency, pg. 112.

[78] Manual of the administration of the Madrass Presidency, pg. 112.

[79] Sagayadoss A. (2015). *South Indian Black's Culture and Religion Academia and Society*, 2(2) ISSN: 2393-9419.

historically as a synthesis of Aryan beliefs with Harappan and other Dravidian traditions that developed over many centuries."

The religion that the Aryans brought with them mingled with the religion of the native people, and the culture that developed between them became classical Hinduism.

These transformations can be extended to ethnic groups in India. For example, to many ethnologists, the Pandyans, Pllavas and the Cheras were non-Dravidians by ethnicity. They were believed to be migrated from the north or elsewhere at a remote period in history that scholars have been unable to determine precisely. However, having migrated to the south, they adopted Dravidian as the language of communication.[80] Subsequently, Cholas, Pandyans and Pallavas became one nationality, giving up their previous identities.

The enrichment of civilisation was subsequent upon the constant and lively interchange of ideas, experiences, and material foundations among these different races.

Rice Culture and Trade.

Early human civilisation evolved in India together with the evolution of agriculture. Settled human life with agriculture began in the western margins of the Indus River approximately 9,000 years ago.[81] The earliest archaeological evidence for agriculture in the region dates back to 8,000–9,000 years before the present (in Pakistan) and involved wheat and barley originally domesticated in West Asia. This gradually advanced into the Indus valley civilisation of the third millennium BCE. It is only during the Iron Age (1500-200 BCE) that rice cultivation became more widely established through north-eastern India and was introduced to Sri

---

80 Anuradha Senevirathna, 2004. Anusmrithi, Pgs. 315-316.
81 Belwood, 2015.

Lanka from the northeast. The wet rice farmers in the Iron Age were the last significant agriculturist migration within South Asia.[82]

The Agricultural Revolution was first applied to northern India and became noticeable in the south only during the second half of the first millennium BCE (Franke-Vogt, 2001). In Sri Lanka, however, rice culture developed around 900 BCE, and iron was used at Anuradhapura between 900 and 600 BCE (Coningham et al., 2006: 648; Fuller, 2008: 765). Sri Lanka was further advanced into rice culture and livestock breeding (specifically cattle and horses). The first settlement at Anuradhapura is dated between the ninth and fifth centuries BCE; it had become a fortified city covering approximately 100 hectares by the fourth century BCE (Coningham et al. 1999: 54). According to traditions, such as by the Mahavamsa, the first Sinhalese kingdom was founded by a prince called Vijaya, who came from Kalinga. The Greek ambassador of Seleucus at the court of the Maurya king Chandragupta (third century BCE), reports that Sri Lanka exported elephants to Kalinga. Kalinga and Sri Lanka maintained links over the centuries.[83]

The following period also saw a significant development in southern India and Sri Lanka. Major irrigation systems were implemented under state control, not only in Maurya India, but also widely in Sri Lanka, around Anuradhapura. Small states appeared in southern India centred on large river valleys that were favourable to intensive rice culture. These states were also sea and trade oriented. Many archaeological sites dating to this period have been discovered in Karnataka, Tamil Nadu, and Andhra Pradesh. The first urban centres emerged in South India.[84]

---

[82] Belwood, 2015.

[83] Philippe, 2019, Worlds of the Indian Ocean, Vol 1. Pg. 439.

[84] Philippe, 2019, Worlds of the Indian Ocean, Vol 1, pg. 445.

Southern Cultural Region.

Indrapala (2007) identifies a naturally formed cultural region that existed from prehistoric times to approximately 1200 AD among South India and Sri Lanka. That was within the modern Indian States of Kerala and Tamil Nadu and the southern parts of Karnataka and Andhra Pradesh together with Sri Lanka. Palk Strait and the Gulf of Mannar was the unifier of this cultural region.

Even after the emergence of states, there was always a two-way flow of influence, particularly in arts, religion, and technology, between Sri Lanka and India. Indrapala claims that Sinhalese and Sri Lankan Tamils eventually descended from the Mesolithic people who occupied all parts of the island in ancient times. The distribution of the Indian Mesolithic peoples is demonstrated by the archaeological evidence scattered across the South Asian landmass from Afghanistan in the west, and east to Assam, from the Kashmir Valley of the Himalayan ranges south to the island of Sri Lanka. There was no displacement of the ancient people by northern newcomers (Aryans) in later times because they were all assimilated.

The trade was the single important factor responsible for the arrival of Prakrit-speakers (Sanskrit-based language) from eastern and western regions of India to this cultural region. Prakrit-speaking traders were also responsible for establishing urban centres and chiefdoms around the Gulf of Mannar (particularly in and around Thambapanni and Madurai) and Brahmanism (Hindu religion). In fact, Mesolithic people spoke different languages, but it was replaced by Prakrit because of elite dominance (or sanskritisation). This new medium was beneficial for communication among different linguistic groups.

Thambapanni (Sri Lanka) and Madurai (South India) emerged as two major chiefdoms that later grew into leading kingdoms in the

71

region. Thambapanni found a permanent place in the Pali chronicles of Sri Lanka and Madurai also grew prominence in South Indian legends.

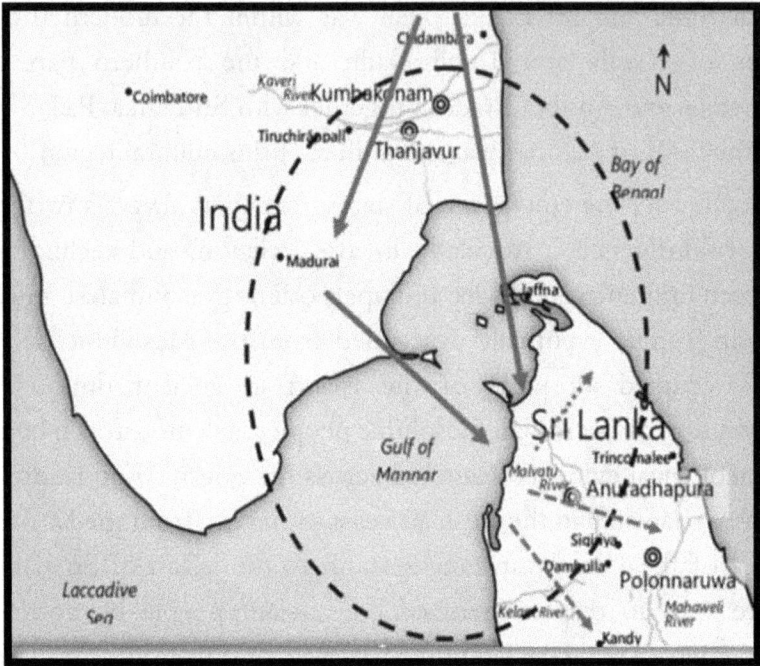

Map 3: Southern Cultural Region

At these two coastal centres, Mesolithic people came into contact with north Indian newcomers (Indrapala, 2007). Eventually, Mesolithic people adopted the North Indian culture. Mendis (1948, pg. 28) states that, "The first point to be remembered then is that from the very beginning, Ceylon formed a unit of Indian civilisation."

The new culture helped local chiefs for wielding authority to assume greater importance and power. At first, there could have been conflicts but later gained authority by either marrying into the families of chiefs or by using their superior military power. In any case the chiefs themselves and other local elites adopted the culture of the traders and opened the way for sanskritisation.

The main aspects of this pattern were the arrival of so-called civilised people, like the Brāhmaṇas and Kshatriyas to the ports (Indrapala, 2007). This arrival, by design or accident, required either conflict or reconciliation. The newcomers were more attractive in terms of their novelty and power. The reconciliation was strategically preferable regardless of the cultural dominance of the North Indians. The marriages of the leaders of the visitors with the leading maidens of the locals established a North Indian style ruling lineage in the Madurei region in South India and the Thambapanni region in Sri Lanka. The rulers adopted the North Indian Brāhminical ideology in the new polity, linked their family with a North Indian lineage, and introduced Brahmminical rituals. The local rulers established the Sanskrit language by the appointment of Brāhmins as court priests (purohits).

It was fashionable to adopt Sanskrit/Prakriti names or to Sanskritise their names by the locals. Even place names got Sanskritised or altered to new Sanskrit names. Thus, the way was opened for the flow of North Indian cultural practices and ideals among the South Indian and Sri Lankan elites.

Thambapanni chiefs gradually grew their principalities in the north-western region and expanded their boundaries into the hinterland along the Malwathu river. Before the establishment of Anuradhapura Kingdom in Sri Lanka some Sanskritised principalities in the region included: Upathissa Gama,[85] Anurardha Gama, Udeni Gama and Uruwela Gama. Eventually, Anuradhapura became the first Sri Lankan empire, uniting small states and principalities of the whole island. The foundation for the Sri Lankan

---

[85] Regarded as the first Brāhmin settlement.

history commenced. However political, cultural, technological, and commercial bonds between Sri Lankan kingdoms – Anuradhapura, Polonnaruwa, Dambadeniya, Yapahuwa, Kurunegala, Kotte and Sithawaka – and South Indian states continued for another two millennia.

In the preceding chapters (9 to 12), I briefly trace other South Indian migrations which occurred by accident or otherwise, frequently or infrequently, throughout Sri Lankan history. I try to focus on leading streams of migrants that formed Indian roots in the ethnic formation in Sri Lanka. Despite strong north and south Indian influence, Sri Lankan independently evolved into a nation with a unique identity.

I will include a brief description on Kerala migrants, as it is a place where many migrants came to Sri Lanka in addition to Tamil Nadu, and I highlight one method of migration, which is through mercenary influx.

Kerala Migrants.

Sri Lanka attracted migrants mainly from South Indian states of Kerala, Tamil Nadu, and Karnataka during medieval times.

Kerala migration to Sri Lanka occurred throughout the history. But prominent Kerala migrants to Sri Lanka can be identified at two phases. One phase was the Kalinga Magha (himself from Kerala) invasion and the Kerala mercenaries that helped to overthrew Magha occupation. The Magha followers and the mercenaries were assimilated to Sri Lankan society. The second phase was the peaceful Kerala chieftains (Malala Bandaras) who migrated to Sri Lanka since the Dambadeni kingdom and accelerated during the Kotte kingdom.

The most famous Karela invader to Sri Lanka was Kalinga Magha. Kalinga Magha landed in Karainagar in 1215 AD with a large army of 24,000 Kerala and Tamil soldiers. This army later became more than 44,000 including Chola, Pandya and Kerala soldiers. First, he brought the Jaffna principality under his control. Then he marched to Polonnaruwa and defeated Parakrama Pandyan II and ruled the kingdom for twenty-one years. He was expelled from Polonnaruwa in 1236 and withdrew to Jaffna. He ruled Jaffna until 1255. After Magha, Aryachakrawarthi, another Kalinga lineage, established his powerful kingdom in Jaffna, and he was influential in Sri Lankan politics (Liyanagamage, 1988).

The Magha's army have been described in the *Culavamsa* to be ruthless, and to have destroyed the Buddhist religion, ransacked, and destroyed many stupas. However, late mercenaries and peaceful merchants from Kerala kept foothold in Kandy, Matale, Gampola and Kotte. Kerala merchants emerged as powerful groups, not only in the economic but also in the political arena. For example, Alakeswaras (or Alagakkonara) of Kerala origin,[86] a powerful ruling group in Raigama and later in Kotte, derived their power from their ability to control sea-borne trade. They were instrumental in restricting the southward expansion of the Aryachakrawarthi of Jaffna, who were also interested in controlling these trading activities in the Indian Ocean. Mehenawara is another family group who came from Kerala and settled down in Dedigama, Gampola and Kotte. Although the Mehenawara family were initially merchants, they became powerful as royal officials.[87]

Apart from invasions and invitations from the local kings, some South Indian families including Kerala move to island first as refugees and then as peaceful migrants. They also embraced Buddhism. The Alakeswaras family was originally a trading family

---

[86] G Obeyesekere, 2004.

[87] G Obeyesekere, 2005.

and they accumulated considerable political power and reached the climax when he led the forces against Jaffna becoming triumphant.

Indrapala (2007) reiterates that Alakeswaras were not the only Keralas that came to Sri Lanka, there were also others who came from South Indian territories who settled in the northern parts of the island in increasing scales. Sinhalese in the north became a minority and eventually submerged.[88] They became Tamilised in the course of time. The reverse order took place in the south. Tamil minorities living among the Sinhalese were Sinhalised with the passage of time. Alakeswaras were no exception to this historical process.

Lona Devarajah (1972) identifies that the peaceful migrants who settled down in uninhabited places, such as Puttalam, Mannar and Nuwarakalawiya (largely Anuradhapura District) in the 13th and 14th centuries were people from Kerala. As already noted, the origin of Bandarawaliya was a deviation from Tamil *"Paththaram"*, and she says that these people belonged to the Wellala caste in Bharatha. Further, from the end of 13th century, stone inscriptions and literature reveal that the titles of honour, such as *Epa* and *Mapa* were replaced by *Bandara*. From the 17th to 18th centuries onward, Bandaras was used to call the people in the highest echelon, and the children of the second wife of the King or aristocrats.

Palm-leaf manuscripts reveal peaceful migrations by a few Kerala princes and nobles. They are famously known as Malala Bandaras as well as Malala Kumaras (princes). As stated elsewhere, they appeared to be experts and hardened warriors. Their migration has been recorded by a few palm-leaf manuscripts with different variations. It appeared that Malala Bandaras settled in Sath Korale (particularly in Vanni Hathpattu) or adjoining principalities. Some

---

[88] Fernando, Denis A. 1987.

Malala Bandaras developed marriages with the descendants of Brāhmin families, who were early settlers or compatriots. Descriptions of Malala Bandaras who settled in Sath Korale Vanni Hathpattu are provided in Chapters 9 and 12.

South Indian Mercenaries.

South Indian mercenaries often made Sri Lanka home after marrying local women. This was one dominant avenue from which the invited Indian migrants became Sri Lankans. Sri Lankan kings regularly sought South Indian mercenaries during internal conflicts and when foreign invasions occurred. The mercenaries came to Sri Lanka in thousands at a time.

The Mukkara Hatana ("The Mukkuvar War") palm-leaf manuscript[89] provides comprehensive details about the manner the mercenaries were hired and employed in local battles. This manuscript is written in Sinhalese, the work celebrates the victory of the Karaiyars, also known as Karavas, over the Mukkuvars, who invaded the western coast of Sri Lanka in the 15th century. The Mukkuvar were led by their leader, Nala Mudaliyar. About 7700 Karaiyar chieftains from Kanchipuram (Karnataka), Kaveripattinam (Tamil Nadu), and Kilakarai (Tamil Nadu) arrived in Sri Lanka following the invitation of the King Parakramabahu VI of Kotte to flush out the Mukkuvar invaders.

This event and what followed are examples of the grand mercenary adaptation model in Sri Lanka. When Mukkaru invaded, the King asked his chieftains, "Who do you think are mighty enough to fight Mukkuva hosts?" To which the nobles replied, "If we would engage them in battle, it would be best to summon here the armies from three countries (rata) namely, Kanchipura,

---

[89] Raghavan, 1961; Mukkara Hatana.

Kaveripattanam, and Killakkarai." Consequently, the Karaiyars army was brought in from India for the war.

The South Indian Karaiyars chieftains who led the mercenary army were: Vammunatta Dever, Kurukulanattu Devar, Manikka Thalavan, Adiyarasa Adappa Unnahe, Varna Suriya Dombaranada Adappa Unnahe, Kurukula Suriya Mudiyanse, Paradakula Suriya Mudiyanse, and Arasakula Suriya Mudiyanse.

The Karaiyars chieftains overthrew Mukkara garrisons of Puttalam and Nagapattinum with a loss of 2500 troops. They also lost one of their leaders: Manikka Thalavan. Manikka Thalaivan's sons were eventually adopted by King Parakramabahu VI, and one of whom is known as Sapumal Kumaraya, who later captured the Jaffna kingdom and became the regional king, or the governor, of Jaffna.

The Karaiyars chieftains and thousands of soldiers settled after the victory in the area between Chilaw and Negombo. More details about Karaiyars settlements are provided in Chapter 11 under the section on the Karava community.

This chapter presented an account of how the human civilisation evolved in the Indian subcontinent, providing an insight into the current demographic landscape. As an island located at the southern tip, the civilisation in Sri Lanka formed with the continuous influence from India. Sri Lanka was influenced initially through trade, but later from cultural domination (Sanskritization). Even though Sri Lanka developed its own character but the waves of immigrations from India from time to time refreshed the cultural developments. An ongoing Kerala migration to Sri Lanka was noted together with the trends of South Indian mercenaries making Sri Lanka Home.

The next chapter describes the historical phenomenon of Brāhmi migration (general) to Sri Lanka and the way they were absorbed into the Sri Lankan scheme of things. That account will assist in examining if the seven Brāhmin families had to go through the same process, or not, in their assimilation.

Chapter Eight

Brāhmi Migration to Sri Lanka and Their Fate

The arrival of the seven Brāhmin contingent was not something new. There has been influx of Brāhmin to Sri Lanka throughout history, including some acceleration during the medieval times. This chapter takes a brief account of different groups of Brāhmi immigrants to Sri Lanka in the history with the assistance of palm-leaf manuscripts and identify their fate.

Brāhmins Migration to Sri Lanka.

Gananath Obeyesekere is one of the key scholars who identified and popularised the information about Brāhmi migration to Sri Lanka during medieval times and about their subsequent flight. He organised many unpublished traditional records such as palm-leaf manuscripts or vitti books, kadayim books and Bandaravaliyas, published them, and brought our attention to the emerging information in these new group of chronicles. He revived our academic interests into hidden historical realities in the medieval times through these manuscripts.

Brāhmins resided in Sri Lanka from the beginning of Thambapanni cultural era. Brāhmins were used as royal advisors for state administration, and they played a role in establishing and maintaining cultural connections with India.[90] For example, the delegation from King Devanampiyathissa to Ashoka was led by Sali Pabbatha and Thiwakka Brāhmins. They were instrumental in bringing in Ven Mahinda[91] and Sangamiththa[92] to Sri Lanka to establish Buddhism. These Brāhmins established the friendship between Ashoka and Devanampiyathissa and their knowledge in state affairs and diplomacy were useful. There are records related to Brāhmins conducting the coronations of Sri Lankan kings. If local senior Brāhmins were not available, the Brāhmins were brought from India to conduct these ceremonies.[93]

Brāhmi Migrants During the Dambadeni Period.

Palm-leaf manuscripts glorify the history of Brāhmin arrivals in Sri Lanka at various stages in the history. Vanni Kadayim book (pg. 87) and Srilak Kada Ayuru vitti book (Bandarawaliya, 2005, pg. 77) records an event about a group of Brāhmins settling in Sri Lanka during the Dambadeniya Period and demonstrated their mystical powers. That is, a group of seven Brāhmins landed at Munnaswaram and built a few *devala* or gods' shrines. Next, they travelled to Lindapitiya and dug a well and stayed for seven days, and then travelled to Annaruwa. At this place, they performed puja and showed the magical power of making milk out of a rock. The king of Dambadeniya met these Brāhmins, and the eldest Brahman Rala was awarded Annaruwewa village and seven "amuna" of paddy land with a royal decree. Other Brāhmins were arranged to settle at Bamunupola, Brāhmaṇagama, Bamuna Kotuwa, Brāhmaṇa Daluwa, and Bamunu Gedara.

---

[90] Obeyesekere, Mirandor. (2014). *Brāhmins in Sri Lanka.*

[91] King Asoka's son as a Buddhist monk lead the delegation who brought in Buddhism.

[92] King Ashoka's daughter who brought in a Bodhi sapling.

[93] Obeyesekere, Mirandor. (2014). *Brāhmins in Sri Lanka.*

According to Malala Vittiya (pg. 81), another group of seven Brāhmins landed at Mutupantiya established a *devale* or shrine for God Vishnu on Munnessarama cliff. For their skills, the Sitavaka-Kotte king granted villages of Bamunavala, Bambara-gedara, Brāhmaṇagama, Bamunu-gedara, Bamini-golla, Bamunakoṭuva, Itana-vatta, Divulgas-piṭiya, Kalgaha, Mirihan-piṭiya, Konanattava, Magula, Ganvarala and Mamunuva.

Kurunegala Vistharaya[94] lists various locations where Brāhmins lived in the Kurunegala Kingdom. There had been five hundred Brāhmin houses in Kurunegala historic city limits alone. This city had a street called " Brāhmin Street" (Bamunu-vidiya) and another street called "Street of the Gods" (Deviyo-vidiya). It is possible certain parts of the city had been allocated to Brāhmins. Those two streets are remaining. The Kurunegala Vistharaya also provides names of Royal villages like Bamunugedara, Bamunugama. Bamunkotutva, Bamunussa, and Bamundvela to which amounts of paddy lands were allocated by the kings.

Arrival of Brāhmins to Matale.[95]

The Matale Vitti book (M1) written in the Kandyan era, provides details of the Brahman chiefs who settled in Matale. In fact, they claimed that they were the seventh generation of Brāhmaṇa chiefs who brought the Bodhi tree. For example, a poem in the vanni vitti (pg. 63) says that the king was kind enough to grant land to settle in Sri Lanka when the new migrants claimed that they were the seventh generation of descendants of the great grandparents who accompanied the sacred Bodhi tree and received land. The new migrants made a request to grant those ancestral lands and re-establish their legacy:

---

94   Modder, F (1893), Kurunegala Vistharaya
95   This section presents materials primarily from Obeyesekere, 2013 and 2016.

"Sathveni mutththa ape kiyanne,
wadina bo raja samagawa enne,
wunder labuna rata denda kiyanne,
emawita rajugen karuna wenne."

"(Translation) We belong to the seventh generation of those who brought the Holy Bo Tree here. We ask the king to be kind enough to return our land".

Among the Brāhmi land winners include: Somadanta-Brāhmaṇa-Rala, Srivisṇu Brāhmaṇa-Rala, Srirama Brāhmaṇa-Rala, Solamgiri Brāhmaṇa-Rala, Kotudeyiya Brāhmaṇa-Rala, and Sridanta Brāhmaṇa-Rala who came from Sridanta Desha region in India. According to the Matale Vitti book (M1) Somanada [Sonadanta Brāhmaṇa-Rala] was placed in charge of Nagapaṭṭalama, Srivisṇu Brāhmaṇa-Rala settled in Aluvihara, Srirama Brāhmaṇa-Rala settled in Ratvatta, Kotudeyya Brāhmaṇa-Rala settled in Kotuvegedera. Sridanta Brāhmaṇa-Rala built a *dagaba* (Buddhist stupa) in the south, and enshrined the relics brought by him, and settled down in Monaravila, while Vadande Brāhmaṇa-Rala settled down in Vabodapola, Madiva Viramesvaraya settled down at Madipola. Matale Brāhmins appeared to claim that they came from Madya-desha. Madya-desha in Sri Lankan topography of the period mostly refers to the area of the present-day Buddha Gaya in Bihar.[96]

By contrast, the kadayim book (the second book, Matale Kadayim book, we call it M2) written during the reign of King Kirthi Sri Rajasinghe, does not list the Brāhmins as a collectively as defined in the M1, but mentions ten Brāhmanas, none of whom make any direct reference to the mythic ancestry of the previous Brāhmins of Matale.[97] Only four families have even indirect connections with the

---

[96] Obeyesekere, 2013. The Comings of Brāhmins.
[97] Obeyesekere, 2013.

Bodhi tree. *"Sonaka Brāhmanaa Rāla, who came from Madya-desha lives in the village of Hulangamuva."* He is a descendant of Somanada Brāhmaṇa Rāla who settled down in Nagapaṭṭalama.

According to M2, a woman named Brāhmaṇa Ran Manika, daughter of Kopuru Brāhmaṇa Rāla, resides at Ratvatta. Obeyesekere (2013) thinks she is clearly a descendant of Sri Rama Brāhmaṇa Rāla because she has inherited the village of Ratvatta originally belonging to her ancestor. However, the male member of that line seems to have at least retained the name of his ancestor, for example, "Sri Rama Brāhmaṇa Rāla resides in Atipola". The preceding account indicated that some of the most distinguished Sri Lankans such as the Ratvattes to which former Prime Minister Sirimavo Bandaranayaka originally belonged to this line of Brāhmin settlers (Obeyesekere, 2013).

M2 recognises that Vadandee Brāhmana Rāla lives in Vaudapola and this is the second Brāhmaṇa Rāla, whose name is unchanged from the M1, implying a continuous family tradition.

A new set of Brāhmi dignitaries, however, emerged in the second Matale Kadayim Book (M2). For example, the "son of Hirugot Brāhmaṇa Rāla is settled in Kappitipola." Obeyesekere (2013) believes that this family might be the ancestors of the very distinguished family of Kappetipola, one of whom led the great rebellion against the British in 1817-1818.

Hirugot is an old usage meaning Suryagotra or Rivigotra (Solar dynasty), namely Brāhmins claiming descent from the sun. This indicates the potential migration of people from Indian Solar dynasty. Therefore, Mundukondapola kings with lineage to Solar dynasty had no problem welcoming migrants form their own lineage.

M2 identifies that one Brāhmaṇa Rāla appears to be in poor states: "The son of Hirugot Brāhmaṇa Rāla lives in the *makaral hena* (a swidden plot that and grows long beans) at Kahagala in the Sat Korale". Despite solar origins, M2 explains Hirugot's second son was really poor because he lived in a *hena*. This son had moved from Matale (Sathara Korale) to another large district known as Sat Korale, looking for more hopeful future. That suggests there have been movement of Brāhman Ralas between Matale (Sathara or four Korale) and Kurunegala (Sath or seven Korale).

M2 also provides information about Brāhmans who descend from Lunar dynasty (Sandagot or moon gotra). For example, a "son of Sandagot Brāhmaṇa Rāla lives at Pahindena-Galagama." That means there were some Brāhmins belonged to a group that contrasts itself to Hirugot (Solar dynasty). Obeyesekere (2013) suggests that Sandagot Brāhmins adopted well known dynastic names associated with Sri Lankan and South Indian kings and/or with Brāhmaṇa gotras coming down from ancient times. Puranic literature identifies Sandagot as Kshatriya Dynasty (kings), and therefore, Hirigot and Sandagot Brāhmins hold similar high social status (Obeyesekere, 2013).

M2 has information about the intermarriage relationships with formally settled and well-established seven Brāhmi migrants. For example, the daughter of Kalahagala Brāhmaṇa Rāla was married to Kandulawa Herat Bandara, implying that this Brāhmaṇa woman was married to a distinguished Sinhala aristocrat who held extensive properties (Obeyesekere, 2013).

Kandulawa is where the Kandulassa Brāhmaṇa Rāla settled according to the Nikawagampaha Vitti Book (N1). That means the seven Brahman Ralas came before the Matale Brāhmins who were stated in M1 and M2, and they were well established. The

Kandulawa Brāhmin family had already gained recognition, accumulated wealth, and enjoyed high aristocratic status. Their descendants would be the Herat Bandara family.

Can a Brāhmin Royalty Claim be Mythical?

Rasanayagam (1926) suggests that Brāhmin and Arya terms apparently have been attributed to great kings and nobles in the Indian History and Sri Lanka History for secondary reasons. It is possible these mythical labels could have been used by some rulers to grab power, stay in power, or validate their authority.

Rasanayagam (1926, pgs. 293 - 297) claims that the Kalinga kings calling themselves Aryans were reigning in the 10th to 12th centuries. And also, in early part of the 13th century in Jaffna, these names were visible with the rulers. They called themselves Arya Chakravarthi and claimed they were descendants from two Brāhmin kings who were appointed by Lord Rama himself after his conquest of Ceylon and the establishment of the Rameswaram temple to rule over the Northern District of Ceylon. They had connected to a Brāhman origin.

Rasanayagam claims that the Kalinga kings were descendants of Chola or Pandya origin and not connected to any Aryan descent. The Brāhmin origin of these Kalinga kings was certainly mythical. They adopted this origin after they attained power and fame. It appeared that some of the Indian royal dynasties manufactured a Puranic genealogy to trace their origin back either to the Sun or to the Moon dynasty. That the kings of Jaffna wore a sacred thread over their shoulders not worn by any other kings of South India or Sri Lanka, was to stamp their Aryan origin.

It is possible in some contexts in India and Sri Lanka had adopted mythical connections to align with the holy Puranic genealogical tradition. We must be cautious about whether some rulers or dynasties attributed mythical identities to raise their social status.

Brāhmin Flight in Sri Lanka.

Obeyesekere (2013) tends to suggest that by the mid-thirteenth century (potentially during the Dambadeniya period) the Sri Lankan caste system had been formalised into four broad classes or kula aligning with the Indian system of things. However, the traditional caste system as prevailing in India, was not strictly speaking operational in Buddhist Sri Lanka as the country was more liberal.

Denis Fernando (1986) claims that the four-caste system was subject to modification and could be attributed to some local conditions. For example, there were only a handful of purohits and the priest around who delegated the teaching of morals, religion, and ritual practices. The peasants represented what was equivalent to the workers (*sudras*), but all communities cultivated land as farmers, irrespective of their specialised occupations which were passed from father to son. The caste system operated only in a very subtle way and was not as oppressive as it was prevailing in Hindu India.[98]

The new migrants, including so called Brāhmins and Kshatriyas, who settled in Sinhala areas embraced Buddhism and assimilated into Sinhala society. Exemptions existed in the coastal areas and in the north.[99] The migrants who became Buddhists continued to worship Hindu Gods and conducted Hindu rituals e.g., offering puja to gods, seeking heavenly interventions from gods, and conducting "yaga and homa [sacrifices]" for divine interventions and healing. Ariyapala (1969, P184-185) states that Kings employed

---

[98] Dennis Fernando, 1986, pg. 91.

[99] Some people who settle in coastal areas embraced Catholicism due to Portuguese and Dutch influence. The people settle in the North continued Hindu practice and spoke Tamil.

purohits to perform Hindu and Brāhministic practices at the palace along with Buddhist rituals.

Obeyesekere (2016) says that these foreign migrants are not only indigenised, but they also brought with them their own gods and religious practices that eventually become part of the mainline beliefs of Sinhala Buddhists. Most of the gods, magical practices, and folk rituals that prevailed in Sri Lanka had their origin in South India but were transformed and often given Buddhist validation and significance. The Buddhism tolerated Hindu fundamentals and permitted these heretical practices to go side by side. Venerable Upali Thero, the Burmese chief monk who came to Sri Lanka to establish Upasampada, with the patronage of Kirthi Sri Rajasinghe (1747-1782) in 1753, was surprised to see many popular Hindu shrines in Kandy and Hindu influence in the ruling class. He apparently discouraged Buddhists to worship Hindu Gods.[100] Gananath Obeyesekere (2016) says it was natural for Buddhism and Hinduism to coexist (particularly during medieval times) due to historical bonds and shared mythical belief systems.[101]

Obeyesekere (2016) notes that Brāhmins had an important role in the Sinhala kingdoms as purohits or gurus/advisors of the royal palace along with Buddhist monks. Many of the vitti books refer to princes, merchants (hetti) and Brāhmins eventually being absorbed into aristocratic "govigama" (cultivator's caste). Obeyesekere (2016) observes that some vitti books that can be assigned to the Dambadeniya and Kurunegala kingdoms, simply account for the presence of Brāhmin families in their midst and gives traditional histories of their origins.

---

[100] Wikipedia, Sivaratnam, 1968.
[101] Gananath Obeyesekere. 2013.

Obeyesekere also notes that most migrants, not just Brāhmins, were males and they presumably married into the local population. It is less likely that they often obtained their wives from India. Given their notions of ritual purity, a few Brāhmins did bring their women with them. They might have brought some women after their arrival to Sri Lanka. Vanni Vitti books mention the arrival of noble Brāhmin women (Bamini Brāhmaṇa Rāla) and men. Many of the

Brāhmins assimilated into the aristocratic segment of the Govigama (Obeyesekere, 2016):

> "...they have dropped their Brāhminic names and become part of the radala or aristocratic segment of the large broad-based caste, the farmer or Govigama. This capacity to absorb the two classic varnas of the Indian scheme has been going on for a long historical period such that the highest varna in the Indian scheme of things, that of the Brāhmins continue to exist as a sub-caste of Govigama which is also the sub-caste or varna of the Kandyan kings. Remember once again that the category sub-caste is our convenient invention and does not exist in empirical reality anywhere in the Matale district or for that matter anywhere in the Kandyan kingdom..." [102]

Eventually, the Brāhmins were absorbed into radala and aristocratic segments of the Govigama caste in Sri Lanka.

This chapter provides an insight into Brāhmin migration that took place throughout history but focused on some groups of Brāhmins who migrated during Dambadeni, Kotte and Kandyan kingdoms. All were absorbed into the Sri Lankan society without trace of their origins. The next chapter presents another community of South Indian migrants who settled in the western and northern parts of Sri Lanka. They are generally known as Vanniars or Vanniwaru.

---

[102] G Obeyesekere, Caste conflicts and discourses during the Kandyan Kingdom: evidence from the Matale District, ACES conference 2016.

Chapter Nine

Vanniyars and South Indian Migrants in the North

This chapter identifies a community of South Indian migrants, from historical regions of Kerala, Pandya and Chola, known as Vanniyars or Vanniwaru, who settled in the western and northern parts of Sri Lanka. Some parts of this region are known as Vanni. It is to be stated that any details of the kingdom that existed in Jaffna is not within the scope of this publication.

Vanni Region and Vanni People.

As previously stated, the dominant North Indian culture originally transformed South Indian states as well as the southern cultural region that included the northern Sri Lanka. An initial historical event that the Sri Lankan chronicles have recorded regarding the North Indian involvement in Sri Lanka is Prince Wijaya, who had ousted from the Kalinga Desha in the 6th BC. However, the South Indian influence was inevitable for many centuries.

Vanniwaru

The history tells us about a particular community group known as Vanni people, Vanniars, Vanni chieftains, and "Vanniwaru". This group appeared to have South Indian connection and evolved as a distinguished Sri Lankan community group. The event of the seven Brāhmins migration provided an account of their interactions with Vanniyars (fluent in Tamil) who had already settled in north-western regions and offered assistance to seven Brāhmins (including Malala Princes though with reasonable contrasts of the periods), giving directions and working as language and other interpreters.

South Indian people settled in the region which can be generally identified as Vanni during the ancient times. These people settled down in the southern region, from Jaffna to Daduru Oya in Kurunegala district, and then spread to Anuradhapura and Trincomalee and to the south to Batticaloa.

Let me illustrate the accounts of the information, regarding these settlements, with the assistance taken from Vitti books, Tamil and Sinhalese chronicles, accounts recorded by historians, and the European records.

Indrapala (2007) and Liyanagamage (1988, 1963) provide a comprehensive insight into Vanni and the origin of northern Vanni chieftains in Sri Lanka. Palm-leaf manuscripts also throw additional information on how the later South Indian migrations had enriched this community from the Dambadeni Period onwards.

As stated earlier, the King had absolute control and rights over all lands. This included not only the lands given to his subjects but the royal officials, officials, and peasants to farm as well. This includes all the forest lands and their produce, including minerals and gems. To prevent the Vanni from falling prey to foreigners at times, he appointed Vanniyas or petty chiefs in charge of forest areas who administered these lands and the king's territory (Fernando, 1986).

It is also important to understand that vanni is also a caste name in modern India. The Vanniyar caste of today in South India follows the profession of cultivation. However, when turned further back in time, these Vanniyar had been warriors rather than cultivators and that the Vanni chieftains enjoyed the status of feudal lords. In the twelfth and thirteenth centuries, several Vanni chiefs were in the service of the Chola and Pandya kings. In the eleventh, twelfth and thirteenth centuries, the Vanniyars were associated with martial pursuits rather than with agriculture. Some of their chiefs were in the service of kings and enjoyed a status like that of other feudal officials of that time.[103]

Traditions relating to the later Vijayanagar period refer to them as a "forest race, a tribe of low cultivators", who built forts and those who had "paid tribute to the sovereigns of Andhra, Karnataka and Dravida (Tamil) segments." The vanni term occurs in the South Indian sources earlier than in the Sri Lankan records. It is difficult to trace back where this name originated and the application to Sri Lankan chieftains.

Indrapala (2007) suggests that one possibility is that the term "vanni" had been consolidated to chieftains in the sparely populated regions of Rajarata and in the forested regions after Vanni chiefs from South India established themselves in the northern parts of Sri Lanka. Another possibility is that the term was introduced and became established within the island before the migration of the South Indian Vanni chiefs.

Sivaratnam (1968) takes the Vanniyars settlement back to the early Anuradhapura kingdom. The first batch of fifty-one families of Vanniyars with their seven chieftains came from Pandya coast in 493 AD for the noble purpose of cultivating the land at Tambalakamam. They were experts in agriculture and known as the *palli* in South India, who claimed to be Kshatriyas. Another batch

---

[103] Indrapala, K. (1970). Sivaratnam, C. (1968); Wikipedia.

of sixty Vanniyars came from Tarunipuram Kulam of the Pandya country, along with Samathuthi, a pandya princess. These Vanniyars increased in number and populated the Vanni districts between Kalpitiya and Punakari in the west, and Kottiyar and Mullaitivu in the east. The Vanniyars from Trincomalee spread out towards Batticaloa and Badulla districts, from central Vanni districts they gravitated towards through Anuradhapura to Kurunegala to become Sinhalese Vannis in Sinhalese districts (Sivaratnam, 1968).

The earliest Sri Lankan work in which the name Vanni occurs is the Pujavaliya, written in the third quarter of the thirteenth century. In the account of the Maghas occupation of the Rajarata (1215 AD), Pujavaliya refers to the Maha-Vanni areas and the chiefs of those regions who lived in fear of Magha.

However, there is a question about Tamil and Sinhalese Vanniyar who live in Vanni regions. Indrapala points out that Sinhalese and Pali chronicles do not refer to the Tamil Vanni chieftaincies. The references to "Sinhalese Vanni kings" (Sihale Vanni-rajha means Vanni chieftains of the country Sinhala) in the Chulavmsa and to 'Sinhalese Maha-Vannis' (Simhala maha-Vanni means tribe of the clan of greater Vanni of the country Sinhala) in the Pujavaliya imply that there were also Vannis who did not belong to Sinhalese. The Tamil sources and the later European works give much information about the Tamil Vanni chieftaincies. As in the Sinhalese sources, the name Vanni is applied in the Tamil chronicles to the chieftaincies of northern and eastern Ceylon. The Tamil chronicles – Yalpana Vaipava Malai (written in 1736) and the Konesar Kalvettu (written in 1750) – refer to a time when invaders and settlers from South India, including the Vanniyar occupied parts of the present Northern and Eastern Provinces and set up chieftaincies there. These were undoubtedly the chieftaincies which were later came to be known as the Vanni.[104]

Indrapala emphasises that there is no evidence to suggest that there were such Vanni chiefs or chieftaincies, in number in the Rajarata before the fall of Polonnaruwa kingdom. The fall of Polonnaruwa and the consequent breakdown of central authority seem to have led to the establishment of regional power by South Indian military chiefs who were employed by Magha and his associates. These military chiefs had the probability of being the Vanni chiefs mentioned in the Tamil sources. It is possible that Vanniyar soldiers were brought to Sri Lanka as mercenaries at the end of the twelfth century and in the first quarter of the thirteenth by South Indian invaders and other aspirants to the Sinhalese throne.

During the medieval times, the Vanni provinces in the North were partially under the Portuguese and subsequently under the Dutch regime (Fernando, 1986). It was the border territory between the colonial maritime province and the King's undisputed territory. These far northern pattus of the Vanni became a sort of buffer zone, which later became the Dutch Vanni and is described by Commander Antony Mooyaart, commander of Jaffna Patam in 1766 in his Memoir to Noel Antony Lebeck:

> "[T]he Vanni which consists mostly of large forests, and is an extensive, but, for the greater part barren and uncultivated territory, which as said above, separate our domain from that of the Kandyan King. This territory is on account of its great extent divided into eight provinces, which are placed in temporarily possession of some mayoral, under the name of Vanniyars."[105]

---

[104] Indrapala, 2007
[105] Quote from Dennis Fernando, 1986.

Some of the names of the Vanniars recorded the Pattus they were appointed to, and the Disawa they reported to, are mentioned in the Rajawaliya. In fact, some of them were Muslims and Roman Catholics as well according to Doyly's records. There was a Nuwara Vanniya at Anuradhapura under the Dissawa of the Nuwarakalaviya, a Kumara Vanniya (a Muslim) of Marikkar Pattu and a Raja Vanniya (a Roman Catholic) of Pandita Pattu, both of whom were under the Disawa of the Seven Korale. The names of the Vanniyas in the northern areas who paid tribute to the Dutch are recorded in the Governor's reports (Fernando, 1986).

Palm-leaf (Vitti) Manuscripts on Vanni People.

The manuscript called *Rajasingha Rajuge Prothugisi Wirodi Satana pilibandawa sandahan Vitti* (pg. 75) provides symbolic stories about Malala Bandaras and a prince called Samasinghe who lived in Rajarata originally from the time of King Davanampiyathissa. They oversaw 360 Vanni Pattus. When there were no kings, they controlled the region and survived brutal famines. They were known as Bandara Kumaras, or Bandara Princes, but also named as Vaddhas.

This manuscript goes into details and provides a list of those surviving Vaddhas chiefs in Vanni regions (including current Vanni Hathpattu). They were: Hurulle vadda, Kalawala vadda, Prince Sangabodi, Utro vadda, Kiralo vadda, Mulleriyaye Kumarasinghe vadda, Wilawa kumaragajasinghe vadda, Kakunawe Sinhanada vadda, (three belong to the same tribe) Hathlispahe Labunoruwe vadda, Galawawe vadda, Helgoma vadda, Labunnoruwe Mahakatahoruwaya, Nikapitigama liyana vadda, Wara gammana Adipathi vadda, Wendakaduwe Wanasekara Gajanada vadda, Sulugalle Sulugulu vadda, Hathigammana Mahasekara vadda, Magalle Olupokune Sundaraya, Kumburupitiye Irugal vadda, Magulagama vadda, and Dunupothagama Rathna Malla vadda (pg.

75). These Vaddhas chiefs were warriors and apparently participated in various war games during the Sithawaka kingdom. We can speculate that these Vanniyars could be the descendants of early Pandya migrants and late Kerala Malala princes (Kshatriyas) who mixed with early residents.

Vanni Upatha manuscript (pg. 25) provides details about several South Indian royal families who come down to Sri Lanka during the Buvanekabahu 1 (Dambadeniya Period). They were the regional princes who had lost battles and fled to Sri Lanka with their families and their fortune. The group included seven princes and ministers accompanied by several skilled labour groups (castes). One prince was Kalu Kumara Bandara who was from Madurai (Madurapura) royal family. The list of princes and the countries (*ratas*), and Vanni chieftain titles awarded to them in Vanni region, which include:

- ❖ Kalu Kumara Bandara was given Kaluwila and twelve villages and he was honoured as "Kalu Kumara Vanniya."
- ❖ Ilangasinghe Bandara was given nine villages including Kattaman Kulama. He was honoured as "Ilangasingha Vanniya."
- ❖ Diwakara Kumara Bandara was given eighteen villages in Jaffna including Suriya Damana. He was honoured as "Kumara Vanniya."
- ❖ Rajakaruna Bandara received Kalawewa and thirty-eight villages including Amanaya Kunchikulama and he was honoured as "Rajakaruna Vanni."
- ❖ Wanaviraja Bandara was given nineteen villages including Puthalum rata and Munneswaram. He was honoured as "Wanawiraja Vanniya."
- ❖ Ilangasinha Diwakara Bandara was another prince. The rata and title awarded to this Bandara are not stated.

Vanni Upatha (pgs. 25-26) provides a list of chieftains who accompanied the group with different technical skills.

In addition to *Vanni Upatha*, the manuscript called *Kandure Bandarawaliya* (pg. 45) records seven South Indian nobles (Bandarawaru) who migrated to Sri Lanka and settled in the upcountry and in the Vanni region of Nuwarakalawiya. Similar to the reasons explained in *Vanni Upatha*, some of these royal family members left India when they were defeated by opponents or due to disputes in the royal family. Kandure Bandarawaliya records an event where the kingdom was given to the legitimate heir, but a group of seven cousins (mentioned as "Bandarawaru") decided to sail to Sri Lanka looking for better opportunities. They travelled to "Sinhale" (upcountry) and three of them, Disa Bandara, Monarawila Nawarathna Bandara, and Akuranboda Rala settled there. The rest, Herath Bandara, Kandure Bandara, Megoda Bandara, travelled to Nuwarakalawiya.

There are extensive details about Kandure Bandara's fortune in the Vanni Upatha palm-leaf manuscript. He received rata from the Kotte King in Nuwarakalawiya which included Paspaththuwa (five Paththus – five demarcated larger regions of the country) of Kahalla, Parawaha, Undurawa, Kiralawa and Dunumadalawa. In addition, he was given the honorary title of "Rajapaksa Mudiyanse" and crowned as a "Vanniyar" (Ruler) in that part of Nuwarakalawiya. The descendants of Rajapaksa Mudiyanse also inherited prestigious ruler class of "Vanniyar" positions. They established marriage relationships with the families of Sathara Korale and Sath Korale elites. This information indicates that these elite migrants received titles and privileges specific to the areas they settled. They can be regarded as specific group appointed Vanniyars.

Vanni Upatha (pg. 30) also emphasises the high social status given to the newly crowned "Vanniwaru". The term used to enlist them as "Rajaperuwe attho" which inherit the royal bloodline to be kings. Further, this manuscript condemns the local "govigama" caste as the people who held Vidana (petty officers) posts under the Vanniwaru and collected revenue for the Vanniwaru.

According to Gira Sandesha,[106] the area between Jaffna kingdom and Kotte kingdom was named as Vanniya and it was divided into eighteen pattu (sub-districts). Nuwarakalawiya was under a disawanni (maha Disawa)[107] during Kandyan kingdom but this chieftain was regarded as a junior Disawa (sulu Disawa)[108] compared to other Disawanies of Kandyan Kingdom. The person who controlled Nuwarakalawiya under a maha Disawa called "Maha Vanniya." He had held the custodianship off eight holy religious places (Atamasthana) of Anuradhapura main Buddhist shrines. Eighteen Vannivaru reported to the Maha Vanniya. Karunananda (2005) says that the Maha Vanniya posts always had got filled by the Nuwarawewa family of Anuradhapura[109].

Assimilation Patterns of Vanni People.

Indrapala (2007) notes that the Vanniyar of the nineteenth century were divided into two different communal groups. Those who lived in the Vavuniya district were Tamil – speaking while those who lived in Nuwarakalawiya district were mainly Sinhalese-speaking persons or families. He believes that these Sinhalese-speaking Vannis were in fact descended from Tamil Vanniyar who had become assimilated to the Sinhalese population after the Nuwarakalawiya district was re-colonised by the Sinhalese. Indrapala suspects that these people in Nuwarakalawiya were descendants of Tamils.

---

[106] Gira Sandesha, 130 verse.

[107] In 1815, this disawanni was under the control of Galagoda Disawa, who was the Maha Disawa.

[108] Karunananda, 2005, Nuwarakalawiya, pg. 11.

[109] Karunananda, 2005, pg. 11, Descend from the Prince Bodhiguptha who brought Sri Maha Bodhi to Sri Lanka

Northern Vanni people lived either in Tamil dominated regions or close to the border of Sinhala dominated country. This settlement pattern distinguished their community character which was a result of a unique assimilation process. The European writers identified southern Vanni people with close resemblance to the northern Tamils. A nineteenth-century writer makes the following observation on the Sinhalese of the Vanni region:

> "They have adopted the Tamil system of personal names, thus a man has his father's name prefixed to his own and does not take his name from the village or family he belongs to or the land he owns, as is the common Sinhalese custom elsewhere. Many of their names, too, are Tamil in a Sinhalese shape. The older generation have taken to wearing earrings. but this practice has been discouraged by the present Sinhalese headman. The Sinhalese villagers have as much faith in the Hindu god Pillaiyar as have the Tamil villagers whose favourite god he is... As regards dress the Sinhalese keep generally to their own customs, but they often wear the Jaffna cloth (chayaveddii) and fasten the handkerchief on their heads after the Tamil manner."[110]

Vanni chieftains and Vanni people who lived in Vanni region inherited a localised assimilation process. They originated from the early Pandya Kshatriyas (migrated as cultivators) or later migrants from Kerala (Malala) or Tamil Nadu (army chieftains and mercenaries). They could have subsequently mixed themselves with local chieftain families. The language base was decided by where they lived for many years. If they were living close to the northern Tamil speaking dominant region, they spoke Tamil, and if they were living close to the buffer zone near Sinhala region, they spoke Sinhalese (or bilingual). The next chapter also continues with the South Indian migration topic but focuses on the Kandyan Era.

---

[110] Anonymous, "The Vanni", MLR & NQC. II, No.5, May 1894, pgs. 98-99.

Chapter Ten

Migration Patterns During the Kandyan Kingdom

South Indian migration continued during the Kandyan kingdom in different forms, especially through mercenaries and marriages.

The Kandyan Nayakas from Madurai (Madurapura) and Tanjore.

It appeared that the Kandyan kings had marriages with contemporary Nayakas (or Nayakkars) dynasties of South India – Nayakas of Madurai (Madurapura) and Nayakas of Tanjore.

The Nayakas belong to the Vaduga caste and the speakers of Telugu language. Obeyesekere (2017, pgs. 29-32) states that they were a warrior clan from Andhra Pradesh and Karnataka and hence were labelled "Vaduga", meaning "northerners" by the people in Tamil Nadu. They were governors of the regions in the Vijayanagar Empire. According to Tripathy (2017), the Nayakas were a group of Dravidian people, who descend from a mixture of pre-Dravidian tribes, Dravidian, and Indo-Aryan people[111]. However, the Nayakas were allies of Kandyan kings.

---

[111] Tripathy, et al. (2017).

Kandyan kings started seeking assistance from Nayakas from time to time to fight against the invading Portuguese. For example, King Wimaladharmasuriya (I) and King Senart brought down Nayakas from Thanjavur and Madurai to fight the Portuguese. When King Rajasinghe (II) fought the battle at Gannoruwa against Portuguese there have been a thousand of Nayakas in his army. With them came their families too, who later intermixed with the Sinhalese population in the hill country.

The Nayaks of Kandy established marriage relationships with South Indian nobility. These relationships helped them to stabilise their power. They were heavily reliant on the support from the Madurai and Thanjavur branches of the House. Many Nayakas marriages brought brides with their entourage from South India and settled in the new country. Many entourages of bridal parties came down from South India had settled in Kandyan regions with their extended families. These royal relationships established another breed of South Indian aristocracy in Sri Lanka. Eventually, four Nayakas kings ruled Kandy from 1739 to 1815.

Bridal Sources for Kings.[112]

The first South Indian marriage connection starts in the Kandyan Kingdom from King Rajasingha (II) who reigned from 1635-1687. The King's Chief Queen was from Madurai, and she bore him one son that was named Wimaladharmasuriya. After King Rajasinha's death, his son ascended to the throne as Wimaladharmasuriya (II). He reigned from 1687-1707. He also followed his father's example and married a princess from Madurai. She gave him one son

---

[112] De Silva, 2005, Devaraja, 1985, Obeyesekere, 2017. I am also thankful to websites of: https://www.jaffnaroyalfamily.org/kingdomkandyhistory.html, Agiya Katha, http://aagiyakatha.blogspot.com/2012/07/12.html , https://en.wikipedia.org/wiki/Madurai_Nayak_dynasty , https://en.wikipedia.org/wiki/Nayaks_of_Kandy for the information for Nayakkar marriage relationships with Kandyan kings.

named Sri Wira Parakrama Narendrasinha, who reigned from 1707-1739. Sri Wira Parakrama Narendrasinha had a Kandyan wife, but her son died at a young age. Later, he married Princess Udumala Devi of the Nayak dynasty. The king had subsequently married her two sisters as well. None of them had given him an heir. King Sri Wira Parakrama Narendrasinha was the last Sinhalese king to rule the kingdom of Kandy. His queen used a custom that was practised in South India which grants the queen's family the right to claim the throne in the event of there being no legitimate heir from the king's side. One of the queen's brothers had come from South India. On his deathbed, the king nominated his chief queen's brother, Sri Vijaya Rajasinghe, to succeed him.

Sri Vijaya Rajasinghe was the first Nayaka King of Kandy without any Sinhalese blood. He was a pure Hindu and Dravidian. His three successors were four members of the Nayak dynasty, who traced their origin to Madurai. Marriage relationships played an important role in cementing the relationship between Sri Lanka and South India. King Sri Vijaya Rajasinghe married again after seven years to another princess from Madurai. The King died on 11th August 1747.

After the death of King Sri Vijaya Rajasinghe, his brother-in-law, his wife's eldest brother, came from Madurai and ascended the Kandy throne as Kirti Sri Rajasinghe, and reigned from 1747-1780. King Kirthi Sri Rajasinghe married two daughters of Vijaya Manan Nayakar, the grandson of Vijaya Raghava Nayakar of Thanjavur. He also married another South Indian wife from Madurai, the daughter of Nadukattu Sami Nayakar, in 1749. But he had no children by any of his queens.

Nayakas Influence During the Kandyan Era.

It is important to note that the Nayakas embraced Buddhism and learned the Sinhalese language and made every effort to naturalise themselves. However, they avoided marrying into the local Radala families. Kirthi Sri Rajasinghe built a Raja Maha Vihara, a palace complex and the Dalada Maligawa Temple. He reconstructed the existing inner temple of the Tooth Relic. He was responsible for bringing the Siamese monks who arrived in Lanka in 1753 to re-establish the higher ordination of monks.

As a result, Siyam Nikaya was established. The Siyam Nikaya evolved into two major divisions, the Malwaththa chapter and the Asgiriya chapter. These chapters started to play a greater part of the old temples and of their temporalities. During the Nayaks rule Hindu temples and shrines flourished. According to C Sivaratnam (*The Tamils in Early Ceylon*), as mentioned earlier, the Siamese monks were quite shocked to find many Hindu temples like the Natha, Saman and Vishnu devales in the capital of the Buddhist country.

Sri Rajadhi Rajasinghe ascended the throne of Kandy and reigned from 1780-1798. King Sri Rajadhi Rajasinghe had come to Ceylon during his childhood, and he had his education in Kandy. He had three wives from Madurai. The King Sri Rajadhi Rajasinghe died on 16th July 1798, leaving no sons. Prince Kannasamy took the name of Sri Vickrama Rajasinghe, and he reigned from (1798-1815). He was a member of the Madurai Nayak dynasty and the nephew of Sri Rajadhi Rajasinghe. King Sri Vickrama Rajasinghe had four wives and two of them were sisters (Venkata Ranga Ammal Devi and Venkata Ranga Ammal). Later, early in 1813, he married the two daughters of Degal Sami of Madurai. They were Muttu Kannamma Devi Degal Sami and Venkata Ammal Degal Sami. King Sri Vickrama Rajasinghe who reigned for seventeen years from 1798-1815 was the last Monarch of the Kingdom of Kandy. The whole island became part of the British empire in 1815.

According to C Sivaratnam (*The Tamils in Early Ceylon*), the Dravidian cultural influences had intensified during the Kandyan kingdom. When a prince or a royal bride came from Madurai to Kandy, they did not come alone. They were accompanied by their parents, brothers and sisters, kith and kin and a whole entourage. They were accommodated in mansions in Kumararupe Vidya (present day Malabar Street) in Kandy.

The Nayakkar elite families also had recognition during the British rule[113].

Nayakas Settlements in Kandy as Described in Palm-leaf Manuscripts.

There are at least two manuscripts that provide specific information about the waves of Nayak families flowing into the Kandyan society during the Kandyan kingdom. One manuscript is the *"Madurapura Rajaparampara Rajawaliya"* written by Munamale Malhami Vidane Rala.[114] The other is "Sathara Korale Nayakkar Vittiya" (Marambe, 1926, pg. 43).

Madurapura Rajaparampara Rajawaliya contains information about marriage relationships, migration of extended families, and other Nayak immigrants. The following are some examples:

✧ With a request from King Narendrasingha, the king of Madurapura, Arya Chakrawarthi, sent his daughter Sumiththa for marriage. She was sent with Swaminatha and Hemanatha who were two sons (princes) of his brother Pantara Chakrawarthi.

---

113 De Silva, KM. (2005)
114 Peradeniya University library index number 277456.

✧ King Narendrasinghe offered a chief minister position to Swaminatha and a deputy minister position to Hamanatha.

✧ Pantara Chakrawarthi's other son, prince Sumedha, came to Sri Lanka with his two sisters, Kaushalya and Suparna, and stayed at the Anuradhapura Nuwara Wawa residence. Kaushalya married Tikiri Banda of this Nuwara wawa family (due to an unexpected pregnancy).

✧ Prince Sumadha was given a village called Alakola Anke and a treasurer position (*Gabada Nilaya*) at the royal palace.

✧ Princess Suparna married to Manpitiya Bandara (a local elite).

✧ During this time, many princes came from Madurapura. They settled at villages like Aludeniya, Kempitiya, Kaballa Pitiya.

✧ Prince Sumedha (Gabada Nilame) married from Dullewa and had one son and six daughters. They all married to local elites. The daughters married to the sons of Lewuke Bandara, Urulawaththe Bandara, Kempitiya Bandara, Unambuwe Bandara, Rathwaththe Bandara, and Kappetipola Bandara. The son was married to the daughter of Mayadunne Bandara.

This manuscript is evident of the intimate relationships between the Kandyan kings and Madurapura Nayakas royal families. It indicates how the elite Nayak families migrated to Sri Lanka and established their legacy in the districts of Kandy and Matale.

Sathara Korale Nayakkar Vittiya also lists many Nayakkar elites who migrated to Sri Lanka and settled down in Matale potentially during the early period of Kandyan kingdom. The list includes 942 elites as aristocrats in various divisions like Korale and Pattus. The list appears to be from the records of the king's military services, but certainly contain numerous names of aristocrats with the Nayakkar label (Nayakkar Radalawaru).[115]

Both manuscripts openly recognise the Nayakkar influence and foothold in Sri Lanka during the Kandyan kingdom. They provide symbolic information about Nayak base in Kandyan region.

Many Nayakas descendants had royal patronage during the Kandyan kingdom, helping them to join the Kandyan form of radala and aristocratic class.

The next chapter focuses on the South Indian migration during the recent past.

---

[115] Royal families or aristocrats.

Chapter Eleven

South Indian Migration in the Recent Past

The South Indian migration continued during the European rule, but mainly changed into trade communities and migrant workforce.

Other General South Indian Migrants in Later Periods.

There are other prominent Sri Lankan communities in coastal areas and southern parts of Sri Lanka who are descendants from the South Indian origin. They are: Karava, Salagama, Durawa and Chetties. They are powerful community groups economically, socially, and politically in the modern era. De Silva (2005, pgs. 421-426) provides an account of the rise of these communities economically with the blessing of the booming plantation sector which was established by the British since mid-1800s. They involved in managing infrastructure facilities like clearing forest for plantation, owning carts and dominating transport industry, owning mines for exports, controlling toll rents of bridges and ferries, becoming owners of liquor (arak) industry, and purchasing Crown land and controlling real estate industry etc. They (particularly the Karava) became most affluent segments of the new capitalist class creating an elite domination, a caste rivalry, and setting out to claim high caste hierarchy displacing traditional Govigama elite domination.

A very brief account of the origin of these communities is provided below to give a complete picture of the potential South Indian phenomenon that had taken place in Sri Lanka. I am mainly focusing on the potential South Indian connections of these communities.

The Sinhalese costal community known as Karava, or Kara and Kaurawa, is the Tamil equivalent of Karaiyar[116]. They are traditionally occupied in seafaring, fishing, and naval warfare. Many Karava communities in Sri Lanka claim an origin from the Kuru kingdom and the Kauravas tribe of the Hindu epic *Mahabharata*. There is an extensive study carri9ed out on Karawa community in Sri Lanka and therefore, I am not going into details.

A major portion of Karava people were mercenaries. As previously mentioned, the *Mukkara Hatana* reveals that there were thousands of Kaurava mercenaries brought from South India to fight *Mukkara* invaders. Raghavan (1961) explains that five hundred years ago, the Karavas were pure Tamils and Hindus, who came to Ceylon at the special invitation of the Kotte king from South Indian principalities to defend Ceylon against an invasion by the Mukkuvars.

Due to the economic collapse resulting from the war, the king had difficulties with making payments but wanted to keep them in Sri Lanka. They were given fertile land along the south-western seacoast. Since they had had been used to the coastal life in their own country, they comfortably settled in these areas. The king gave them eighteen harbours, tax free, for sea-going trade. These soldiers did not come with wives, so the king arranged the marriage of

---

[116] Raghavan, 1961, 1964

Sinhalese brides potentially from the Govigama caste, which always formed the largest constituent of the Sinhalese people (Sivaratnam, pg. 35). Obeyesekere (2004) says that there is no doubt that Karaiyar-Karawa were fishermen. But like the Sinhalese Govigama, they had other occupations, and were known as sailors and sometimes soldiers. However, these so-called seafarers were not affiliated with the traditional Sinhala land tenure system attachment to land.

The Karavas who lived north of Negombo became Catholic and bilingual in Tamil and Sinhalese. The Karavas of the south of Colombo became Buddhist and Sinhalese.

The community of Salagama was traditionally associated with the cultivation of cinnamon, and were found mostly in southern coastal areas, as well as in the area from Negombo northwards to Chilaw. A small group of the Salagama community that lived in the Kandyan areas were involved in weaving. This community shares similarities with the "Saliya" or "Chaliya", the weaver's caste, of Kerala, Karnataka and Tamil Nadu.[117] The Salagama have a belief, crediting to them 'higher' caste roots, that they originated from Saligrama Brāhmins of Kerala.

According to Jan Schreuder,[118] an 18th century Dutch Governor of Ceylon, the Salagamas the weavers were brought over from the Coromandel coast on the Tamil Nadu side as opposed to Kerala by Muslim merchants. But they were forced to become cinnamon peelers by the king of Kotte in the 15th century. The Portuguese continued the tradition of using Salagamas as cinnamon peelers. Many Salagama people adopted Portuguese names. Cinnamon peelers were a handful of families living in

---

[117] Raghavan, 1964
[118] Johann Schreuder, et al. (1946).

Sinhala areas and directly interacting with the majority Sinhalese. This process made them to be low country Sinhalese.

Obeyesekere[119] names another caste as *oli* because they supposedly came from *oli-rata*, an alternative name for *soli rata*, the Chola country.

> "A huge multitude of oli people have been shoved into the district of Dumbara. They are agantuka, or outsiders, because their origin myths state that they were brought here by king Gajabahu, a famous king (with some mythical anecdotes woven around) who brought them over from the Tamil country in retaliation along with the twelve thousand Sinhalese captured in a previous reign by one of the Tamil kings."

There is another southern Sri Lankan community known as Durave or Durava or Durawa.[120] Their traditional occupation is toddy tapping. They trace their ancestry to medieval period migrants from South India. They were converted to Catholicism soon after the arrival of the Portuguese. They, along with other southern Sinhalese castes such as Karave and Salagama, have played an important role in the historical political parties. They are mostly Theravada Buddhists today and were instrumental in the revival of Buddhism during the British colonial period.

Sri Lankan Chetties were also a class of Tamil speaking traders who migrated from Tinnevelly of South India during the Portuguese rule and continued such migration during the Dutch period. Women did not come with them, and they married among high caste local women. They came to Sri Lanka as Indian Catholics. They absorbed into Sinhalese community in the western and Southern regions and to Tamil Vellalar in the north.

---

[119] Obeyesekere, G (2016). Caste and conflict.
[120] Wikipedia.

Many Sri Lankan community groups (castes) appeared to have South Indian connections, but they were largely assimilated with the locals.

Since the arrival of the Portuguese to Sri Lanka also saw the migration of various Southern Indian and Tamil speaking groups. Several hundreds of converted Christians were brought from the Indian mainland to the western shores of Sri Lanka by the Portuguese to wrest control on the pearl trade. They eventually became Sinhalese.

During the European periods in Sri Lanka, the Indian Ocean was intensified with trading activities and regular travel between countries in the sub-continent, and in the South-East Asian regions. This trade influenced to bring some migrants from the South-East Asian regions. The migration during this time was influenced by either internal wars or growing international trade or economic activities.

South Indian Migration During the British Period.

Similar to the Portuguese and Dutch periods, the South Indian migration during the British period was intensified on economic reasons. The British colonial economic policies at the time contributed to attract many south Indian migrants to Sri Lankan to work in plantation sectors.

The Colebrook-Cameron Commission abolished the feudal Rajakariya system (involuntary royal service) in 1833 to boost commercial cultivation activities and to release labour force from the traditional duties. However, the British were unable to attract the low country or up-country Sinhalese to newly started coffee plantations.

There were a few factors restricting Sinhalese to join newly found commercial agricultural activities. The lifestyle of villagers was composed of daily routines related to their simple agricultural activities. A prominent feature of the Sinhalese in the Kandyan kingdom was that, irrespective of their caste, everyone engaged in their own subsistence agriculture. "Unlike South India, there were no landless agricultural labour castes in Kandy" (Bandarage, 1983, pg.174). Every family unit had their own home garden, a plot of land for vegetables, a tract of wet land for paddy cultivation. In the low country, Sinhalese and Sri Lankan Tamils (who were more exposed to colonial influence over two centuries) were heavily engaged in various economic activities in addition to paddy farming and fishing. Hence colonial landowners were unable to dissolve the paddy peasantry to become plantation labourers.

Like the Portuguese and Dutch, the British colonial period saw the transportation and migration of Tamils to Sri Lanka, but on a much larger scale. Indian Tamils were brought to Sri Lanka as labourers during the 19th and 20th centuries to work on coffee, tea and rubber plantations owned by the British. Workers were recruited from around the Tamil Nadu cities of Tirunelveli, Tiruchirappalli, Madurai, and Thanjavur. These regions were traditional roots of migration to Sri Lanka for many centuries.

Conditions in the South Indian economy encouraged this labour migration (Guilmoto, 1993; Shirras, 1931; Jayaraman, 1967). Many socially low-caste agricultural workers lived in difficult economic conditions. Indebtedness of ordinary villagers to land magnates was high. There were episodic famines and deprivation during this period. Bonds of debt continued to exist between landlords and ex-slaves, even after the official abolition of slavery.[121] The combined impact of these conditions was a "communalised destruction," with the creation of a large pool of poverty-stricken workers. They

---

[121]   Slavery was abolished in the possessions of the East India Company by the Indian Slavery Act, 1843.

needed to find some means of survival during abnormally depressed periods.

This background provided opportunities for British cultivators of India, Sri Lanka as well as in other British colonies. Between the years 1839 and 1859, there were as many as 917,171 labourers who arrived in Ceylon, and some returned to India (Jayaraman, 1967). It was estimated that between the years 1843 and 1877, an average 10,300 women and 8,000 children came to Sri Lanka to work on coffee estates. By the end of the epoch of the coffee plantation era, there were over 100,000 South Indian labourers living in Sri Lanka.

When these groups arrived on the estates, they were isolated, having little social contact with the rest of Sri Lankan society. In 1871, only 3.3 percent of the resident population on the estates were local Sinhalese. These Indian Tamils were separated from an already existing trading community of Indian Tamils (upcountry) who were not part of the plantation economy. The "foreign" Indian work force that served the needs of plantations, were kept isolated from the rest of the society, maintaining Tamil language and Hindu religion.

In 1962, nearly 975,000 people were living in the tea estates, classified by Sri Lanka as "Indian nationals" and as "stateless" by India.[122] The Sirima – Shastri fact signed in 1964 (between two Prime Ministers Sirimavo Bandaranayake and Lal Bahadur Shastri), 525,000 Indian Tamils were to be repatriated and 300,000 were absorbed into Sri Lanka. The number repatriated by 1974 was 85,000. In 1981, it was estimated that only 280,000 had been repatriated to India, and 160,000 had been granted Sri Lankan citizenship. The problem of statelessness among Indian Tamils citizenship issue was finally resolved in 2003, with the Grant of

---

[122] Wikipedia, Sirima–Shastri Pact.

Citizenship to Persons of Indian Origin Act. This Act granted Sri Lankan citizenship to those of Indians who had lived in Sri Lanka since the Sirima–Shastri Pact agreed in October of 1964.

However, the assimilation of the plantation workers into the local Sri Lankan community were difficult because the plantation workers were in larger groups such as thousands in group residence buildings (hostels like lane residences). They settled in clusters in proximity like large camps. They were in large groups who could help themselves. They established marriage relationship with their own fellow families. Their settlements were in large tea estates, and they were geographically distanced from the Sinhalese settlements or traditional Tamil settlements. They involved in routine-based work activities in restricted geographical area. Therefore, they maintained their own identity without largely mixing with the locals for over a hundred-and-fifty years.

Unlike other migrants that came down from South India, the assimilation of Indian estate workers into the Sri Lankan community was restricted but was not largely deprived.

Chapters 8 to 11 described different patterns of South Indian migration to Sri Lanka and the way those migrants were absorbed to the Sri Lankan society in many parts of the country.

The next few chapters survey the seven Brāhmin groups settlement further in detail to understand the social and political environment through which they had to evolve in Sath Korale. These chapters will examine the local conditions they had to adjust to, community groups they had to interact with, challenges they had to deal with, and the transformations they had to undergo. The final chapters focus on the in-depth study of Kambuwatawana Brāhmi village and their Brāhmi legacy.

Chapter Twelve

Compatriots of Brāhmi Migrants in Sath Korale

This chapter examines the early years of the seven Brāhmi families, and their expansion within the new land of the Mundukondapola kingdom of Sath Korale. This section also provides information about their compatriots as revealed from the palm-leaf manuscripts and other historical documents.

N1 and N2 are sketchy about the chronology of events since the arrival of seven Brāhmins and their relationships with the locals who had been living in the area. The close examination of the information reveals that there had been other South Indian (and probably also some North Indian) migrants settled in Sath Korale before and after the arrival of seven Brahmans.

Compatriots of Seven Brāhmin Contingent.

It is reasonable to assume that the South Indian migration was intensified during the periods of the Kotte and Sithawaka kingdoms. The migrants not only settled in Sath Korale, but they also settled in other parts of Sri Lanka (e.g., Demala Hathpaththuwa, Siyana Korale, Nuwarakalawiya, and in Tamil countries in the North and the East). As mentioned early, there were contextual issues in South

India to encourage the outflow of migrants to Sri Lanka. N1 and N2 provide hints about the arrival of waves after waves of new migrants. The Sri Lankan rulers warmly welcomed the influx of new migrants. We can assume that the Mundukondapola and Kotte kings wanted to attract many subjects as much as possible to strengthen their manpower as there were continuous wars between divided kingdoms. It is also possible that Sath Korale was scarcely populated at that time and there was a lack of human strength to promote economic activity together with forming strong security forces.

As mentioned early, according to traditional palm-leaf manuscripts (bandaravaliyas, vitti books, and kadayim books), the South Indian migration sped up in the Dambadeniya and Kurunegala periods, but further intensified during the Kotte and Sitawaka periods. Already we have referred to Brāhmi migrants, but there were other migrant groups like Kshatriya or Malala Bandaras, Hettis or merchants and other skilled professions settled in Sath Korale during the time of seven Brāhmins.

Vanni Malala Bandaras in Sath Korale.

N1 provides incidents of interactions between seven Brāhmins with Uduweriya and Eriyawa Malala Bandaras in Sath Korale. The details of these compatriots need further examination.

The Malala migration to Sath Korale is recorded in several palm-leaf manuscripts with slightly different variations. It is difficult to separate the accounts in each manuscript because they contain similar information, myths, similar Malala names and similar adventures of the migrants in the new country they have settled.

Malala Vittiya (2005, pgs. 15-44) explains about seven Malala Princes who lost the battle with a Maravara king and decide to seek refuge in Sri Lanka. As mentioned early, this group included five princes and two monks. They joined with two other ships carrying Brāhmins and Hetties. They caught up in a storm, drifted around, and landed at three different ports on the northwest coast of Sri Lanka. The ship carrying Brāhmin landed at Karathive port, the ship carrying Malala landed at Welparrapu and the ship with Hettis on board went to Muthupanthi. But later, all groups met at Welparrapu and celebrated the escape from their ordeal.

The Vaddah chief (local indigenous leader), Panikki Vaddha of Eriyawa provided the translations of Tamil to Sinhalese. The Vanni Vittiya (pg. 33) has a verse about this activity.

"මලලුම වැද්දන් ළඟට ගොසින්නේ
සුරතල් බස් දී පාර අසන්නේ
දෙමලෝ ඔය බස් මොකද කියන්නේ
පනික්කි මැතියෝ තෝරා දෙන්නේ"

"The Malalu approached the Veddas
After pleasant word and inquires for the road
Who inquires in Tamil what the words were
The Panikki Chief did translate them."

Malala Bandaras, as princes and war-harden warriors, appeared to be arrogant and overconfident about their background. They wanted to know if the ruler and the inhabitants in Sri Lanka were Aryans, and also from the Solar dynasty. They did not want to meet any other ruler or any corrupt Sinhalese. The Vanni Vittiya (pg. 33) has a verse to demonstrate this attitude:

"සිංහල දේසේ කවුද බොලන්නේ
ආරිය වංශයේ අයද බොලන්නේ
සුරිය වංශයේ අයද බොලන්නේ
අනිත් කෙනෙක් අප නොතකමින් නේ"

"Who are the inhabitants of this Sinhalese country,
Do they belong to the Arya race,
Are they of the Solar race,

We shall not care for any others.

Or sometimes in corrupt Sinhalese".[123]

The Malala princes travelled to the Sithawaka palace, and the king granted land and titles to these five Malala princes and two Malala monks:

- ✧ One prince was named Raja Wanniya and given land, including three-hundred-and-sixty villages around Puththalama.

- ✧ Another prince was named Kumara Vanniya and given land around Munneswaram temple, including sixty-four villages and olagams.

- ✧ Another was given the name of Malala Bandara and given land around Uduweriya region, including twelve villages.

- ✧ Another prince was given the Anuradhapura region and named Nuwara Wawe Suriya Wanni Kumarasinha Bandara. He was also given the Kaluwila region and named Kaluwila Kumarasinghe Bandara.

- ✧ Another Prince was named Samasinghe Rajaguru and received Sina Korale.

- ✧ The two monks, Budhamithra and Saranankara, were given Thotagama and Widagama.

Eriyawe Vanni Pannikki Rala, who brought the princes to the palace, was given the name of Sinha Prathapa Mudiyanse probably to acknowledge his effort.

Malala Bandarawaliya (pg. 54) also gives a comparable account of a similar group of Malala Bandaras settling in the same areas. Interestingly these migrants were given Sinhala aristocratic names,

---

[123] Translation by De Silva, WA (1927).

and in effect divested of their Kshatriya status and converted into the Sinhala aristocratic class (Bandaras).[124]

The Vanni Vittiya (pg. 31), and Vanni Vitti (pg. 66), records a potentially early group of Malala Bandaras and their settlements. They have been identified as Indian princes but provided similar processes of granting similar names. Vanni Vithiya further refers to a group of Malala Bandaras as Commanders (Senavirathdura) of the Elephant Army. On one occasion, Sithawaka Parakramabahu king organised an event to celebrate their elephant handling skills. This ceremony was organised and performed by Eriyawe Panniki Rala, including a group of Malala Bandaras.

It seems that the challenge was to tie up a wild elephant's foot.

⬥ One Malala tied one front leg, and he was given honorary title of *Eriyawa Wanninayaka Mudiyanse*.

⬥ Another Malala tied one back leg, and he was given the title of *Rathna Malala Irugal Bandara Mudiyanse*.

⬥ The next Malala who tied a back leg was given the title of *Uduweriye Panankanthi Hetti Bandara*.

⬥ Another Malala Bandara had gone to a herd of elephants and without fear and tied a foot of an elephant. He was honoured with the title of *Threerajaguru Mudiyanse*.

As mentioned early, all vanni manuscripts records similar elephant handling events with slightly different versions. Eriyawe Pannikki Rala (or Eriyawa chieftains) could have organised several of similar events and similar groups participated. According to Vanni Vittiya (pg. 36) Eriyawe Pannikki Rala had the leadership of four Vanni Vaddha chieftains.

---

[124] Obeyesekere, 2013.

It is possible these events were regular or annual. Always a chieftain from Eriyawa was responsible for organising these "Malala sports". The king participated in these events and every time the king rewarded the people who showed their warrior skills of handling elephants. Their titles were re-established, or slightly different titles were given after every event. For example, the Malala Bandara of Eriyawe Vadiraja Panniki Rala who rode the elephant was initially given Wanaraja Wanasinghe Prathapa Mudiyanse, and secondly Wanninayake Mudiyanse changing the earlier title. According to Ferguson (Tropical Agriculturalist), elephant kraaling events continued during the Kandy period and extended into the British Rule. The Disawas of Sath Korale were the people responsible for organising these events.

The Vanni Vitti (pg. 67) provides extensive details about a country given to Uduweriye sward held Malala Bandara. He was later honoured as Uduweriya Rathna Irugal Bandara. Apparently, he descends from Surya Malala (Solar dynasty) royalty.

Malala Bandarawaliya (pg. 55) provides information about an influx of more Malala migrants to the Vanni hathpattu region (Sath Korale) during the reign of King Buwanekabahu of Sithawaka Kotte. The king wanted to settle more migrants in this area. But both Uduweriya and Eriyawe Ralas had pleaded at one point not to give away the countries inherited by them from their great grandparents.

Eriyawa Sannasa,[125] attached to Appendix 3, gives the details about the rata awarded to Eriyawe Range Bandara Wanninayake Sinha Prathapa with a "mudali" title on shaka warsha 1540 by the Sithawaka King Buvanekabahu.

---

[125] Hand copied sannasa was provided by Chandana Bandara Wanninayake.

The traditional Eriyawa Bandara(s) surname is *"Adi Dunna, Vadi Thilaka, Vadi Sinha, Vadi Raja, Sinhapathapa, Range Bandara, Wanninayake Mudiyanselage".[126]* This illustrious surname is still used by some families of Eriyawa origin. That signifies their Vaddha, Vanni, Malala, and Bandara connection.

It appears that Vanni region (of Sath Korale) was controlled by Malala Bandaras for centuries since Dambadeni period (apparently the chieftains who controlled the Nuwarakalawiya and the area towards Jaffna were named as Vanniyas). During the peace time they could have involved in farming and kraaling elephants for international trade. Malala Bandaras had been traditionally given Vanni Hathara Pattuwa (four larger divisions of Vanni) together with gifts, titles, and elephants. According to the Vanni Vitti (pg. 66), these four divisions were Uduweriya Udugaha Malala Paththu, Kirindigalla Othota Malala Paththu, Kumara Vanni Paththu, and RajaVanni Pattu. The four Vanni chiefs were also given Nindagam called, Atapaththu Ganwasan, Kottal Baddha, Radha Badda, Berawa Badda, Nawa Badhdha, and the title of Vanni Unnehe.[127]

Vanni Upatha (pg. 44) identifies several (Sath Korale) Vanni chieftains who had responsibilities for local elephants. Eriyawe Pannikki Rala or Sinhappu Pannikki Mudiyanse appeared to be one such chieftain. He had been given seven *mandukamba* (rope with noose or loop at the end to catch elephants) and three-hundred soldiers. Wilawa Gajasinghhappu Pannikkirala also received seven madukamba and three-hundred soldiers. Eriyawe Range Bandara is also mentioned as a chieftain with skills in elephants handling. He had been rewarded with the villages of Atharagalla and Eriyawa by the Sithawaka king for his skills in elephants handling (Eriyawa

---

[126] ඇදී දුන්න, වැදි තිලක, වැදි සිංහ, වැදි රාජ, සිංහපුතාප, රංගේ බණ්ඩාර, වන්නිනායක මුදියන්සේලාගේ

[127] Unnehe means a respectable chieftain.

Sannasa). Further, Galgamuwa village had been given to Gajanada Pannikkirala, who was another chieftain responsible for elephant handling. The names Gajasinghe and Gajanada are related to chieftains of the royal elephant's army. These locals must have contributed to the international elephant trade. It was also observed that the early residents of Kambuwatawana village also had connections with capturing and taming elephants.

KMS Rakogama emphasises that Malala Bandaras were rulers in Vanni regions and some of their descendants were related to Sri Lankan royal families and kings in the Kotte and Sithawaka kingdoms.[128]

South Indian Merchants/Hettis and Skilled Migrants.

The Malala Vitti (pg. 25) provides information about some ships carrying only Hettis or merchants and various skilled professionals. However, merchant settlements are not as clearly defined, but they seem to have been dispersed over a wider area. Their leader Semasinha was a merchant prince, and his entourage had been given lands in Siyana Korale, that is, in the very area of Sitavaka, which is close to the port of Colombo.

The Malala group and Hetties accompanied various skilled migrants. Some of these skilled migrants according to the Malala vitti (pg. 25) were:

- ✧ Koṭṭa Vaḍuva: the ship builder for the merchant prince Semasinha of Telingapura (Telegu city),
- ✧ Palingu Irugal Vaḍuva (crystal–worker),
- ✧ Samukka Vaḍuva (spyglass maker),
- ✧ Abharana Baḍala (goldsmith),
- ✧ Kapuru Heṭṭiya (camphor merchant),

✧ Vettila Heṭṭiya (betel merchant),

✧ Pakku Heṭṭiya (areca nut merchant),

✧ Sunnambu Heṭṭiya (lime merchant),

✧ Adu Heṭṭiya (maker of shackles),

✧ Mati Liyana Paṇḍita (the craftsman who decorates pots),

✧ Sankhanada Guruva (conch blower),

✧ Tala Viridu Suddanavali Viriduva (bard of melody, eulogy, and praises)

✧ Naḍagam Panikkiya (maker of plays),

✧ Dali Samanna Cakravartiya (specialist barber in trimming and shaping of beards) and

✧ Suddahaluva (washerman).

This is an extensive list of various skilled professions. The Malala migration was an addition to the Vanni region and Sath Korale to reinvigorate the economy, along with artistic, spiritual, and social life.

According to the Malala Vitti, Hettis settled at Hettikulam paththu without giving specific villages mentioned. They must have spread out.[129]

Disputes Between Seven Brāhmins and Malala Bandaras.

N1 indicates that some migrants who had come to the Dembatogama country did not stay permanently. For example, Katupiti Madampe Rala,[130] did not consider Dembatogama conducive to settle in, as he thought the Dembatogama region was dry, as it had no reservoirs, no rivers, and no irrigation facilities. After the refusal by Katupiti Madampe Rala, some parts of Dembatogama had been occupied by Uduweriya Malala Bandaras

---

129 According to Maha Sammatha Vitti book (Dharmasena, 2011).

130 Probably Katupiti Madampe Rāla went to Madampe and established a Regional Kingdom (where Prince Thaniya Yalla Bahu of Madampe ruled, HCP Bell, 1920).

as an addition to their country. That means Malala Bandaras have come to Sri Lanka before the Brahmins group. It is possible to identify one disputed village as Nambadewa village. It was a part of Vanni Hathpathuwa, but later handed over to Dembatogama Rala by the king. Further, there had been some land disputes rose between Uduweriya Malala Bandara and Parawamapami for Mapegamuwa area.

The Vanni Vitti (pg. 64) introduced a sword-holding-Malala-Bandara as Uduwerye Rathna Irugal Mallawa Bandara. He had offered a gold chair to King Buvanekabahu and Uduweriya obtained twelve villages and Udukahapaththuwa division by a sannas. The Vanni Vitti (pg. 67) reveals that an additional country received by this Malala Bandara. He descended from the Solar dynasty and regarded as a prince.

N1 portraits Uduweriya Bandara as a violent leader who had involved in killings and creating conflicts with other landlords in the region. His behaviour had been tolerated by the local king. Maybe he was a warrior in the royal army or could have been a confidante of the local king. He had sold many villages he had acquired, including some parts of Dembatogama. Since the custody of Dembatogama by the Purohit Brāhmaṇa Rāla, nobody had sold any parts of Dembatogama according to N1.

N1 provides evidence related to the award of villages or gamas to several other South Indian elites with new honorary names. For example, Thalandapitiya village including: Palugaswewa, Balasuriya gama, Weerasangiliyagama, Katta Kaduwa and Hambakkarayagama had been awarded to a Brāhmaṇa Rāla. The elite who had received Herathgama was introduced as Prince Ranasinghe. He was given the honorary title of *Herath Bandara*. He could have been a Kshatriya prince connected to the seven Brāhmin families.

Settlers of Nikawagampaha Korale Before the Arrival of Brāhmin Contingent.

N1 is largely silent about the indigenous people who lived in the area but maintains the names of existing villages. It is possible that the area must have been thinly populated at the time of the arrival of seven Brāhmins and some "olagams" (empty villages) must have existed. Since the vitti books glorify the legacy of the new migrants and their aristocracy the locals could have been exposed to unfair recognition.

A close examination of the vitti books provides hints of some locals in the area. *Mahasammatha* vitti book (Pohorawaththa palm-leaf manuscript or N3) is a good source. It provides conflicting information about the seven Brāhmins and their legacy, while promoting an aristocrat who lived at Pohorawaththa. His name is Pohorawaththe Sri Chandrasekara Purohitha Brāhmaṇa Rankadu Bandi Wijesingha Senewirathna Mudiyanse. It is obvious from his name that he was also from Brāhmin origin and would have come from the same area in India. Apparently, he was a commander of a large army which fought against the Portuguese for the king of Kotte. This vitti book tries to relate Wijesinghe Seneviratne Mudiyanse to one of the descendants of Prince Wijaya. Seneviratne Mudiyanse claimed to oversee a vast country which extend from Kala Oya to Mee Oya, including sixty-four olagams. His second generation was awarded the *Adhikari Herath Mudiyanse* title. A group of Adhikari Mudiyanse currently live in this locality.

It is not clear whether this aristocrat and his entourage arrived after or before the arrival of the seven Brāhmins. However, this manuscript hints that villages where the seven Brāhmins settled were empty and he settled some of his army in those villages. N1 provides continuous history for a several generations of Brāhmins in these villages, probably up to the 1750's. On that basis, I think the Pohorawaththa manuscript refers to a group of migrants who came before the seven Brāhmins.

Seneviratne Mudiyanse had distributed villages and lands to the soldiers of his army in his area of control (e.g., Nikawagampaha Korale). These soldiers appeared to have come from various castes and skilled labour categories. The descendants of these people still live in these villages.[131] The following are the villages where Seneviratna Mudiyanse's army settled:

- ✧ Tamil Hettis who migrated with him were given villages and awarded the "Sri Narayana" name for their services. Currently, there are people with this surname in Mapegamuwa and Rakwaana.

- ✧ Five Naides (also called "Hiththaru", "Acharis", "Nawandanna", or "Gurunnanses") were given land next to his location of residence at Pohorawaththa. The descendants of this group still live at Pohorawaththa.

- ✧ Villages of seven purohits were given to seven chandalas (people of low caste). No trace of this group is found. And must have been gradually vanished or assimilated.

- ✧ Thuthiripitiya village was given to a *waala* (servant). Currently, this locality is a farmland without people.

- ✧ Athuaththa village was given to the person who carried branches for the army elephants to eat. This village still exists as Wathuwaththegama.

- ✧ Galgiriyawa, Dewala Viharagama and Rambawa were given to washerman. Some descendants of washerman families live in this locality.

---

[131] On the basis of individual accounts provided by AM Herath Banda, Pohorawaththa and YM Dharmasena, Nikawewa, verified the information including the current descendants.

✧ Kambuwatawana for Hambakara who ties elephants. Vanni Upatha (pg. 44) also refers to the elephant connection to this village. It refers to a person who helped by giving a rope to Achari Asuri Appu to tie elephants, and he has been named Kambuwatawanaya. This village was named Kambuwatawana by Devamadda Palace. There is no trace of this family currently, but probably must have been assimilated.

✧ Borawewa, Dikweheragama and Ganegama were given to three Hetti (merchants) groups. There is no trace of these families probably they were assimilated.

✧ Konwewa was given to a goldsmith. The descendants still live in this locality.

✧ Gonalagama was given to a metalworker. The descendants still live in this locality.

✧ Kubukkalla (Kubukkadawala) was given to Hettis. It is difficult to distinguish this origin and appears to have been assimilated.

✧ Bulnewa was given to Kara naide. The descendants still live in this locality.

✧ Kaduruwewa for a servant (waala). It is difficult to distinguish this origin appears to have been assimilated.

✧ Pothanegama was given to Hettis who carried books. It is difficult to distinguish this origin and appears to have been assimilated.

✧ Elipichchegama for a Giruwa. No people live in this locality currently, it is a farmland that belongs to Borawewa.

✧ Habarawaththagama for the Hetti who gave "habarala" (giant taro) leaves. There is no trace of people from this origin, they could have been assimilated.

❖ Siyambalewa for the Hetti who blew conch shell . It is difficult to distinguish this origin and appears to have been assimilated.

❖ Paththinigama, Paththini Dewalegama were given to a poem writer. It is difficult to distinguish this origin appears to have been assimilated. Probably, they were custodians of the Goddess Paththini.

❖ Moragollagama for a lime Hetti. It is difficult to distinguish this origin and appears to have been assimilated.

❖ Kumbalporugama was given to a clay worker (potter). This village is closed to Madagalla. It is difficult to distinguish this origin and appears to have been assimilated.

❖ Kadahathawewa was given to a "thala wiriduwa" (drama artist). Currently, there is no trace of this group.

❖ Kongahawaththa for Kirwula Kumari. This village is situated next to Herathgama. There is a mythology related to this noble woman in Nikawewa village history which is described later in the book.

❖ Hambakaragama was given to a Muslim "naide". This village is closed to Thlandapitiya. The descendants still live around this locality.

It appears that the composition of the Senewiratna Mudiyanse's army was multicultural in addition to the various social classes of traders who had accompanied the Brāhmins, Malala Bandaras, and Hettis. However, it is not clear if the people on the above list were the South Indian migrants who came with Senewirathna Mudiyanse and Malala Bandaras or the people who joined the Senewirathna Mudiyanse's army from other parts of Sri Lanka to fight against the Portuguese.

Vanni Upatha manuscript (pg. 44) also gives clues about the inhabitants surrounding Kambuwatawana village before the arrival of seven Brāhmins. Some evidence suggests the existence of an ancient people called "demons". For example, Vanni Upatha (pg. 45), discloses a regional king who was named as Marasinghe in Nikawagampaha division who was able to use humans as well as demons (yakku) to perform duties for him. Coincidently, there is a story about this warrior who was awarded the name Marasinghe Mudiyanse, and he was associated with Ulpotha village. Apparently, Ulpotha Herath Banda's second son had joined the army of the King Rajasinghe (Sithawaka) and killed Portuguese soldiers ruthlessly[132] in the battle. He was nicknamed "Yuddaye Maraya" (demonic celestial king of war) and given the title Marasighe Mudiyanse. The King Marasinha could be the Ulpotha Herath Banda's second son. Madagalla Sannasa[133] provides details about the paddy land (twelve ammuna) given to Marasinghe by the King Rajasinghe in 1644 AD, for his heroism displayed in the war against the Portuguese (Madagalla Sannasa is attached to Appendix 4).

KMS Rakogama (2019) states the existence of small regional kingdoms at Galgiriyawa and Madagalla.[134] Marambe (1929) also states a principality called "Galgiriyawa Devamadda Wasala" operated from Galgiriyawa. They were small principalities potentially within the larger regional kingdoms like Mundukondapola. Marasinghe could have been a local king of a small principality of either Madagalla or Galgiriyawa. There are descendants with the Marasinghe surname in villages like

---

[132] According to Vanni Upatha, Marasinghe brought two heads of Portuguese soldiers who were killed by him to the King's army camp.

[133] 26 February 2014, Divayina Newspaper provides a copy of the Madagalla Thalpotha (ola-leaf), No 2, 189.S.1566 (AC 1644) quoting from the evidence by HCP Bell, Director General Archaeology).

[134] Also known anciently "Kallaggama".

Nikawewa, Rambawewa and Halmillawewa in Nikawagampaha Korale.[135]

New Settlements During the Time of Seven Brāhmins.

N1 records the following settlements in addition to the villages and rata awarded to the seven Brāhmins. Apparently, the author of N1 was a Mohottala who had the responsibility to keep records of vitti, land grants and boundaries. These land grants may have been given with or without the sponsorship of the Dembatogama Purohit. To identify any potential surviving descendants in these locations[136], this information is to be combined with Senevirathna Mudiyanse's allocations to his army soldiers within the same or similar localities:

✧ Madagalla guard posts were given to Muthukutti Arachchi and Edirisinghe Arachchi by the Sithawaka Rajasinghe Palace as hewawasama.

✧ Thibbatuwewa, Gonalagama, and Ranamukgama were also given to soldiers of the royal army.

✧ Aluthgama, Wambatuwewa, and Kathikandawewa including Galgiriyawa were donated to Venerable Bogoda Thero (who followed the group of seven Brāhmins from South India).

✧ Karagaswewa was given to Rathnayaka Mudiyanse.

✧ Gatilewa was given to Mappuwa as hewawasam.

✧ Galgiriya Konwewa was given to Ganelrala as "aththapaththu mure"[137] by the Devamadda royal court.

✧ Palugaswewa, Balasurigama, Weerasangiliyagama, Kattakaduwa, Hambankarayagama, including Thalandapitiya were given to another Brāhmaṇa Rāla by the

---

[135] Dharmasena book pg. 20.

[136] Current descendants were verified on the basis of individual accounts provided by EM Sunil Bandara, Dembatogama and YM Dharmasena, Nikawewa.

[137] Service men at guard posts.

Sithawaka royal court. His son was titled as Jayasundara Mudiyanse.

✧ Tharanagollagama was given to Adikari Mudiyanse.

✧ Katupathwewa was awarded to Rajapaksha Mudiyanse.

✧ Horowwawa, Adune Wewa, Kiralabokkagama including Thalawa were given to Wijekoon Mudiyanse by the Sithawaka royal palace.

✧ Mapegamuwa was sold by Parawamapi to Madappu Arachchi who came from the low country.

✧ Hatangoma, Paththinigoma including Thibbatuwewa were given to Ekanayaka Mudiyanse.

✧ Gonalagama, Moragollagama including Pohorawaththa was given to Mapa Rala by the Sithawaka palace. That Mapami sold Moragollagama to Rajapaksha Wijayasuriya Kuruwita Nawarathna Mudiyanse.

✧ Athawudagama was given to Athawuda Rala who came from the low country by the King Rajasinghe as hewawasam.

✧ Herathgama was given to Prince Ranasinghe by the Sithawaka Royal Court. Prince Ranasinghe was awarded the name Herath Bandara. This Herath Bandara sold Halmillawewa.

✧ Nambadawa was given to Rathnayaka Mudiyanse by the Devamadda palace.

✧ Dambe Siyambalawa, including Kiriwula, were given to Rajaguru Mudiyanse.

✧ Pambadenigama was given to the person who narrated poems to the Devamadda palace and named Wijayasuriya Mudiyanse.

✧ Ulpotha and Nagollagama were given to Wijayasundara Mudiyanse by the Devamadda palace.

- ✧ Bamunugama, Pathirannagama including Pahalawewa were given to Waththeseda Arachchi by the Sithawaka palace as hewawasama.
- ✧ Pahalakale and Mamunugama were sold by Uduweriya Bandara to Koralegama Rala and Mamunugama Rala. Koralegama Rala's son was named Hitihamy Mudiyanse.
- ✧ Ihala Thimbiriwawa and Kandubodagama were sold by Uduweriya Bandara to Kandubodagama Rala. This Rala's son was named Rathnayaka Mudiyanse.
- ✧ Palu Rambawa and Halmillawawa were given to Diwakara Mohottala by King Rajasinghe. That Mohottala's son was named Basnayake Mudiyanse (potentially this family is from Dembatogama family).
- ✧ Pahala Thimbiriyawa was given to Wijayasundara Bhumipala Rajakaruna Mudiyanse of Dembatogama (potentially another member of the Dembatogama family).
- ✧ The Sithawaka Palace awarded Athawudagama to Athawuda, Wicharanagama to Wicharanna, Ranamukgama to Ranamukaya and Thennakongama to Thennakona as hewawasam. They had come from low country.

It appears that Thennakongama, Ranamukgama, Athawudagama and Wicharanagama previously had been given to Dembatogama Purohit Brāhmana Rāla. Ihala Thimbiriyawa was previously part of Athawudagama. It was known as Dekanduwala. Previously, Wicharanagama was known as Palalagoma and Ranamukgama was known as Demaddegama.

It appears that several villages have been awarded to notable aristocrats by the royal palace. For example, Prince Ranasinghe who settled at Herathgama, and a Brāhmana Rāla settled at Thalandapitiya. The king had promoted an internal migration as well. To recognise their services, the king awarded land and settled his soldiers from the low country in Nikawagampaha Korale.

Other Settlements in Sath Korale

Sath Korale Kadayim saha Vitti manuscript provides specific information about how the other parts of Sath Korale were populated by internal (domestic) migration during the Kandyan Kingdom.

At one stage the King Kirthi Sri Rajasinghe failed to conquer Colombo Fort from the "*Parangi*"[138] (the Dutch) despite fighting for months. He learnt that the people in Nawa (nine) Korale around Colombo were supporting the Dutch. To weaken the Dutch power, the king lured these people to come to Sath Korale and Kandyan regions by offering attractive incentives. The manuscript records the offers of 970 swords, 469 golden necklaces and the ownership of lands in empty villages in Sath Korale. Examples of the land grants and the settlement of these people in various locations in Sath Korale included:

✧ Mahara Mohottala received 100 *amunas* of paddy land between Nikawewa and Madagalla villages.

✧ Lansi Sudu Arachchi settled at Polpithigama while Dompe Gamayo at Madagalla and Naidu Rala at Kubukulawa.

✧ Muhandiram positions holders of Hetti clan including Ramanayake Hetti who came from Hetti Street settled at Udalupola, Galatanwewa, Katiyawa, Thalpathwewa, Migaswewa and Hettimulla, Hettipola, Dambagaha Gedara and Barube.

---

138 This term was originally used by the Sinhalese to brand the Portuguese as strangers or foreigners in a derogatory manner. It appears that the term was also used for the Dutch.

- ✧ Sri Ramanayake Andiya who came from Andi Street settled at Angurugolla, and other Andis settled at Kahathilagoda, Kurunegala, Pusgala and Dekanduwala.

- ✧ Guruwo (conch blowers) settled at Kandubodagama, Gokaralla, Udugalpola and Daramitipola.

- ✧ Mukkaru and Parawaru who came from Mukkara Mulla in Puththalam also settled in various parts of Sath Korale.

- ✧ Marakkala (Muslim) people who came from Colombo Street, Negumbo, Puthalama and Kaluthota settled in the areas of Thelambugala, Thelimbiya, Thalgaspitiya, Badagamuwa, Dikwela, Thelatiyagala and Thiththawalgala.

- ✧ Madinnos (toddy tappers) settled in Kiribamuna, Bellanwila and Kandulawa.

- ✧ The people who came from Biyagama settled at Hiripitiya, Dalupotha, Barube, Malagamuwa, Dalunyaya, Nabiriththa wawa, Dodanwatawana and Konwewa.

- ✧ People originated from Masan Gas Street, Balapiti Modara and Kalani Modara settled in various parts of Sath Korale.

- ✧ People who came from Katupiti Madampe settled at Kambuwatawana, Borawewa, Rakwana. Galgiriyawa, Kandulugamuwa and Kallanchiya.

- ✧ People who came from Kollupiti settle at Gaharagama, Malluwagara, Konwewa and Seruwawa.

The manuscript also states that those subjects who wanted to avoid various taxes imposed by the Dutch had chosen jungle hideouts and wanted to live as Veddas. The manuscript lists several Sath Korale Vedda chieftains including Kanchi Vedda at Kallanchiya, Lasan Kada Vedda at Kubukkadawara, Kam Vedda at Katupathwewa, Nikapath Vedda at Nikawewa, Paki Vedda at Kandulugama and Elakada Vedda at Elipichchegala. It is not clear if they were new internal migrants or not.

The manuscript provides specific numbers of vocational and other community groups who newly settled in Sath Korale. They included 300 Radawu (washermen), 275 Arhari (metal workers), 85 Badahala Durayo (clay workers/ potters), 108 Madinnos (toddy tappers), 58 Hali ("Sali" viwers with South Indian origin), 299 Karawos ("Karaiyar" fishermen or sailors with South Indian origin), 475 Mukkaru ("Mukkuvar" fisherman and mercenaries with South Indian origin), 200 Wadakaruwo (domestic workers/ servants), 180 Marawaru ("Maravar" a community originated in South India), 299 Parawaru ("Paravar" - dwellers of seacoast, originated in South India), 400 Guruwo (conch blowers), 85 Yakdehi Naides (devil dancers), 500 Berawayo (drum beaters), 64 Ewaduwo (arrow makers) and 700 Marakkayos (Muslims).

These people could have settled in scarcely populated villages or on the fringes of the established villages. It is possible this was a new sort of colonisation scheme initiated by the Kandyan rulers. The descendants of these communities may still live in these locations or may have been assimilated into the broader community. It appears that this internal migration has helped to create a diverse community composition in Sath Korale.

The next chapter discusses the expansion of Brāhmin villages in Sath Korale, including the shifting of the Dembatogama generation to villages like Wathuwaththegama, Galgiriyawa and Kambuwatawana.

Chapter Thirteen

Expansion of Seven Brāhmin Families in Sath Korale

This chapter provides detailed information about the expansion of the seven Brāhmin families in Sath Korale, highlighting how they established themselves in clusters of villages and divisions. Over time, each cluster developed its own unique identity and a specific network of connections and interconnections not only among themselves but also with other South Indian elite migrants within the region. This expansion and the development of distinct clusters are explored up to the period of the Kandyan Kingdom and beyond, shedding light on the historical and social dynamics of the Brāhmin communities in Sath Korale.

Emergence of Nikawagampaha Korale.

Originally, Nikawa Gampaha Korale was the country (or division) awarded to Purohit Brāhmaṇa Rāla of Dembatogama. Then, this country was termed "Dembatogampaha" (five principal added constituents to Dembatogama) which included the principal villages of Dembatogama, Rakwana, Borawewa, Herathgama and Walpaluwa. N1 explains that Walpaluwa village was given to the

Tamil drummer caste servant (or Sinhala Wiriduwa) who came with the seven Brāhmaṇa Rālas. The purohit wanted to include Walpaluwa as a main constituency to the Dembatogama division to acknowledge his services.

The name of this administrative division has been changed several times. Dembatogampaha later became Nikawagampaha. Nikawagampaha officially included the principal villages of: Dembatogama, Borawewa, Rakwana, Herathgama and Nikawewa. In this new transformation, Nikawewa village had been included to the division and Walpaluwa had been excluded. N1 provides an intriguing story about how Dembatogampaha became Nikawagampaha.

Two brothers who carried Nawagaththe Mudiyanse titles lived in Nawagaththegama, close to Puttalam. One Nawagathe Mudiyanse committed a high crime that enraged the Kotte king. As a result, this Mudiyanse was accused of high treason and executed, and his portion of the land was given to nine *gaththarus* (potentially to de-casted criminals) as a punishment. This was a kind of condemning form a caste or de-casting. Obeyesekere[139] (2016) has several examples of the king "de-casting" a person guilty of some fault. The important technical term is *gattara*, whereby owing to some offense the king can place a person and his family in a lower position from the caste they belonged to. And then given a new name to commensurate that degraded status. This seems to be a high level of insult. Obeyesekere explains that he used the term de-casting because no one can really be "out-casted" and indeed no such category is found in palm-leaf text. There is no way to escape from *jati* (the original cast one belonged to) unless one becomes a renouncer. However, this punishment appeared to be very harsh,

---

and he must have done a serious crime. Potentially, he was the Nawagathe Rala who killed Irugal Bandara, the divine king of Mundukondapola.

The other Nawagathe Mudiyanse (the other brother) did not want to live with these *gaththarus* due to the shame. He heard about the Nikawewa village, which was without a village headman in Dembatogama country. He had chosen to live at a place far away from Nawagathegama village. N1 states that at that time, Nikawewa was without a landlord as the Bandaras of this village had died and there was nobody to represent. However, the village had a boundary issue with the descendants of Uduweriye Malala Bandaras. Therefore, this Nawagathe Mudiyanse obtained permission from the Devamadda (Mundukondapola) King to acquire the village and settle at Nikawewa village. He was able to resolve the boundary dispute with Malala Bandara's with the royal backing.

According to N1, it appeared that the elite Brāhmin families in Dembatogama country did not treat this Nawagathe family who came to Nikawewa village equally or fairly. One reason could be that the Nawagathe family was involved in a horrendous high crime. Another reason could be that Nawagathe Mudiyanse was of Malala or Hetti origin. However, the Nawagathe Rala's "son-in-law", Samarakkodi Appuhamy, attended a crisis resolution meeting ("kula haba" or caste dispute) at Gonalagama, where other elite position holders (Mudalis) in the country, the Mudiyanses of Dembatogama, Rakwana, Borawewa, Herathgama, and Mataluwawa were attending. The registrar (liyanarala) for this trial was Pohorawaththa Rala. The elite attendees treated Samarakkodi Appuhamy in an inferior way not giving an equal status of a seat. Malala Vittiya (pg. 93) records the incident differently. "When a Mudiyanse tried to sit on the mat in which Dematagama Diwakara Mohottala[140] was sitting the Mudiyanse was physically kicked out of the mat" (pg. 93).

According to N1, he complained about the treatment to his father-in-law Nawagathe Rala. Following this incident, Samarakkodi Rala fled to South Indian Tamil State (Soli Desha) in a Portuguese ship and stayed there for seven years with a Hetti (merchant) called Kapurunada. He brought gifts to the king and pleaded to give back Nikawagampaha for his leadership.

According to the Malala vitti (pg. 93), he brought valuable gifts, a golden parrot, and a stature of Yama daughter (Yamaduwa) to the Dewamadde King. The king established his superior recognition in the Dembatogama country. Consequently, Dembatogampaha became Nikawagampaha. The king honoured Samarakkodi Rala as Adhikari Mudiyanse and granted the custody of Dembatogampaha country and renamed the country as Nikawagampaha. The "Nikawagampaha" name has been used for this Korale Division up to now.

It is possible that Samarakkodi Rala was a Hetti Mudiyanse[141] as he was a merchant. This incident also suggests that there was regular travel and close relationships between South India and Sri Lanka.

Kandulawa and Kiribamuna Legacy.

Kandulawa village is located at approximately 7.570800 degrees North latitude and 80.446920 degrees East longitude, while Kiribamuna village is located at approximately 7.589399 degrees North latitude and 80.441965 degrees East longitude.

The manuscript N1 is silent on the legacy of Kandulawa and Kiribamuna Brāhmin families other than their original connection to seven Brāhmins. As noted elsewhere, these two Brāhmins settled

---

[140] It appears that it was a son or a grandson of Dembatogama Purohit.

[141] He sold coconuts to Nikawewa residents.

in close villages but away from the rest of the Brāhmins, who migrated as a group. It is likely they were brothers.

Legends in the Kiribamuna and Kandulawa villages acknowledges the Brāhmin origin but unravels different accounts.[142] Seven Brāhmin migrants led by a Brāhmin called Pandulawa (also known as Kandula) and a Bamini (woman) Brāhmaṇa called Keerashta stayed in a cave in the Puwakkanda hill[143] after their arrival. After an incident,[144] they settled in different villages with the blessing of the king. Pandulawa settled at Kandulawa, Keerashta Bamini at Kiribamuna and other Brāhmaṇas settled at different villages including Bamunawala, Bamunakotuwa and Bamunapotha. All these villages exist to the present day. It is possible that this legend combines the two events[145] of how the Brāhmins came to Sath Korale. It is possible the folklore refers to two groups of seven Brāhmins, one as stated in N1, and another group who settled in Bamunawala, Bamunukotuwa, and Bamunapotha. The second group also had settled nearby.

Kurunegala Vistharaya (Marambe, 1926, pg. 81) gives a different legendary origin to Kiribamuna. That was the place where milk was extracted from a rock to feed baby Irugal Bandara, who later became the legendary king of Mundukondapola. Because of the

---

[142] Mr Ajith Kiribamuna (from Kiribamuna village) and HM Gunasiri (from Kandulawa village) explanation about Kiribamuna and Kandulawa origin based on mythology.

[143] HM Gunasiri stated the area is Bandarawaththa close to Thalaheenna.

[144] Apparently, the villagers misunderstood this as a polygamy and complained to the king. The king ordered to tie and starve them for seven days on a rock. The Brahmans performed "sathyagraha" and survived. After seven days the villagers found they were happy and healthy, but Kirashtika Bamini was crying shredding milk from one eye and tears (kandulu) from the other. The king ordered to name tears direction of the land as Kandulawa and milk (kiri) direction of the land as Kiribamuna.

[145] The seven Brāhmins as stated in Vanni Vitti books and another group who came before or after settled at villages including Bamunawala, Bamunukotuwa and Bamunapotha.

milk extracted from the rock to feed the prince (Sinhalese term "*kiri bima*") this village became a legendary place.

However, the Kandulawa family became very prominent in Sath Korale, and they acquired wealth and connected to elite families in Sathara Korale (Matale). Both Matale vitti and kadayim books reveal marriage relationships between Matale elites and a Kandulawa Herath Bandara family. For example, Matale kadayim book two (M2) has information about the daughter of Kalahagala Brāhmaṇa Rāla married to Kandulawa Herat Bandara, implying that a female partner belonged to a Brāhmaṇa family in Matale married a distinguished Sinhala aristocrat of Kandulawa whose extensive properties are listed in the text (Obeyesekere, 2013), which accounts that seven Brahman Ralas had migrated before the Matale Brāhmins and were well-established. The Kandulawa Brāhmin family had already gained recognition and enjoyed high aristocratic status.

There is some information given in Matale Vitti book revealing that this matrimonial disclose had damaged the traditional family status of Kandulawa. Herath Bandara Brāhmaṇa Rāla had given his plot to a farmer to cultivate, but the farmer's daughter secretly ran away with a man of the *rodiya* (chandala – a down caste). Because of this incident, the Brāhmaṇa Rāla gave the farmer a new plot on the other side of the stream (äla – water supplying stream). The implication is that from the Brāhmaṇa point of view the former plot has been polluted by the unacceptable marriage of the farmer's daughter with a male partner who belonged to the caste of *rodiya*. Despite this unlawful union there is no reference in M2 to any punishment inflicted on the errant couple (Obeyesekere, 2013). It is also to be stated that a few palm-leaf manuscripts, including the Laggala kadayim book (pg. 114) records additional scandalous marriage relationships to low caste women and illegitimate children born to Kandulawa Herath Bandara descendants in the Matale region.

It seems that Kandulawa became the one connection of the seven Brāhmin legacies with Matale aristocrats who belong to the same tribe. It also appears that the vintage legacy of seven Brāhmins stood out during the Kandyan kingdom as well as within the British rule. Subsequent events of the 1818 Rebellion reveals that these clan connections and standing for each other in their fight against the British. Kandulawa Mohottalas played a leading role in Sath Korale during the rebellion.

Further, Matale aristocratic connections and the seven Brāhmin legacies also demonstrated in the leadership of Malwathu Chapter during the Kandyan kingdom and during the British rule.

N1 does not disclose detailed information about Kandulawa Brāhmin legacy. This is mainly due to N1's focus on the legacy of Brāhmins settled in Nikawagampaha Korale.

Currently, there are at least four clans of families at Kandulawa connected with the early Brāhmin origin. Kandulawa early residents established marriage relationships with: Kambuwatawana, Thanawa, Wataddana, Nikawewa, Borawewa, Aranayake, Mawanalla and Matale. Current surnames of the residents in the village include: Herath Mudiyanse, Hitihamy Mudiyanse, Ekanayake Mudiyanse (origin either Hathigamuwa or Thiththawalla villages), Rajapaksha Mudiyanse, Bannaka Mudiyanse, Maha Mudannaka Mudiyanse, Sri Narayana Bamunu Brāhmaṇa Mudiyanse, Bandaranayake Mudiyanse.[146] Kambuwatawana genealogical records in Chapter 19 disclose extensive marriage relationships between Kambuwatawana families and Kandulawa Herath Mudiyanse families (clan).

---

146 Obtained from HM Gunasiri from Kandulawa.

The Kiribamuna descendants use Hitihami Mudiyanse, Herath Mudiyanse and Ekanayake Mudiyanse surnames. Kiri Bamuna village traditionally established marriage relationships with Kandulawa, Manapaha, Gokaralla and Ambagaswaththa.[147]

Mataluwawa Legacy.

Mataluwawa village is located at approximately 7.863839 degrees North latitude and 80.392008 degrees East longitude.

N1 records one Brāhmaṇa Rāla of the recognised seven-member team settled at Mataluwawa. This Brāhmaṇa Rāla's original Indian name was Jothipala Brāhmaṇa Rāla. He was a cousin of other six Brāhmaṇa Rālas. He was awarded the custodianship of villages of Amunakole, Gal Kandegama, Kumbalporugama, Henawagama including Mataluwawa by the Mundukondapola Palace with awarding of the honorary hierarchical name of Ekanayake Mudiyanse.

According to the Nikawewa vitti book,[148] Mataluwawa family had a relationship with Kumbaldiwela Bandara of Sathara Korale (Matale). He was a grandson of Senewirathna Bandara who came from Malwila Desha of India who was another compatriot of seven Brāhmin families. It says the Ekanayake Mudiyanse of Mataluwawa is a grandson of Kumbaldiwela Bandara. The manuscript has been satirical of Ekanayake Mudiyanse for having many marriages (stated as sixty to be precise). One marriage was from the village of Bamunakotuwa. A daughter from this marriage was given to Loku Rala, who was one of the sons of Herath Banda of Ulpotha. Loku Rala's brother married from Udakandawala. A son called Appuhamy, was born to this family who was a warrior of the army

---

[147] Obtained from Ajith Kiribamuna.

[148] YM Dharmasena has written a book about Nikawewa and Nikawagampaha Korale which provide additional details about this village.

organised by Giragama Disawa to fight Portuguese. He served this battalion as a commander.

N1 is silent about the subsequent flight of Mataluwawa Jothipala Brāhmana Rāla. It appeared that this family had marriage relationships from Matale and Ulpotha. However, the surnames of Jothipala Mudiyanse and the Ekanayake Mudiyanse prevail at Mataluwawa village confirming the historical succession.

Nikawewa Legacy.

Nikawewa village is located at approximately 7.883626 degrees North latitude and 80.417153 degrees East longitude.

Nikawewa village[149] is historically termed as "Nika-athu-kadawala", "Manikya Wewa", or "Mahanikawewa".

As previously stated, Nikawawa became a powerful and leading village in Nikawagampaha Korale under Nawagathe Rala or Nawagaththe Adikari Mudiyanse. His son-in-law, Samarakkodi Appuhamy, was a wealthy merchant (potentially Hetti) from Yakkawita (a place close to Narammala) who travelled from one village to another selling coconut.[150] He was used to camp at Nikawewa. Later, his hunting skills and intelligence had impressed Nawagathe Rala and allowed him to stay in his "walawwa" (residence) during his visits.[151] Nawagaththe Rala arranged his daughter to be married to Samarakkodi Rala. This is the time Samarakkodi attended a "kula haba" trial, a dispute of caste, at Gonalagama. As stated previously, due to the shame of the treatment received from the local elites (mudalis), he went back to South India and brought gifts to the Mundukondapola palace and gained the recognition from the elites of Nikawagampaha Korale.

---

149 Ibid.
150 Ibid.
151 YM Dharmasena book 2011.

He married Nawagaththe Rals's daughter. The name Samarakkodi Appuhamy was also used the name Nikawewa Mudiyanse.

Nawagaththe Adikari Mudiyanse's sister married to Kumbaldiwala Bandara of Sathara Korale (Matale). They had two sons with the names of Kalugal Bandara and Irugal Bandara. After their parent's death they came back to Nikawewa. Irugal Bandara married to the daughter (Kumarihamy) of Panaliyadde Diwakara Mohottala from of Sathara Korale. The King Buwanekabahu of Kotte awarded the title of *"Appuhamy Ekanayake Mudiyanse"* to Irugal Bandara.[152]

For some reasons, Pohorawaththa manuscript has been unkind to Nikawewa village. It claims Nikaweawa or Nikathu Kadawala had been notorious for its high crimes. Level of crimes considered as high crimes were done nine times since King Wijaya. It is reasonable to identify one crime as the killing of King Irugal Bandara of Mundukondapola potentially by Nikaweawa Nawagaththe Rala's brother.

According to Dharmasena,[153] generations of Nawagaththe and Samarakkodi later taken to be Rajakaruna Mudiyanse, Rajapaksha Mudiyanse, Samarakkodi Mudiyanselage, Senawirathna Mudiyanselage, and Adhikari Mudiyanse.

Herathgama and Rambewa legacy.

Herathgama village can be found at approximately 7.874059 degrees North latitude and 80.430501 degrees East longitude, while Rambewa village is situated at approximately 7.870077 degrees North latitude and 80.433315 degrees East longitude.

Herathgama has been listed as a Brāhmin village in the Malala Vittiya manuscript. It included five villages of Dembatogampaha

152 YM Dharmasena book 2011.
153 YM Dharmasena Book 2011.

under the Purohit Brāhmaṇa Rāla. It is believed that it was occupied by a Brāhmin family who came to Sri Lanka during the same period of time and is closely related to the seven Brāhmin families. N1 states that an elite called Prince Ranasinghe received a title of *"Herath Bandara"* from the Sithawaka Palace. Because of the Herath Bandara, this village got the name of Herathgama (where Herath lives).

Legends of Herathgama[154] disclose that there were two grandsons of King Buvanekabahu VII residing at Herathgama and Rambawa. This grandson of Herathgama held the name of Senarath Durandara Parasekara Bandara Herath Mudiyanselage. It is possible that this royal or Brāhmin connection helped Herathgama to include in the supreme villages of Dembatogampaha. It is unlikely that Herath Bandara was a Malala Bandara. Residents of Herathgama held higher positions in Kandyan Buddhist sangha hierarchy. The residents hold predominantly the Herath Mudiyanse surname and any other surnames (like Ekanayake Mudiyanse) in the village because of *"binna vivaha"*.[155] As far as the tradition is concerned, Herathgama is an unspoiled village.

Rambawa village is situated next to Herathgama village. Rambawa people have surnames of Herath Mudiyanselage and Rajakaruna Mudiyanselage. Herathgama and Rambawa had intensive marriage relationships with Kambuwatawana, Borawewa, Nikawewa, Rakwana and Dembatogama.

There is a legend about a "Kiri Ula Kumarihamy" (a foster mother or "milk mother") from Kiri Ula who fed a newborn baby of the queen of the King Buvanekabahu VII.[156] Apparently, a baby

---

[154] YM Dharmasena's book 2011, pg. 50.

[155] Males from outside villages marrying maidens and settling in the maiden's village.

[156] Refers to YM Dharmasena book for the details.

was born to the queen at Nikawewa while she was travelling via Rambawa and Herathgama.[157] The queen had inadequate breast milk to feed the baby prince. After a test for a suitable mother with suitable milk[158] to feed the prince, this noble woman was selected from Herathgama or Rambawa who had a royal connection. Vanni Vittiya (Marambe 1926, pg. 35) suggests that Kiri Ula Kumarihamy was a sister of a Range Bandara. There is a lack of information about this Range Bandara and if he was a Malala Bandara or any other descent. However, according to the manuscript, Ranthimbirigahawila, Kadawila and Kiriula villages were awarded to this noble woman.

Nikawewa vitti book states that the noble woman and her son were taken to the King's palace and the woman was named Kiri Ula Kumarihamy and her son was named Rajapaksha Mudiyanse.

Kiri Ula is situated between Herathgama and Rambawa. There is a reservoir called Kiri Ula Wewa and includes two parts of the locality called Maha (greater) Kiri Ula and Kuda (minor) Kiri Ula. No people live in Kiri Ula presently, the original residents had been moved to Herathgama, Rambawa and Nikawewa.

Nambadewa Legacy.

Nambadewa village is located at approximately 7.882723 degrees North latitude and 80.375102 degrees East longitude.

Vanni Vittiya manuscript lists Nambadewa as one village where one Brāhmaṇa Rāla out of the seven settled. He was the youngest in the group. As previously stated, N1 does not list the Brāhmaṇa Rāla who settled at this village. This village is in Vanni Hathpathtu which belonged to Uduweriya Malala Bandara. N1 states at one

---

[157] There has been a road from Matale and Dambulla via Palle Kale Sanctuary according to YM Dharmasena's book.

[158] A milk drop was formed a shape of a dagger or "ula."

stage that Devamadda Palace had given this village to a Ratnayake Mudiyanse. One Purohit Brahman's grandson was appointed for the Mohottala (registrar) position for Nambadewa. Dembatogama and Nambadewa had close relationships. Angamugama Buddhist temple was under the custodianship of this village for centuries. There were intensive marriage relationships between this village and Dembatogama, Kambuwatawana, Wathuwaththegama, Galgiriyawa, Nikawewa and Herathgama.

Current surnames of the village include Wanninayake Mudiyanse (predominantly), Rajakaruna Mudiyanse, and Ratnayake Mudiyanse.

Parawahagama Legacy.

Parawahagama village is located at approximately 7.688095 degrees North latitude and 80.500251 degrees East longitude.

Vanni Vittiya manuscript lists Parawahagama as a village where one Brāhmaṇa Rāla settled in and identifies this person's name as Mapa Brāhmaṇa Rāla. However, N1 is silent about Parawahagama, and states Dunuwila village[159] instead as a place where one Brāhmaṇa Rāla settled. The families from Nambadewa and Walathwewa had marriages with Parawahagama.[160] There could have been a Brāhmin connection to Parawahagama. The legendary leaders of the 1818 Rebellion, the supreme leader Kappetipola, and the deputy Pilimathalawe were arrested at Parawahagama Walawwa.[161] The other leader, Madugalle, fled from the backdoor of this Walawwa. According to the legend, the Walawwa belonged to a chieftain called Mapa Mudiyanse, consistent with the Vanni Vittiya record. According to another legend, Mapa Mudiyanse had

---

[159] This village is in Matale District, and I did not follow up that information.
[160] Information was provided by EM Sunil Bandara.
[161] Tennakoon Wimalananda, 1818 Udarata Great Rebellion, (part 11).

married to a close relative of Kappetipola from Matale. It appears that Mapa was in the cycle of Brāhmi supporters of the Rebellion and Kappetipola, at the end, withdrew to his enclave. Parawahagama currently has almost none of its traditional landowners.[162]

Pohorawaththa legacy.

Pohorawaththa village is located at approximately 7.910411 degrees North latitude and 80.412982 degrees East longitude.

There are two different accounts in N1 and Mahasammatha Pohorawaththa vitti (N3) books about Pohorawaththa residents. According to N1, Gonalagama, Moragollagama including Pohorawaththa, had been given to Mapa Rala by the Sithawaka Palace. That Mapa Rala sold Moragollagama to Rajapaksha Wijayasuriya Kuruwita Nawarathna Mudiyanse.

The *Mahasammatha Pohorawaththa* vitti book is devoted to Pohorawaththa's legacy. As stated elsewhere, the manuscript is dedicated to an aristocrat named Sri Chandrasekara Purohitha Brāhmaṇa Rankadu Bandi Wijesingha Senewirathna Mudiyanse. Obviously, he is also of Brāhmin origin, but he was a commander of a large army that fought against the Portuguese for the King of Kotte. N1 is silent about this aristocrat. The *Pohorawaththa* Vitti book states that part of Gonalagama was given to the "Achari Naide" (metal worker or technocrat) who came with him from India. He was later awarded the name of "Wijesinghe Patabanda" by the royal authorities.

Senewirathna Mudiyanse's son was Sri Chandrasekara Purohitha Rathnapala Herath Adhikaram Mudiyanse. He also served in the royal army of Sithawaka Rajasinghe. Mahasammatha Vitti book

---

162 Information provided by Chandana Wanninayake.

provides information about marriages of this generation with Perawaththa, Doratiyawa, Dodanwatawana, and Mapegamuwa. The manuscript also admits that there was no person remaining who can claim the heritage of Senawirathna Mudiyanse after a few generations. Subsequently, claiming the relationship from his paternal side, Dodanwatawana Mohottala's son, Pinhamy Mudiyanse, who came from Siriwardanapura, obtained the title of "Muhandirum for Nikawagampaha Korale" and settled at Pohorawaththa. The area awarded to this elite is stated in the vitti book.

The current Adhikari Herath Mudiyanse generation in Pohorawaththa descends from Rathnapala Herath Mudiyanse.[163]

Dembatogama Legacy.

Dembatogama village is located at approximately 7.885239 degrees North latitude and 80.385710 degrees East longitude.

Dembatogama village can be considered as the supreme residence of Brāhmin generation of Nikawagampaha Korale from where Purohit Brahman ruled the rata – the region. The role and responsibilities of the authorities who held this office is not exactly clear, but N1 hints that they resolved conflicts, kept peace and security, informed the king of any significant events, organised labour for royal duties, including supplying troops for wars etc.

N1 records that Purohit Brāhmin selected Dembatogama because the area was secure and peaceful. The adjoining rata (parts of Vanni Hathpattuwa) was under the control of Uduweriya Malala Bandara. He was powerful and domineering in the region. As stated early, according to N1, Malala Bandara was killing people and creating disputes between landholders and selling land. The generation of Uduweriya Malala Bandara had come to Vanni

---

Hathpattu before the immigration of seven Brāhmins. He also had owned some villages in Nikawagampaha Korale.

Purohit did not want to settle in that Vanni country (Vanni Hathpattu) because of Malala Bandara's unruly and violent behaviour. Dembatogama rata was safe from three sides and the only land dispute had taken place from one side which was the country of Uduweriya Malala Bandara. However, the dispute with Uduweriya Bandara for Ranpathwila, Walathwewa, and Nambdewa territories were later resolved in the favour of Dembatogama Purohit Brāhmaṇa Rāla.

The information in relation to the prolongation of Dembatogama Purohit family available from at least three vitti books,[164] but the sequence of the family events lacks consistency.

The Purohit Brāhmaṇa Rāla had an illustrious generation, as evident from the Nikawewa Vitti book. The Purohit Brāhmaṇa's son was Appuhamy Bandara Brāhmaṇa Rāla. His son was Appuhamy Rajakaruna Mohottala (grandson), his sons (Appuhamila) were Loku (senior) Mohottala and Kuda (junior) Mohottala (purohit's great grandsons). One daughter of a Dembatogama Mohottala married from Eriyawa, and she was given Hettigama village, and another daughter married from Galmaduwa. According to the Nikawewa vitti book, several subsequent young men of Dembatogama Mohottala married from Mahabole, Galgiriyawa (a daughter of Maha Yapahamy), Ambogama, Kandubodagama, and Rakwana villages.

N1 also states slightly different information about the descendants, titles, and marriages of the Dembatogama family. A son of the purohit (or perhaps a grandson) held a custodian position

---

[164] N1, N2, Vanni Vithiya etc.

at the royal treasury (Kotte or Kandy) and gained the Registrar (Mohottala) position of Nambadewa. He was also honoured as Rajakaruna Mohottala. His son, Purohit's grandson, was given the honorary title of Rajakaruna Mohotti Mudiyanse. His son, Purohit's great-grandson was given the title of Wijesundara Bhumipala Mudiyanse. He was awarded the custody of Dembatogama including the villages of: Walpaluwaththa, Kongama, Ranamukgama, Wicharanagama, Archirigama, Hettigama, Mawidalupotha. Later Pahala Thimbiriyawa village was added to his village portfolio by the King of Sithawaka.

N1 provides some contradictory information about Wijesundara Bhumipala's family. One section of the record states that he had two sons, a Mohottala and a Kuda (junior) Mohottala. One Mohottala was honoured as Kambuwatawana Ekanayake Mudiyanse and the other as Basnayake Mudiyanse. N1 is silent about Ekanayake Mudiyanse's legacy. However, Basnayake Mudiyanse's son was awarded the title of Rajakaruna Maha Mohottala (Mohottala means registrar) by King Sithawaka Rajasinghe. N1 had been potentially written by this Rajakaruna Mohottala. He proclaims in N1 that Purohit's children and grandchildren are the only people entitled to demarcate boundaries and certify statutory declarations in the Dembatogama country. This indicates the continuous recognition of the Purohit Brahmans superiority, the power, and the legacy. His dignity and supremacy enjoyed the region, and he is honourably called "Dembatogama Muththa" (supreme elder or the elder of the Dembatogama rata) even to the present day. He is respected as a regional deity (reincarnated as a regional spirit) by the locals.

As stated in N1 Walpaluwa village was given to Tamil Nakathiya or Sinhala Wiriduwa who has come down from South India with Purohit Brāhmaṇa Rāla. The descendants of this family still live in

155

this locality. One descendant of this family, Sinha Wiridualage Hapuwa, has legendary memories of Purohit Brāhmaṇa Rāla as a fair and gracious elder.[165]

The descendants of Dembatogama hold surnames such as Rajakaruna Mudiyanse, Basnayake Mudiyanse, Ekanayake Mudiyanse and Ratnayake Mudiyanse.

Eventually, the leadership of the Dembatogampaha rata was transformed into Nikawagampaha and came under the control of Nikawewa Nawagaththe Rala and his family with a royal decree. The decline of Dembatogama supremacy was due to several factors. Dembatogama lost the leadership to Nawagaththe Adikari Mudiyanse of Nikawewa. And some Dembatogama villages were given to Hewawasam or soldier leaderships of the royal army. Dembatogama's irrigation facilities were gradually abandoned due to a lack of reconstruction or repair. Eventually, the original heir family members shifted to farming villages such as Wathuwaththegama, Galgiriyawa, Rakwana, Eriyawa, Ambogama, and to Kambuwatawana, built up with marriage relationships etc. Only a handful of families remained at Dembatogama to the present time.

After the 1950's, some lands at Dembatogama had been given to commercial estate developers and the people who had come to work in these properties from various parts of the country settled down permanently. Dembatogama is a living example of shifting of traditional power and creating the foundation for modernisation and commercialisation at the end.

---

[165] Interview evidence

Rakwana and Galgiriyawa Legacy.

Rakwana village can be found at approximately 7.913731 degrees North latitude and 80.395781 degrees East longitude, while Galgiriyawa village is located at approximately 7.916561 degrees North latitude and 80.387260 degrees East longitude.

The Brāhmaṇa Rāla who settled in Rakwana was introduced as "Rakkandu Bandi". Brāhmaṇa Rāla, which means the Brāhmaṇa Rāla or chieftain of Brahman, who was wearing Rakkandu (bangles or earrings of gold). His name is not specifically mentioned in vitti books, but N1 hints he could be another Mahipala. That is not strange because Borawewa Mahipala and Rakwana Rala were brothers of a family. According to N1 Rakwana Mahipala's son was Bandari Brāhmaṇa Rāla. It is interesting that the second generation had also carried the same identity as Brāhmaṇa Rāla to stamp their Brāhmin origin. He had three children:

- ✦ Maha Yapa Mudiyanse,
- ✦ Undiye Rala, and
- ✦ Madiya Mahage[166] (the lady called Madiya).

Bandari Brāhmaṇa Rāla died after giving Rakwana village to Maha Yapa Mudiyanse. This was the time a land dispute had arisen between Rakwana Mudiyanse and Pohorawaththa Udugedara Rala.

Rakwana Yapa Mudiyanse had two marriages. The first marriage was to a woman from Dembatogama, and they had two children – Kadumuluwe Rala and Pissi (psychotic) Rala. Both Kadumuluwe Rala and Pissi Rala had no children. After Dembatogama wife died he married a lady from Walathwewa. She had two daughters and one was married to a man from Undurawa. The other married to

---

[166] Mahage was used to address Vidane's or Mayoraal wife (KD Pasranawithana).

Gamage Rala, who was the son of Galgiriyawe Maha Yapa Mudiyanse.

It is important to note the legacy of Galgiriyawa at this point. As stated before, the Devamadda Palace had granted Galgiriyawa including the villages of Aluthgama, Wambatuwewa, Kathikanda Wewa, and Dalupathkota to a monk called Bogoda who potentially followed the seven Brāhmins to Sri Lanka. A close relation of this monk (a grandson) had been introduced as Maha Yapa Mudiyanse of Galgiriyawa (in N1). This Maha Yapa Mudiyanse could have been the person who married the daughter of Rakwana Yapa Mudiyanse. It is possible this monk had siblings who had migrated with him.

The Galgiriyawe Bogoda monk could have maintained prestigious status because of his Brāhmin origin. He could have established a Galgiriyawa monks order that combined with Malwaththa Temple in Kandy during the Kandyan kingdom (or he lived at Malwaththa temple). There had been two Mahanayaka (chief incumbents) of Malwaththa Chapter from Galgiriyawa which could be considered as a significant contribution from Galgiriyawa Brāhmin legacy.

Galgiriyawe Maha Yapa Mudiyanse's son Gamage Rala had six children:

- ✦ Neththipola Rala,
- ✦ Undurawa Rala,
- ✦ Liyana Rala,
- ✦ Gokarelle Mahage,
- ✦ Porapola Mahage, and
- ✦ Hanwalle Mahage (who married to Hanwalle Wijepala Mudiyanse).

This information indicates that this family expanded to other elites in other parts of Sri Lanka outside the territory of seven Brāhmaṇa Rāla cycle in Sath Korale.

The remaining surnames of Rakwana and Galgiriyawa villages include Yapa Mudiyanse, Rajakaruna Mudiyanse, Sri Narayana Bamunu Midiyanse, and Herath Mudiyanse in addition to other professional groups (castes) living in this area.

Borawewa and Kambuwatawana Legacy.

Borawewa village can be found at around 7.922833 degrees North latitude and 80.403586 degrees East longitude, whereas Kambuwatawana village is situated at approximately 7.937990 degrees North latitude and 80.392371 degrees East longitude.

As mentioned previously, the seven Brāhmaṇa Rālas who migrated to Sath Korale had been blood relations or first cousins. Purohit Brāhmaṇa Rāla, Rakwana Mahipala Rala, and Borawewa Mahipala were brothers. According to N1, their cousins lived in Kandulawa (Kandulassa Brāhmaṇa Rāla), Kiri Bamuna (Kiri Brāhmaṇa Rāla), Dunuwila in Matale, and in Nabilikumbura. However, N2 does not record Dunuwila and Nabilikumbura connection but includes Mataluwawa and Nambadewa, which are villages in proximity to Dembatogama.

Mahipala received eleven villages (names given previously). Wanni Upatha records that he had been also given seven olagams (abandoned villages) and are not clear as to which villages they were.

Mahipala Brāhmaṇa Rāla was honoured with a Sinhala authoritative name of Chandrasekara Maha Basnayake Mudiyanse (N1). He had a son, and he had been honoured with the name of Maha Basnayake Mudiyanse and given Kambuwatawana village. This son could have joined Mahipala later coming from India with his mother. N1 hints that Mahipala could have had another son who lived at Borawewa but no specific information available.

Mahipala's sister (who also had come from South India later) had married to Ekanayake Mudiyanse of Parakumbura (in Kegalle District). According to N1, when Mahipala was old and fragile, he heard that his sister and brother-in-law had died, and they had a daughter called Bingumalethana and a son called Sirimalhamy. Mahipala asked his son Maha Basnayake Mudiyanse to go to Parakumbura and accompany them to Borawewa which he complied. Mahipala gave Kambuwatawana village to Bingumalethana and Ahatugaha Dalupotha village to Sirimalhamy.

Bingumalethana married to Hanwalle Wijepala Mudiyane's brother Appuhamy Rala (Galgiriya connection). It appeared that this Appuhamy Rala settled at Kambuwatawana which was his wife's heritage. They had three children:

✧ Pothuwe Mahage,
✧ Unnassa Mahage who married to Unnassa Rala of Borawewa, and
✧ Mahappu Maha Korala.

Kambuwatawana village had been transferred to Mahappu Maha Korala. The "Maha Korala" is a position that could control a few divisions or many villages. This award of Maha Korala position mentioned for the first time among the descendants of seven Brāhmaṇa Rālas recorded in N1. With this position, Kambuwatawana appeared to be evolved as a new centre of power for local leadership.

Mahappu Maha Korala married to Kapu Mahage,[167] who was the daughter of Borawewa Herath Mudiyanse. Herath Mudiyanse was the son of Maha Basnayake Mudiyanse (who had the right of Kambuwatawana village previously) and the grandson (or great grandson) of the famous Mahipala Brāhmaṇa Rāla. It appeared that the Mahappu's marriage was to a blood relative or to a cousin from Borawewa. This marriage restrengthened the Borawewa connection.

Mahappu Maha Korala had three children:

✧ Dambagaha Mahage or Hinkendahamy (a daughter),

✧ Yammepala Mahage (a daughter), and

✧ Borawewa Arachila (a son married from Borawewa and had held an Arachchi position).

Mahappu Korala appeared to have transferred the ownership of Kambuwatawana land to Dambagaha Mahage. N1 provides some information to suspect Dambagaha Mahage married to Ekanayake Mudiyanse, a grandson of Dembatogama Rajakaruna Mohottala. By this marriage Dembatogama family kept foothold at Kambuwatawana.

Dambagaha Mahage had five children:

✧ Sepalahamy or Basnayake Mudiyanse,

✧ Sooryahamy (potentially later honoured as Ekanayake Mudiyanse),

✧ Gamthiha Rala,

✧ Appuhamy Arachila, and

✧ Konwewa Mahage (who married from Konwewa).

---

[167] According to KD Paranawithana and Ekanayake, the names ending with Rāla, Mahage and Mahathmo attributed to Sinhalese govigama elites. Rāla and Appuhami, and Mudiyanse for men and Mahage, Hamy and Mahathmayo to introduce women who married to title holders like Arachila, Rāla, Korala, and Mohottala.

The name of the Sepalahamy's (Basnayake Mudiyanse's) wife is not stated but he had three children:

- ✧ Kudawewa Mahage (who married from Kudawewa)
- ✧ Karagaswewa Mahage (who married from Karagaswewa), and
- ✧ Maha Korala (potentially "Korala" position was later transferred to him through Basnayake Mudiyanse senior who was his father).

Gamthiha Rala had only one son – Dunumani Rala. Appuhamy Arachchila had two children: Aluthwawa Rala, and Loku (senior) Rala.

Ekanayake Mudiyanse (potentially Sooryahamy) had five children:

- ✧ Nikawewa Rala (who left to settle down in Nikawewa or married from Nikawewa),
- ✧ Muhandiram,[168]
- ✧ Nakath Rala,
- ✧ Maha Korale (Probably, he became a Maha Korala), and
- ✧ Mahage who was married from Galgiriyawa.

Nikawa Rala had two children: Halamba Rala (who settled at Halambewa), and Ramba Rala (who settled at Rambawa).

Muhandiram had five children:

- ✧ Kambuwatawana Rala,
- ✧ Pothanegama Rala (who settled in Pothanegama),
- ✧ Kandubodagama Rala (who settled at Kandubodagama),
- ✧ Thalakolawawe Mahage (who married from Thalakolawewa),
- ✧ Mahathmoyo (lady) married from Rakwana.

---

168   This is a village headman position that reports to a Korala. This position started by Portuguese and continued by the Dutch and the British.

Maha Korala's children:

- ✧ Kuda (junior) Korala,
- ✧ The Mahathmayo (lady) who married from Kuda Herathgama,
- ✧ Nikawewa Rala (who settled in Nikawewa),
- ✧ The Mahage who married from Herathgama, and
- ✧ The Mahathmayo (lady) who married from Rakwana.

N1 manuscript concludes with this Maha Korala's children. N1 hints that the Kambuwatawana legacy became strong and Borawewa supremacy started to wane. It also appeared that Kambuwatawana Maha Korala had renewed marriage relationships with surrounding divisions of Rakwana, Herathgama, Nikawewa, Galgiriyawa, Rambawa, Kandubodagama, Thalakolawawa, Dembatogama and Pothanegama.

N1 covers at least five to six generations of the seven Brāhmaṇa Rālas legacies. This manuscript has potentially been written towards the middle of the Kandyan kingdom; therefore, I have used other historical records to provide a reasonably uninterrupted genealogical history of Kambuwatawana and other Brāhmi villages. This information is presented in Chapters from 14 to 19.

The next chapter is allocated to follow up the Brāhmins legacy during the British rule and beyond.

Chapter Fourteen

Seven Brāhmin Families During the British Rule

Palm-leaf records conclude towards the middle of Kandyan era, and no similar records exist that are applicable to the British rule or beyond. To trace the Brāhmin legacy to the present day, I had to rely on other historical records. The 1818 Rebellion was a major event in which descendants of seven Brāhmin families emerged in playing a foremost role.

1818 Rebellion.

The 1817-1818 Rebellion described as the *Uva Wellassa* Rebellion or *Udarata* (up country) Karalla of 1818 is the height of the people's anger and dissatisfaction over the British rule which did not keep promises of the convention signed on 2nd March 1815 with Kandyan chiefs. The local chiefs wanted to revert and regain the Kandyan Kingdom. The turning point for the uprising was the appointment of a non-Kandyan chieftain to a position in Wellassa by the British undermining the authority of the Kandyan chiefs.

However, the rebellion was ill planned and showed signs of failure from the start. However, Kandyan chiefs fought together potentially a failing war.

The rebellion was led by Kappetipola and Pilimathalawe Maha Adikars (prime ministers). The Kambuwatawana and Borawewa families, together with Kandulawa family, are noticed among many other leaders from Sath Korale to have fallen into this unplanned and unsuccessful rebellion.[169]

Governor Brownrigg declared Marshall Law and issued a Proclamation on January 1st, 1818, that leaders engaged in promoting rebellion and war against His Majesty's forces, were "Rebels, Outlaws and Enemies to the British." Their lands and properties were confiscated by the Crown.[170]

During the time of this rebellion, Seven Korale had been divided into two parts for administration – Ihala Dolos Pattuwa (Upper Twelve Pattus) and Pahala Dolos Pattuwa (Lower Twelve Pattus).

Using the British military records kept at National Archives Sri Lanka (records 6/543 and 6/543A), in his book, *1818 Prathama Nidahas Satane Purogamiyo* (Pioneers of 1818 Freedom Struggle), Anura Manatunga, lists 104 rebel leaders from Sath Korale who were involved in the insurrection.

The rebel leaders from Kambuwatawana and Borawewa were:

❖ ***Kambuwatawana Mohottala.*** He was named as a rebel leader from Pahala Dolos Paththu of Seven Korale and his properties were confiscated by the Crown. He was surrendered mimself to the British army on 29th October 1818.

❖ ***Kambuwatawana Kuda (Junior) Mohottala.*** He was named as a rebel leader from Pahala Dolos Paththu of Seven

---

[169] I do not suggest that other community groups and caste groups were not in the rebellion. The focus is isolated on the Brāhmi leaders for the purposes of this publication.

[170] Palitha Kohona, Daily news 8th December 2018.

Korale and his properties were confiscated by the Crown. He surrendered to the British army on 2nd November 1818.

✧ ***Kambuwatawana Loku (senior) Mohottala.*** He was named as a rebel leader from Pahala Dolos Paththu of Seven Korale. The Crown proclaimed on 20th November 1818 that his properties were confiscated by the Crown. Apparently, he died in the battlefield.

✧ ***Borawewa Korala.*** The Crown proclaimed on 14th November 1818 that he was a rebel leader from Pahala Dolos Paththu of Seven Korale and his properties would have been confiscated. There is no record to indicate if he surrendered or killed. Most probably he escaped any penalty.

✧ ***Borawewa Kuda (Junior) Mohottala.*** The Crown proclaimed on 14th November 1818 that he was a rebel leader from Pahala Dolos Paththu of Seven Korale and his properties would be confiscated. There is no record to indicate if he surrendered or was killed. Most probably he escaped any penalty.

✧ ***Borawewa Loku (Senior) Mohottala.*** The Crown proclaimed on 14th November 1818 that he was a rebel leader from Pahala Dolos Paththu of Seven Korale and his properties would be confiscated. He surrendered to the British army on 2nd November 1818.

Among the rebels from Kandulawa and Delwita villages included:

✧ ***Kandulawa Kuda (Junior 1) Mohottala.*** The Crown proclaimed on 31st October 1818 that he was a rebel leader from Seven Korale and his properties were to be confiscated. There is no record to indicate if he surrendered or was killed. Most probably he escaped any penalty. He was a brother of Kandulawa Senior Mohottala.

✧ **Kandulawa Kuda (Junior 2) Mohottala.** The Crown proclaimed on 31st October 1818 that he was a rebel leader from Seven Korale and his properties were to be confiscated. He joined the rebellion while working as Pussalle Korala. There is no record to indicate if he was surrendered or killed. Most probably he escaped any penalty. He was the youngest brother of Kandulawa Senior Mohottala.

✧ **Kandulawa Loku (senior) Mohottala.** The Crown proclaimed on 31st October 1818 that he was a senior rebel leader from Seven Korale and his properties were to be confiscated. He had been labelled as one of the senior rebels who led the fight in the Ihala Dolos Paththu. He was a skilled fighter and a warrior. He also acted as a fair and humanitarian leader during the war. He surrendered to the British army on 20th November 1818 and this surrender was regarded as only secondary to the surrender of Pilimathalawe Disawa.

✧ **Delwita Lekam .** The Crown proclaimed on 31st October 1818 that he was a rebel from Seven Korale and his properties were to be confiscated. He was regarded as a senior rebel, and he surrendered while pleading others to do the same.

There were several other rebel leaders who involved in the rebellion close to Kambuwatawana and Borawewa:

✧ Kubukwawe Mohottala (pg. 25)
✧ Kubukulawe Mohottala (pg. 26)
✧ Giriba Mohottala (pg. 35)
✧ Gokaralle Lekam (pg. 36)
✧ Dodanwatuwana Nilame (pg. 45)
✧ Doluwe Mohottala (pg. 46)

✧ Polpithigama Mohottala (pg. 56)

✧ Bamunapotha Mohottala (pg. 58)

✧ Mahawa Mohottala (pg. 64). A senior rebel.

✧ Makaduwawa Mohottala (pg. 65)

✧ Mapegamuwa Mohottala (pg. 66)

In the book *1818 Udarata Great Rebellion,* (part 11), Tennakoon Wimalananda (1962, pg. 249), states that Kappetipola Dissawe was arrested with Pilimatalawwe on 28th October 1818, by Lt. William O'Neil in a Walawwa at Parawahagama near Manewa. Letter 70 – written by J. Frazer (an army officer) to one of his higher officers on 1818 Oct 29th at Amunakole (somewhere around Kalawewa) informed that Keppetipola and Pilimatalawa had been arrested from a house.[171] Molligoda escaped with a group of senior rebels which included Borawewa Korala, Borawewa Mohottala, Kambuwatawana Mohottala, and Doluwe Mohottala etc. In this same letter, he (Frazer) informs that Kambuwatawana Mohottala had surrendered on the same day (not on this location). This description suggests that Kambuwatawana and Borawewa rebel leaders were with Kappetipola and Pilimathalawe until the last stage.

There is a detailed description about the senior rebels in Sath Korale in *Sinhale and the Patriots 1815-1818* written by PE Pieris in 1950. In Appendix Q,[172] pg. 638. Pieris provides a plausible account of rebel leaders of Kandulawa, Delwita etc. using the British military records (Hook to Lusignan) folklore:

"Kandulawa Mohottala ... considered as to rank, wealth, influence or talents, is the first in the Ihala Dolos Pattu. He

---

[171] Folk tales account that these two leaders were arrested from two villages next to each other, Parawagama (Walawwa of Mapa Mudiyanse) and Kahalla (Walawwa of Wanasinghe Rajakaruna Mudiyanse). Both these chieftains were Vanni Mudiyanses who had marriage relationships to Matale Brāhmi chieftains.

[172] PE Pieris full report regarding rebel leaders in Sath Korale is added to Attached to the Appendix 2.

joined early in the attempt to subvert the English Government established in the Interior. He was one of the most active and formidable opposers we had. He more than once held the highest offices under the English and Kandyan Governments. He says it had been his intention to come in previous to 20th September, but extreme ill health prevented. His personal appearance gives a colouring of truth to this, looking most wretchedly ill. The vast stores of grain in his possession were appropriated to feed the insurgents, and he frequently commanded in person his followers. It is true no act of cruelty stained the rebel career of this leader; he has received praise for his humane conduct to some who fell into his hands. He had no appointments under the Pretender's party. This I consider by no means favourable, because it indicates that no necessity existed to bribe him to exertion. Almost the whole of his properly has fallen a sacrifice, viz. houses, grain and cattle. His lands remain and are very extensive. I am informed he can raise on his lands about 1,000 ammunas of paddy annually including both seasons. Gardens and his most valuable effects remain, though many of the coconut trees have been cut down. The latter, viz. effects, he carried off into Wanni. He has two brothers, the youngest was Korale of Poossalle at the commencement of the Rebellion and joined his efforts to those of his eldest brother, remaining with him until his surrender on the loth instant. The second brother was not in any office under the British Government. His efforts were also joined to those of his elder brothers. They have all three suffered severely during the struggle by the privations sustained in partaking, in common with the Brutes of the jungle."

For this full report, please refer to Appendix 2.

By August 1818, the English army had the upper hand on many fronts and rebels have been in disarray. Delwita Lekam was one leader who encouraged rebels to surrender. Of Delwita Lekama, the English Commander Hook said:

"[W]ho with talents and ambition has been very active in the hostile measures of the rebels and only submitted from conviction of our cause being irresistible. He advised the rebel Chief Mohottalas to submit as the English troops were dispersed like so many mosquitoes over the whole country and not to be opposed."

Kambuwatawana Junior was among a rebel group which was still resisting. Hook wrote to Lusignan, on 10th November 1818, regarding the local talent at the war and the loss to the country:

"After these rebels have suffered the punishment due to their crimes, is it the intention of Government to render them ineligible to any office? It is unfortunate that almost all the chiefs of talents or who had considerable knowledge of the country were among the rebels. I have received more information from them than from our friends."

Kappetipola together with Pilimathalawwe were beheaded on 18th November 1818. Kandulawa Senior Mohottala surrendered on 20th November after Kappetipola had been beheaded. According to the mythology, Kambuwatawana Senior Mohottala carried the battle without surrendering and English soldiers killed him in the battlefield. One Mohottala surrendered and expelled but returned to the country. Another fled and hid somewhere but returned to the village after a few years with a pardon.

Why Did Local Brāhmin Chiefs Support the Rebellion?

It appeared that Kandyan family connections and kinship put the rebel leaders together.

Not only the strength of the army but also the trust and reliability of the local leadership counts in war situations. Matale vitti book brings up a good example of the importance of trusted leadership for military allegiance

During the 1818 Rebellion, Kandyan chiefs provided a strong "chain of connections" through kinship lines. This chain was unbroken with strong biological links. One operational principle of the Kandyan chiefs was the maintaining and prolonging their power for survival.

However, there had some elements of lose connections as well by another group of chieftains who took the British side. That was also for their personal gains and survival.

The core Brāhmin clan was willing to sacrifice themselves for a cause, and for their clan leaders in the 1818 Rebellion. Altruism has long been a topic of interest in the study of both human and animal behavior. Why would individuals be willing to sacrifice anything for another individual or a group of individuals? The logic of natural selection would seem to suggest that altruism should not exist, and yet it is found throughout the natural world. Hamilton (1964) demonstrated that altruistic behaviour (behaviour performed at a cost to oneself for the benefit of another) could evolve if the individuals involved were genetically related and his actions would aid his own genetic kin, then he receives an indirect fitness benefit.

The kinship relationship of Kandyan chiefdom was a reliable operational model. The Kandyan chiefs supported each other based on their primary relationships. The propaganda against the British and rebel strategies were confidentially shared between local chiefs. The family and marriage relationships among local chieftain families played a major role in organising and carrying out the military intelligence in top secrecy. Family network became reliable and trustworthy. It appeared that almost all Kandyan chiefs who fought the war were from Brāhmin descent, including Kappetipola and Pilimathalawe. It appeared that Hetti and Malala chiefs did not consistently support the rebellion. From Vanni Hathpattuwa (of Sath Korale), only tthre chieftains, Mahawa Mohottala and Giriba Mohottala, and Makaduwawa Mohottala supported the rebellion. It could be that they had close family connections with Brāhmi or rebel leaders.

It is debatable if the 1818 uprising was a national freedom struggle or power struggle for domination by Kandyan chiefs.

However, many leaders lost their lives, and their property was confiscated. The British troops were brutal, destroying properties, setting fire to buildings, and killing many domestic animals. Those who were involved in the rebellion lost their social status, wealth, and economic power. Despite all that they had something to sacrifice for. Kandulawa Mohottala family was one rich family who became weak after the rebellion.

Some Mohottala families fled from their villages. Gananath Obeyesekere (2004) identifies an influx of new migrants from Wellassa to Batticaloa and Ampara districts after the rebellion. Many family members of Sath Korale chieftains also fled from their home villages.

Kambuwatawana Generations.

Following the devastating defeat during the 1818 Rebellion, a significant number of descendants of Kambuwatawana chiefs chose to flee the village. This pivotal rebellion marked an event where the stability of the Kambuwatawana social unit began to disintegrate.

Among those who left Kambuwatawana, two prominent lineages emerged and expanded in different regions. The Molagoda and Kirindigala (Balangoda) generations, both of which originated from descendants of Kambuwatawana, played a significant role in shaping their respective areas after the rebellion.

Another noteworthy lineage that can be traced back to Kambuwatawana is the Delwita family. Their connection primarily arises from marriage relationships with Kambuwatawana. It is plausible that many descendants of Kambuwatawana may have dispersed to various parts of the country. However, these particular families, especially the Molagoda, Kirindigala, and Delwita families, continue to honour their roots by incorporating "Kambuwatawana" as part of their surnames, preserving the historical legacy of their ancestral village.

A description of these notable generations is provided in Appendix 3 "Kambuwatawana Generations in other Parts of the Country".

Kambuwatawana Disawa

As already stated elsewhere I gathered information about at least one Disawa of Sath Korale and one Rate Mahaththaya (two bothers) from Kambuwatawana. John Ferguson,[173] who created Ferguson Directory provides extensive details about this Disawa. It appears that Kambuwatawana Disawa was a dear friend of Mr AM Ferguson, OMG, reporter for Ceylon Observer (potentially John Ferguson's father). The esteem friendship between Mr A M Ferguson and Kambuwatawana Disawa is well demonstrated in John Ferguson's record. He introduces Kambuwatawana Disawa as a "fine old Kandyan gentleman" and "a grand old Kandyan Chieftain."

It reveals that Kambuwatawana Disawa had been brought up at the Sri Wikrama Rajasinghe palace since he was a teenager. Ferguson states that he was the first Disawa appointed for Sath Korale after the British occupation of the Kandyan Kingdom (in 1815). The reference to this timeframe is questionable. It is well recorded that the three most senior elite members of Kambuwatawana family were involved at the 1818 Rebellion. Therefore, it is difficult to believe that the Disawa for Sath Korale was a silent participant at the war or a supporter of the British

---

[173] *Tropical Agriculturist*, (1904) edited by the Hon. John Ferguson, CMG, pg. 135.

regime. Looking at the details of the Ferguson report potentially he became the Disawa after 1850. Some unconfirmed reports suggest the last Disawa of Sath Korale was from Kambuwatawana.[174]

Kambuwatawana Disawa had been a veteran public servant under the British rule. Ferguson states:

> "During the time of the Kandyan Kings, the Seven Korale had always a Disawa, having been one of eleven principal divisions or disawanies, into which the ancient Kingdom was divided. The first Disawa, after the British occupation, was Kambuwatawana, the elder. Both he and his brother were Ratemahatmayas. After their death, the name[175] is extinct.

> "Kambuwatawana was, in addition to Disawa, the first Kandyan Justice of the Peace of the Seven Korales and the first President of the Village Tribunal, when Gansabhawas were introduced to the district. He was a fine old Kandyan gentleman, and when a youth of seventeen was in the Court of the last King of Kandy, Sri Wikrama Raja Sinha."

Then the report goes to an elephant kraaling event in which the Kambuwatawana Disawa and Mr. Ferguson participated. At this function, both were enjoying a glass of Scottish beer and having a friendly conversation even making fun of Sir John Doyly:

> "The Kandyan Monarch …. did not take the trouble of going to the kraal as the English Rajjuruwos do. The elephants were actually driven on the esplanade and captured under the eye of the Monarch, as he sat surrounded by his court in the octagon; and mine ancient friend (who insisted on pledging me in a glass of London bottled stout) states that the same custom was pursued in the time of Bishop Heber's schoolfellow, the semi-Buddhistical Sir John Doyly. The old Rate Mahatthaya quite agreed with me that the presence of the Governor and his

---

[174] Folklore found in Sath Korale and what I heard from a gentleman in Polgahawela was that, "the last disawa of Sath Korale was from Nambuwatawana village in the Vanni area". He used the name Nambuwatawana rather than Kambuwatawana.

[175] Refers to the name "Kambuwatawana".

friends, however, pleasant and interesting to them, was an impediment to the kraaling of the elephants; and he added that Lord Torrington's kraal (the one described by Sir JE Tennent) did not succeed until his lordship's platform was removed. The Disawa was in the Court of the Kandyan King at the period of Mr. Ferguson's birth! After a long interregnum, [H]alps, during the closing years of his official career, was appointed Disawa, and he did not live very long to enjoy the honour and dignity of the much-coveted title."

For Ferguson's full report, please refer to Appendix 1.

Kambuwatawana Disawa had this conversation with late Mr AM Ferguson, OMG, in 1866, when both these veterans were present at the kraal at Nelugolla. The former was one of the chief organisers, and the latter was a reporter to the *Ceylon Observer*. The report further states that "the grand old Kandyan Chieftain" (Kambuwatawana Disawa) had taken part in twenty-one kraals under the British Government-twenty successful and one blank". The report is clear evidence of the reporter's friendship with the Kambuwatawana Disawa.

Then John Ferguson goes to talk about another larger-than-life figure, Hulugalla Disawa who replaced Kambuwatawana Disawa for Sath Korale. In fact, Hulugalle Disawa, unlike his predecessors, became the Disawa for the entire North-western Province.[176]

The Ceylon Handbook and Directory 1898-99, compiled and Edited by J. Ferguson, reports the death of Kambuwatawana Disawa on 1891 August 9th - *"Death of Kambuwatawana Disawa, one of the oldest Kandyan Chiefs and the first president of the Village Council of Seven Korale"* (pg. 227).

---

[176] See Appendix 1. for the full report about Kambuwatawana Disawa and Hulugalle Disawa by John Ferguson.

The precise information about this Kambuwatawana Disawa is not available. On one hand, he went to the king's palace around 1800, and was a youngster in Kandy during the 1818 Rebellion. On the other hand, he was probably a son or a family member of one of Kambuwatawana rebel leader and later supported the British regime.

Shift of Authority Among Local Chieftains in Sath Korale.

It seems that there was a shifting locus of power among the elite Brāhmin villages over time. In the Ceylon Government Gazette released on January 27th, 1893, official records detail the appointment of trustees by the British Governor to oversee temples and shrines in accordance with the Buddhist Temporalities Ordinance of 1889. Notably, these appointments reflect a deliberate choice by the British Governor to select local elites and responsible community leaders, recognizing their esteemed traditional backgrounds.

This list of appointees provides valuable insights into the enduring influence of traditional chieftains in Sath Korale as the 20th century dawned. However, it also suggests a subtle shift in the locus of authority away from the traditional centres of power.

Hiriyala Hathpattuwa

(Name of the Trustee, Residencial village of the Trustee and the name of the Temple)

- ✧ Chandrasekara Mudiyanselage Punchirala, Kambuwatawana, Kubukkadawala Temple
- ✧ Chandrasekara Mudiyanselage Punchirala, Kambuwatawana, Borawewa Temple
- ✧ Wijekoon Mudiyanselage Ranhami, Talawa, Bulnewa Temple

✧ Herath Mudiyanselage Punchirala, Herathgama, Herathgama Temple

✧ Ekanayake Mudiyanselage Punchirala Korala, Hathigamuwa, Hathigamuwa Temple

✧ Yapa Mudiyanselage Ukku Banda, Galgiriyawa, Karagaswewa Temple

✧ Herath Mudiyanselage Mudiyanse, Kandulawa, Kandulawa Temple

✧ Disanayake Mudiyanselage Banda, Mapegomuwa, Mapegomuwa Temple

✧ Herath Mudiyanselage Banda, Herathgama, Nikawewa Temple

✧ Ekanayake Mudiyanselage Punchirala Korala, Hathigamuwa, Niyadawane Temple

✧ Tennakoon Mudiyanselage Banda, Malagamuwa, Veragala Barube Temple

Vanni Hathpattuwa

✧ Wanninayaka Panditha Mudiyanselage Kapuruhamy, Nambawewa, Angamugama temple

✧ Wanninayake Mudiyanselage Appuhamy, Embogama, Embogama Temple

✧ Basnayake Nilame, Uduweriya, Gonnawa Devala

✧ Wahala Mudiyanselage Banda, Walpaluwaththa, Kaduruwewa Temple

✧ Rathnamalala Bandaralage Manikrala, Uduweriya, Uduweriya Devala

✧ Kariyapperuma Mudiyanselage Mudalihamy, Rekogama, Walassawa Temple

✧ Disanayake Mudiyanselage Pinhamy, Embogama, Walathewa Temple.

The transformation of power dynamics within Nikawagampaha Korale is readily apparent. An illustrative example is the case of Chandrasekara Mudiyanselage Punchirala, hailing from Kambuwatawana, who held the trusteeship for both Kubukkadawala and Borawewa temples. Notably, the Governor did not appoint a trustee from Borawewa to oversee the Borawewa temple, hinting at a possible decline in Borawewa's leadership influence during that period.

Additionally, it is evident that the legacy of Nikawewa Adikari Mudiyanses had waned, with Herathgama emerging as a prominent figure. Meanwhile, the enduring legacy of Kandulawa continued. Notably, the Uduweriya Malala Bandaras were appropriately entrusted with the guardianship of Hindu Gods' shrines (Devala).

The subsequent chapter delves into another facet of the Brāhmin groups' legacy, particularly their contributions to Buddhist heritage.

Chapter Fifteen

Seven Brāhmin Families Ascend Within the Buddhist Order & Hierarchy

After embracing Buddhism, the descendants of the seven Brāhmin families joined the Sri Lankan Buddhist order, with some even ascending to the highest echelons of the hierarchy. This chapter is dedicated to exploring the enduring Brāhmin legacy within Buddhist institutions.

Malwaththa and Asgiriya temples are the leading monasteries during the Kandyan Kingdom who are the guardian priest of the Tooth Relic. The chief incumbents or Mahanayaka of Malwaththa and Asgiriya chapters of the Siyam Nikaya and the *Diyawadana Nilame* hold the joint custodianship of the sacred tooth relic of the Buddha (Seneviratne, 1983). These monasteries were in proximity of the royal place. Malwaththa chief monks had the privilege to teach Buddhism to Kandyan (Nayak) kings thereby becoming "Raja Guru".[177]

---

[177] Teacher of the king.

Malwaththa and Asgiriya temples followed strict and traditional protocols in relation to who could become monks at these temples and who would be ordained (become upasampada) within Siyam Nikaya down (sect of monkhood with the tradition of whose ordainment descended from the Siamese Bhikkus). The monks of Brāhmi origin and who belong to "Radala" and "Govigama" castes had the privilege to become chief monks or "Mahanayaka" Theros and Anunayaka Theros of this sect of Sangha. Ven Sitinamaluwe Dhammajoti (belonged to Durawa caste before being a monk) thero was the last non-govigama monk to receive upasampada before the new upasampada rule established in 1764 with this sect of sangha. This un-Buddhistic like practice of caste discrimination has been protested by Amarapura Nikaya and the Ramanna Nikayas.

Several descendants from the seven Brāhmaṇa Rālas became monks at Malwaththa temple, obtained upsampada at this temple, and became Chief Incumbents (Mahanayaka) and Deputy Chief Incumbent (Anunayaka) of Malwaththa Chapter[178].

Malwathu Mahanayaka Theros

One Mahanayaka from the Brahmin group's origin was Ven Daramitipola Dhammarakkitha Mahanayake, the third Mahanayaka of Malwaththa chapter (from 1774-1787). He was from Sri Ranga Bamunu Mudiyanse clan from Daramitipola and was closely related to Kandulassa Brāhmaṇa Rāla family at Kandulawa. He was the chief incumbent of Kandulawa temple before moving to Malwaththa Temple and becoming the Mahanayaka.

There were two Mahanayaka Theros from Galbiriyawa village in Nikawagampaha Korale. Ven Galgiriyawe Sri Sumangala Thero was the third and one of a long serving Mahanayaka of Malwaththa Chapter (from 1829 to 1850). He belonged to the Maha Yapa

---

[178] TB Ekanayake, 2015, Malwathu Mahaviharawansa Mahanahimiwaru.

Mudiyanse clan of Galgiriyawa which was an off root of Dembatogama Purohit Brāhmaṇa Rāla family and Rakwane Mahipala Brahman Rala families.

Ven Daramitipola Dhammarakkitha Mahanayaka Thero

The fifteenth Mahanayaka Thero of Malwaththa Chapter was also from Galgiriyawa Maha Yapa Mudiyanse clan. He was Ven Galgiriyawe Sri Buddharakkitha Thero who held the Mahanayaka Thero position from 1913 to 1919.[179]

Malwathu Maha Viharaya originally had only three temples (pansalas) or dwelling places for chief monks.[180] Namely, the Sangaraja Pansala dedicated to Ven Valivita Saranankara Thero.

The adjoining temple is Thibbatuwawa pansala which was to commemorate Ven Thibbotuwawe Sri Buddharakkitha Thero who was the first Chief Incumbent or Mahanayaka of Malwaththa

---

[179] TB Ekanayake, 2015, Malwathu Mahaviharawansa Mahanahimiwaru and Wikipedia.
[180] Anuradha Senevirathna, (1983) Kandy, pg. 99-100.

Ven Galgiriyawe Sri Sumangala Mahanayaka Thero

Ven Galgiriyawe Sri Buddharakkitha Mahanayaka Thero

Chapter after the first higher ordination, which took place in 1753. The middle temple (Made pansala) was dedicated to Ven Morathota

Sri Dharmmakanda Thero who was the fourth Mahanayaka Thero. He was a Rajaguru.

One of these temples was named as "Borawewa Pansala" and "Herathgama Pansala" in the past[181] to commemorate chief monks who were at Malwaththa from these seven Brāhmin villages.

Borawawe Dharmapala Anunayaka Thero.

Venerable Borawewa Dharmapala Thero was the Deputy Chief Incumbent (Anunayaka) of Malwaththa Chapter from 1774. He was the first student of the third Mahanayaka of Malwaththa Chapter, Venerable Daramitipola Sri Dharmarakkitha Thero (1774-1784).

The King Kirthi Sri Rajasinghe (1747-1782) reconstructed Niyadawane temple and awarded to Venerable Borawawe Dharmapala Thero in 1780 by a royal decree (Sannasa).[182] Ven Dharmapala appeared to be the Anunayaka for a long time but was not appointed to the Mahanayaka position potentially because of the two Mahanayakas who succeeded Daramitipola Mahanayaka were Rajagurus, i.e., Ven Morathota Sri Dhammakkanda Thero (1784-1811) and Kobbekaduwe Siri Niwasa Thero (1811-1819). Malwaththa temple once was called "Borawewa temple"[183] in respect of this Anunayaka Thero.

Brāhmin Legacy with Niyadawane Temple.

Niyadawane temple which was originally built by King Walagamba of Anuradhapura Kingdom (103-89 BC) had been neglected for centuries. As stated above, the King Kirthi Sri Rajasinghe (1747-1782) reconstructed this temple and awarded it to Venerable Borawawe Dharmapala Thero, who was the Deputy Chief

---

[181] As described by Ven Danthure Vipassi Theo the current incumbent of Kandulawa temple.

[182] Sri Ranthapala Abhidana, 1995.

[183] Ven Danture Vipassi Thero provided this information.

Incumbent of Malwaththa Chapter in 1780 by a royal decree (Sannasa).[184]

Niyadawane[185] temple is situated within the Polpithigama Divisional Secretariat Division of Kurunegala District.

It appears that for nearly two and a half centuries, the chief incumbents of this temple were from the seven Brāhmin families of Nikawagampaha Korale. Since then, the chief incumbent position of Niyadawane temple had been transferred among monks of Brāhmi origin of Kambuwatawana, Borawewa, Herathgama etc.[186] The following were the Chief Incumbents of Niyadawane temple from 1780 AD:

- ✧ Venerable Borawawe Dharmapala Thero – 1780.
- ✧ Venerable Borawawe Piyadassi Thero – 1816.
- ✧ Venerable Borawawe Medankara Thero – 1850.
- ✧ Venerable Kambuwatawana Siddartha Thero – 1866.
- ✧ Venerable Herathgama Dhammadassi Thero.
- ✧ Venerable Kambuwatawana Saranankara Thero – 1895.
- ✧ Venerable Borawawe Rathanapala Thero – 1935.

From 1943, Venerable Palipana Sri Sumangala Thero became the incumbent. He is from Harispaththuwa Kandy. Two other temples namely Hathigamuwa Gurugoda temple in 1924 and Pethgiyagala Temple in 1930 came under Niyadawane Temple.[187]

Athkanda Vihara of Kurunegala also had a tradition of accommodating monks from seven Brāhmins families. This is a regal temple which extends its history for many centuries from the beginning of the Anuradhapura era. This temple flourished again

---

[184] Sri Ranthapala Abhidana, 1995.

[185] This temple is also known as "Kuda (small) Dambulla" temple.

[186] Sri Ranthapala Abhidana, 1995; Niyadawane ha Bandunu Pethiyagoda Sanga Papapura, 2019.

[187] Niyadawane ha Bandunu Pethiyagoda Sanga Papapura, 2019.

during the Kurunegala and Dambadeni eras. Venerable Borawawe Sri Sumangala was a chief incumbent here in this temple. He also was a Mahanayaka of the North-western Province in early twentieth century.

Ven Kambuwatawana Piyadassi Thero.

Ven Kambuwatawana Piyadassi Thero was among the forerunners who established Vidyalankara Pirivena, Peliyagoda in 1875. This pirivena later became Vidyalankara University and currently known as University of Kelaniya. *The Ceylon Handbook and Directory 1898-99* (pg. 915), compiled and Edited by John Ferguson states:

> "Vidyalankara (Oriental) College, Paliyagoda (near Kelaniya Railway Station) -Established in 1875. Principal - Dharmakirti Sri Dharmarama, High Priest. Assistants - Lunupoknne Dhammananda and Kambuwatawana Piyadassi, Priests."

Ven Rathmalane Dharmaloka Thero (1828-1885)[188] was the key figure who established the Vidyalankara Pirivena. Venerable Rathmalane Dharmakirthi Dharmarama (1853-1918)[189] was a student of Dharmaloka. He assisted Ven Dharmaloka to establish the pirivena together with Ven Kambuwatawana Piyadassi. Ven Ratmalane Dharmarama became the principal of the pirivena after the passing away of Ven Dharmaloka in 1887. The two deputy principals of the pirivena when it was established in 1875 were Ven Rathmalane Dharmarama and Ven Kambuwatawana Piyadassi. Ven Lunupokune Dharmananda (1869 - 1945) also was a student of Dharmaloka and became the principal in 1917.[190]

Punchi Banda Nugawela Disawa (later Diyawasdana Nilame) and Bellanwila Lekam Nilame[191] initiated the establishment of

---

[188] https://en.wikipedia.org/wiki/Ratmalane_Sri_Dharmaloka_Thera.
[189] Samipathayehi Boudacharyawarayo, by Ven Polwaththe Budhadhathta, 1964.
[190] Ibid
[191] Ibid

Bellanvila Sri Widyawardana Pirivena, at Mawanalla, around 1901. Ven Rathmalane Dharmarama Thero appointed Ven Lunupokune Dharmananda as the first principal at this newly established pirivena. However, another pirivena called Vidyarathna was established at Wirahene with the initiation of Mr PA Peris Appuhamy. He invited Venerable Lunupokune Dhammananda Thero to accept its principal position around 1904. Therefore, Ven Kambuwatawana Piyadassi Thero, who was the Deputy Principal at Vidyalankara Pirivena, was appointed to the principal position of Widyawardana Pirivena in 1904. Ven Piyadassi was the second principal at Bellanwila Widyawardana Pirivena.

The names of Ven Kambuwatawana Piyadassi's parents had not been discovered at the time of this publication. It appears that Venerable Piyadassi Thero became a monk at Malwaththa Temple in Kandy and, potentially, was a student of Ven Borawawe Dharmapala Anunayaka Thero of Malwaththa Chapter. He had entered the order with Venerable Ambanwalle Sri Sidhartha Sumangalabhidana Thero who became the Mahanayaka (chief incumbent) of Malwaththa Chapter of Siam Nikaya in 1924 (1924 - 1927).[192]

Ven Walamitiyawe Dharmarakkitha Thero who wrote the book titled *Sri Dharmarama Sahithyankaya* with Venerable Thalakiriyagama Dharmakirthi Thero,[193] providing a heartfelt homage to Venerable Kambuwatawana Piyadassi:

"When Ven [Rathmalane] Sri Dharmarama wanted to bring Ven [Lunupokune] Sri Dharmananda back to Vidyalankara Pirivena, he approved Ven Kambuwatawana Piyadassi who was then the Deputy Principal at Vidyalankara Pirivena as the replacement for the Principal Position at Bellanwila Widyawardana pirivena. Ven

---

[192] Ibid

[193] Walamitiyawe Dharmarakkitha (ed. 1961). Sri Dharmarama Sahithyankaya.

Kambuwatawana Piyadassi became a [brother] monk with Ven Ambanwalle Sri Sidhartha Sumangalabhidana Thero who was the Registrar of Malwaththa Bikku Chapter and later became the Malwaththa Chapter Mahanayaka.

Ven Kambuwatawana Piyadassi Thero was always behind Ven Dharmarama like a shadow, organising everything with utmost care and dedication to the progress of the pirivena. Ven Dharmarama kept Ven Piyadassi at the pirivena with enormous affection since he was doing an immense service. However, he [Dharmarama] unable to refuse the request from the Widyawardana Pirivena and reluctantly released Ven Kambuwatawana Piyadassi. He was sent to Widyawardana with Ven Andugoda Aththadassi Thero. ... Ven Kambuwatawana Piyadassi was one of my teachers at Vidyalankara Pirivena. He was a kind, venerable and disciplined scholar. He provided a magnificent service to the Widyawardana pirivena. At Widyawardana Pirivena, once he organised a prize giving ceremony and invited honourable Hulugalle Adhikaram to attend. Sadly, Ven Piyadassi passed away suddenly."[194]

The untimely demise of Ven. Kambuwatawana Piyadassi, which likely occurred around 1910, brought an abrupt halt to his academic career advancement and the possibility of him ascending to the supreme hierarchy within the Malwaththa Chapter. His brother, monk Ven. Ambanwalle Sri Sidhartha Sumangalabhidana Thero became the Mahanayaka of Malwaththa from 1924–1927.

The next chapter provides a brief account of the transformation of Brāhmin villages including Kambuwatawana in the modern era. It tries to capture the continuity. That brief account will be followed by genealogical records of Kambuwatawana.

---

[194] Ibid.

Chapter Sixteen

Transformation of Brāhmin Villages in the Modern Era

It is important to note that the current social and economic landscape in these traditional Brāhmin villages is completely different to what can be imagined through the accounts of the palm-leaf manuscripts. The Brāhmin domination declined with the influence of European occupation, and these communities have since undergone another phase of transformation.

Sri Lanka underwent rapid changes in line with the western oriented government and civil administration since the British occupation in 1815. Kandyan ruling families had realised that the new authoritative style of the British government was fundamentally different from the ruling of the monarchy. As we saw previously the discontent soon boiled over into a rebellion in 1818. But the British introduced further reforms in changing the traditional economic and administrative system, introducing a new unitary administrative and judicial system for the whole island. English became the language of government and the medium of instruction.

The British removed restrictions on the country's economy by abolishing all state monopolies and eliminating compulsory labour service (*Rajakariya*). They also advocated the liberation of the economy, which led to new economic enterprises. The British released the land for commercial or large-scale plantations to change the economy Under the Crown Lands (Encroachments) Ordinance No. 12 of 1840 (sometimes called the Crown Lands Ordinance or the Waste Lands Ordinance), the British acquired the common land of the peasantry and released them for the commercial sector. The British next introduced a peculiar tax system which was strange to the locals and not known before. For example, on 1st July 1848, license fees were imposed on guns, dogs, carts, and shops. The labour was made compulsory on a plantation unless a special tax was paid. These taxes bore heavily on the traditional lives of the Kandyan peasantry.

A mass movement was launched against the British regime, but this time the masses were without the leadership of their native King or the Kandyan chiefs. The leadership for the peasant uprising in 1848 was provided by the ordinary people. The traditional power structure of the local leadership was in continuous transformation.

Capitalist enterprise introduced changes in agricultural practices and techniques, but these developments were essentially restricted to the urban areas and particularly associated with the plantation sector.[195] The rest of the country continued with subsistence economic activity, using traditional methods. Eventually, Sri Lanka started to shape into a dual economic system which is an existence of two separate economic sectors, modern commercial plantations and commercial sector and the traditional rural subsistence economy. These sectors within one country, divided by different levels of development, technology, and different patterns of demand. New roads and railway systems helped to reduce territorial

---

[195] KM de Silva, 2005.

isolation. Overtime commercial sector rapidly grew creating urban centres and urban way of life.

Economic development and the spread of formal education made substantial changes in the society. These included changes in the relationships between social groups. Upper elements of the dominant castes in urban areas strengthened their positions by taking advantage of new developments. Castes traditionally of lower status also saw the opportunities to move upward, creating tensions within the caste system.[196] A community of capitalist businesspersons and professionals who were proficient in English surfaced as a new class that went beyond caste boundaries. A new middle class was created, who eventually grew to take the country's leadership displacing traditional elite domination.

Historically, Brāhmi villages survived for long within the traditional agricultural sector which provided a subsistence economic infrastructure. This type of agricultural activity, unless the residents have extensive properties, did not support an accumulation of wealth had restricted potential economic power opportunities. Many Brāhmi villages lacked large reservoirs even for consistent farming activity. The Brāhmin villages we have followed were situated in the dry zone and inherited constant droughts, which inflicted economic hardships for the community. People often prayed to the god for good rainy seasons to yield good crops. The inhabitants had to adapt to the arid climate, limited agricultural activity, and a harsh environment. There were lesser signs of a middle class in these traditional Brāhmin villages.

Even under difficult economic circumstances, they maintained a community that was rich socially, culturally, and spiritually. They were happy, healthy, and full of spirit within their own restricted

---

[196] KM de Silva, 2005.

social environments. They were connected to the land and respected the natural environment. The inhabitants were socially cohesive and there was a close unity. Their association with the outside was on commercial activities, taking part in the government related activities and performing assigned duties.

Since then, the breakdown of the traditional systems which had provided Brāhmi descendants an advantage, started to wane. The community progress and the social mobility started to depend on modern requirements and values of the educational qualifications and skills.[197] The succession of power and the leadership of the society was no more dependent on their birth, clan, or the family status. There were no more automatic privileges. The formal education and earned economic power became the basic parameters of social mobility and advancement. Many traditional Brāhmin villages looked for opportunities through formal education.

Social Mobility.

Historical Brāhmi villages like Kambuwatawana, Rakwana, Dembatogama and Mataluwawa did not have government schools within their localities for formal education. Borawewa Government School, which was established in 1887, provided primary and junior secondary education for Kambuwatawana, Borawewa, Rakwana, Pohorawaththa and Galgiriyawa children. There were large secondary schools had stablished in urban areas like Kurunegala but not many families were wealthy enough to send their children to those schools. In early days, when children completed grade 8, they were qualified to find occupations like school teaching. Early teachers who hailed from Kambuwatawana were grade 8 graduates. Borawewa Government School provided education in Sinhalese,

---

[197] Bandaranayake, 2011, *Gamratawa.*

but the grade 8 graduates were also familiar with the English language.

The Central College system, which started in 1940's, offered English Senior Education with residential (hostel) facilities. Most of the students were selected through competitive examinations at grade five and grade eight and they were offered scholarships. The two Central Colleges close to Kambuwatawana were Maho Central College, approximately in thirty kms. and Ibbgamuwa Central College approximately in forty kms. from Kambuwatawana. These colleges assisted to produce college graduates at Kambuwatawana, Borawewa and other neighbouring villages.

Later, the most successful government secondary school to provide higher education around Kambuwatawana was Nikawewa Devanampiyathissa Maha Vidyalaya (Nikawewa school). This school is located approximately 15kms. away from Kambuwatawana. It became more popular and successful since 1960's under the principalship of Mr Hangilipola (Mr RMGB Hangilipola). [198] It had produced many graduates paving way for various government jobs. Borawewa Maha Vidyalaya (Borawewa school) was also improved later and produced university graduates, but Nikawewa was the most successful in producing many university graduates in the area. Later, the government schools of Ehetuwewa Maha Vidyalaya and Polpithigama Maha Vidyalaya which are in the proximity also provided facilities for higher education.

Even though Sri Lanka offers free education to children of poor villages and labourers engaged in agriculture generally do not achieve superior higher education due to their parents' financial constraints. Most of the parents are early withdrawal from the

---

[198] Herath Madana Bandara, Nikawewa MMV, Hangilipola Era, 2021.

education system to engage in the subsistence economy or work as labourers. There is also uncertainty of securing a well-paid job even if qualifications are gained. However, most of the villagers are motivated to provide education to their children to have a breakthrough.

Competition for paid jobs, particularly in the state corporations and the bureaucracy, is high. Entry to fashionable jobs in state bureaucracy, and executive jobs in the trade and commerce sector require higher educational qualifications. However, entering professions and obtaining government employment in the state sector in turn, contributes to the advancement of one's position in the village.

However, the paid jobs and employment structure of the high school graduates had a common pattern. The number of government teachers from Kambuwatawana village grew considerably. All university graduates became teachers. The increased vacancies in security forces due to civil wars provided opportunities for high school graduates. Many young men of the village joined the Police force and the security forces. During the LTTE Civil War between 1983 and 2009, and even after that period, the army and the navy had been the main sources of employment for the youth in these villages.

In addition, some youth went to Middle Eastern countries looking for manual labourer jobs and domestic work to improve their financial status. Since the commencement of industrial zones in Sri Lanka in the 1980's, the garment industry has become another major source of employment for school dropouts. Many village youths that went to work in the industrial zones in the urban areas found marriage partners and settled down in those areas. Several agriculture colonization schemes introduced by the state sector with permanent irrigation facilities had also attracted some families from these villages.

Since the late 1900's, affluent villagers started to move into urban areas, dreaming better educational opportunities for their children to climb the ladder of social status. As a by-product, the traditional Brāhmin villages either shrunk or had very little growth.

As mentioned early, Kambuwatawana did not have large water reservoirs, only inherited small water tanks. People depended heavily on seasonal rain. The inadequate rain meant drought, lesser harvest, and economic hardships. People were yearning for large scale irrigation facilities for decades. There is a proposed large-scale irrigation program called MWSIP-North-western Province Canal (to be completed by 2025),[199] which goes through Kambuwatawana, Galgiriyawa and Wathuwaththegama villages. It is expected that this irrigation facility will help the villages improve their agricultural activities with much certainty. With this irrigation facility, the villages could transform into an economic revival. But it is not quite certain how this scheme of things may transform the community character along a reviving path. This will be another phase of change to the traditional village infrastructure.

Demise of Dembatogama Country.

As mentioned in the chapter under Dembatogama legacy, the supremacy of Dembatogama declined after the emergence and the transfer of leadership to Nikawewa. Dembatogama also lost some villages to Hewawasam. The irrigation facilities of Dembatogama had been also neglected for decades. Eventually the Dembatogama residents shifted to villages such as: Wathuwaththegama, Galgiriyawa, Rakwana, Eriyawa, Ambogama, and Kambuwatawana to live or due to marriage relationships. Some of these residents only

---

[199] Website, Ministry of Irrigation, Sri Lanka.

returned to the village to cultivate paddy lands on a seasonal basis. The neighbouring village Rambawa was known as Paalu (abandoned) Rambawa due to outflux of people. By 1950, the government had allocated at least three large scale land plots to commercial plantation at Dembatogama. These commercial growers brought labour from the other parts of the island. These newcomers also cleared adjoining government land and settled permanently. Dembatogama is currently inhabited by nearly fifty families who came to work in the commercial plantations. They have been branded as *"pitagamkarayo"* (outsiders). Only five families of traditional landowners returned to Dembatogama to live. Some traditional landowners of Dembatogama did not interfere in land disputes or to reclaim their land.

The neighbouring Walpaluwa village where the Sinhala Wiriduwa or Tamil Nakathiya settled by the Dembatogama Purohit is still largely intact. The village currently holds approximately twenty-five families of his descendants. They are involved in agriculture, rather than working as the traditional assistants of Hindu rituals like playing drums.

The traditional land ownership is largely intact at other traditional Brāhmin villages like Borawewa, Kambuwatawana, Rakwana, Galgiriyawa, Herathgama, and Mataluwawa. Therefore, the traditional clan base and genealogical legacy is clearly observable in these villages. However, Nikawewa had attracted outsiders due to the establishment of Nikawewa District Hospital and the expansion of Nikawewa Maha Vidyalaya (School). Another reason was that this village is located by the main road of Ibbagamuwa to Moragollagama. Kandulawa and Kiribamuna also had attracted outsiders as they were located close to the Kurunegala commercial centre. The traditional clan base is very thin in these two original Brāhmin villages.

The next few chapters are an in-depth study of the Kambuwatawana Brāhmin village and trace remnants of the genealogical legacy.

Chapter Seventeen

In-depth Study: Kambuwatawana Brāhmi Village

―――――― ❦ ――――――

This chapter is dedicated to introducing the historical background of Kambuwatawana village before the settlement and expansion of the South Indian Brahmin contingent.

As stated elsewhere Kambuwatawana village is situated at approximately 7.937990 degrees North latitude and 80.392371 degrees East longitude.

The village is bordered by the villages of Kubukkadawala to the north, Pothanegama and Nipunegama to the east, Borawewa to the south-east, and Jayalathgama and Karagaswewa to the south. Galgiriya Mountain stretches to the west.

Village History Before Brāhmi Migration

Kambuwatawana village had existed before the Brāhmins occupation in the 16th century. No reliable historical records are available to clarify the origin of Kambuwatawana as a human settlement. It is reasonable to assume that the village was gradually inhabited and expanded as other parts of the country before the event of the Brāhmi migration in relation to the lengthy recorded history of Sri Lanka. The available evidence suggests that the area around Kambuwatawana was largely populated during the early period to the Anuradhapura Kingdom (337 BC to 1017 AD). But some evidence hint that it could have been populated even before or during the pre-historical times.

The prominent landmark of this village is the Galgiriya Mountain (hill) which is approximately one thousand metres high above the sea level and approximately twelve kilometres long in the North-South direction. This village is one among a dozen of villages established on the slopes around this mountain.

There are dozens of historical stone caves in the banks of this mountain with stone inscriptions. There was a tradition in the early period of Anuradhapura kingdom to decorate caves, engrave them, and offer to Buddhist monks to live (these could have been the caves which had been using by the donors to Sangha).

Also, there are many historical man-made water reservoirs (at different scales) around the Galgiriya Mountain that have been constructed for irrigation purposes. This information also validates the spread of early human settlement in the area. The reservoir-based irrigation is a unique cultural heritage of early Sri Lankan peoples. Every reservoir was associated with a hamlet (village) beside it. The reservoir and the hamlet were the basic format of early agricultural settlement of Sri Lanka. Buddhist temples were also built and maintained in these settlements for worship.

The boundary of the village Kambuwatawana is marked by eight small man-made lakes namely: Madapolayagamawewa, Ulpothwewa, Ambagaha Amuna, Polgahawewa, Gorokgahawewa, Nlunnewa, Jayalathgamawewa, Aluthwewa, Gatilewa, Thammanewa, and Elipichegamawewa. However, the nature of the village settlements generally contrasts with the general layout of the villages found in the dry zone. The settlements are not generally located beside water, in relation with the water body, as seen in other parts of the dry zone. The Kambuwatawana settlement model was mainly influenced by the dominant geographical future of Galgiriya Mountain. The village is placed along the foothill of the mountain.

The Buddhist temple of Kambuwatawana is considered to have been constructed by the king Devanam Piyathissa, renowned monarch of the history of the country, who reigned the country from 307 BC to 267 BC. This information is also indicative of the age of this human settlement.

There is a general possibility that the villages could have been established even before the Anuradhapura Era (before 337 BC). One potential example is the plateau called Kosgasmandiya (jackfruit garden) located on the Mountain mentioned here, approximately five hundred metres above the village level of Kambuwatawana, and approximately in the middle of the mountain. This plateau has some archaeological remains including an ancient water reservoir called "Giant's Reservoir" (*Yodaya's wewa*), a water well called "Giant's Well" (*Yodaya's linda*) and a stone bed called "Giant's Bed" (*Yodaya's anda*).[200]

The people who had lived in this place could have been either physically large in size or strong compared to the general people who settled later. Kosgasmandiya, mentioned earlier, potentially could be a settlement where prehistoric[201] indigenous people lived. These early people, as usually being the authoritative among the rest of the others, could have selected an elevated position of the immediate surrounding of the land under their command to live.

---

[200] The author has seen tall, old jackfruit trees in this plateau besides these archaeological remains to indicate there was an early human settlement there.

[201] Prehistoric is not in the sense of the prehistory uncovered within the country.

They might have wanted to exert their ruling power, authority, and high social status living in an elevated position. Further, places of this nature also provide secure landscape for physical protection from enemies in addition to wild animals. This high mountainous location is also a cooler location. The spot where the Giant's Bed is located called "*Meerawwa*", which translates to "a place that provides a cool and pleasant sun."

Buddhism was introduced to Sri Lanka around 252 BC. There are no signs of Buddhist ruins of veneration is found in Kosgasmandiya and the place could not have been established as a general Buddhist shrine. And the Giant's Bed could be a place of worship or a place of ancient rituals of these people who lived there.

Skilled Wild Elephant Trappers and Tamers.

The term *kombu* stands for a stick or a large timber pole in Tamil language. In the Sanskrit language *kambu* refers to elephants. In South Indian languages, *kombu* also means horn or elephant tusks.[202] It is possible that the inhabitants in this village, and in the surrounding villages, were skilled elephant captors and tamers for trade. The mountain could have provided a geographically secure natural boundary (wall) for building kraal for capture of elephants. The Sinhalese word for kraal is "watawana" (a kraal made of high logs planted in a circle). Kambuwatawana, this traditional elephant kraal,[203] has derived the name of the village.

During the olden days, elephants were heavily used for wars and heavy-duty work. Sri Lanka was also famous for international elephant trade in the past. Again, the geographical location was ideal, safer, and efficient to kraaling elephants for capture.

---

[202] https://sanskritdictionary.com

[203] In other areas the kraal for wild elephant capture is generally termed as Gala. Name Galoya stand for the elephant Krall (gala) build nearby a stream (Oya).

According to this theory, Kambuwatawana was a natural enclosure where elephants (kombu) were captured in early days for international trade.

Vanni Upatha palm-leaf manuscript (pg. 44) provides a more reliable theory about this village's name. The area including Eriyawa and *Galgamuwa* were inherited by the chieftains who tamed elephants and led the elephant army of Kotte kings. It records a person who had helped giving a "rope" (*Kamba*) to *Achari Asuri Appu* to tie elephants have been introduced as *"Kambuwatawanaya"*. The village given to him by Devamadda Palace and probably since then, it was named Kambuwatawana.

As explored above, Kambuwatawana was an old village that was populated and existed before the arrival of Brāhmin migrants. Kambuwatawana people were elephant tamers, in addition to farming. They also served in the King's Army when necessary. Service in the royal army was necessary for men, and there was an established procedure for men to fulfil this service. "In the case of men of war, soldiers, captains, and high officers – these had to come with their own arms as necessity arose and were bound to bring food for fifteen days from homes and when this was finished, they had fifteen days' rest."[204]

Brāhmin migration might have opened a new social era for Kambuwatawana with having new personalities with different skills and attitudes including high social connections and new administrative arrangements etc.

Kambuwatawana Village Settlement.

The old settlement of Kambuwatawana was at the foothill of the Galgiriya mountain. As usually there were no well paved roads to access the settlements except the foot paths. There had been some

---

[204] Writings of Portuguese Historian Ribeirio, in Dennis Fernando, 1986, pg. 90.

rough roads in some parts of the village which were used for bullock carts the main means of transport in the days.

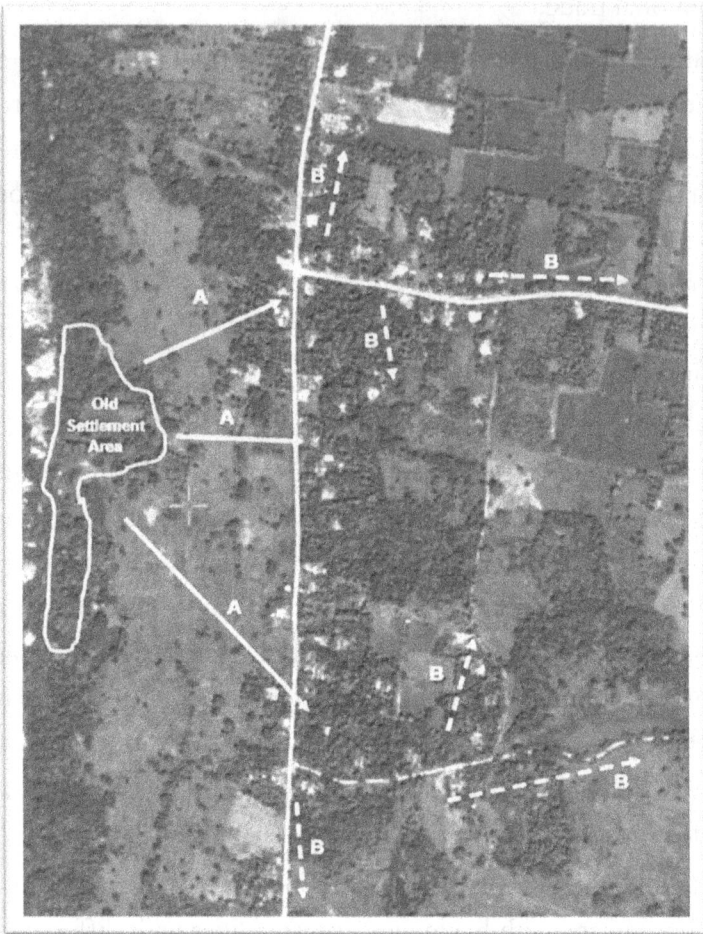

Map 4 – Kambuwatawana village settlement

A= Early shift, B= Later Expansion

The layout of the village had fulfilled the close relationships, security arrangements and collective community needs of the village. The rule of the thumb was to maintain the "community living arrangements" of people living around a distance where a hooting sound could be heard generated from the middle.

This distance helped to communicate urgent messages by yelling or calling aloud. There had been groups of houses close to each other, and some houses were joined together. Some groups of houses had a middle open compound (meadow or midula) to which people gathered by stepping out from the houses. This structure supported mutual interdependence and community harmony. There were no strict fenced boundaries to separate the properties. The lands were transferred or split to the next generation by the word of mouth. Extended families lived in almost every house.

Map number 3 shows the old settlement area of the village as well as the expansion of the new settlement that extended along the road network. The people gradually moved out of the old settlement area and built houses in the new area along the main gravel road starting approximately around early in 1900. By approximately the 1930's, people almost abandoned the old settlement.

The houses were not kept closer to each other from the old settlements. This new settlement layout of the village seemed to have disrupted the traditional communal values, harmony, and collective attitudes that the villagers had enjoyed. People grew into new values promoting the individuality.

Kambuwatawana village is in a constant transformation. For example, with the influence of the modern commercial values, the old system of subsistence agriculture had transformed into a mixture of traditional and small-scale commercial crops.

The next chapter provides a basic framework of name conventions and kinship before introducing the Brāhmins genealogical information at Kambuwatawana.

Chapter Eighteen

Kambuwatawana: Name Conventions and Kinship

This section lays the genealogical foundation of the Kambuwatawana people, which aligns with the ola-leaf or palm-leaf manuscripts. It commences by elucidating the conventions and protocols governing the formation of Kandyan names, serving as the basis for understanding the naming conventions in the village. Following this, the section explores sociological aspects such as family units, kinship patterns, marriage relationships, nicknames, and clan formations.

Naming Conventions.

In general, the name "Bandara" is regarded as a common Kandyan hierarchical family or part of the general surname commonly used in the medieval times and being currently heavily used at Kambuwatawana.

According to Reimers,[205] "*Bandara*" was a word derived from the Tamil word "*Pandaram*" which was used by the Tamils as a general name for the Brāhmin priests. However, this term might have been borrowed by the Sinhalese and applied to the Sinhalese royal

---

[205] Reimers 1930, Some Sinhalese Names and Surnames. pp. 437-452.

families as an honorific title. Afterwards, this became a part of the names of the Kandyan princes. Historically, a Bandara was used to identify the sons of a chief in the Sinhala Kingdom.[206] There are many male names ending with Banda or Bandara in Kandyan villages. A Bandara was also a Great Officer in the Amatya Mandalaya, or Sinhalese Council of State, in the Sinhalese Kingdoms. Generally, the part of the name 'Banda' was commonly used by members of the Govigama caste.

Other form of Sri Lankan name is "-ge" name[207]. Similar to other parts of Sri Lanka, Kambuwatawana people use the "-ge" name tradition. In addition, Ge names appeared with other parts of the names standing traditionally in front sections before the name of the person. These front parts include *"pelapath nama"* and *"variga nama"* (family descending name); *"Vasagama"*: the village or the region where the family had lived or come down (vasa stands for dwelling and gama for the village). However, Kambuwatawana people appeared to be using the *"pelapath"* or *"wariga"*[208] name predominantly as given by the kings for the services for successive generations.

It is necessary to acknowledge that different naming convention existed in the Kandyan kingdom to identify the people who belong to different castes. High class Brāhmins had a tradition of starting their name with the village name.[209] Also, during the Kandyan era, honorary names were given to people to recognise their contribution to the kingdom or to significant loyalty provided to the king. This custom of giving a new name when a subject was raised

---

[206] Wikipedia https://en.wikipedia.org/wiki/Band%C4%81ra.

[207] Perera, B J, (2009).

[208] Honorary names given by the king.

[209] Mirandor Obeyesekere.

to a dignity is very ancient and seems to have prevailed in many eastern countries.

We can observe from the vitti books where father and son have different honorary names due to the recognition of their services to the king separately at different times. For example, the father's honorary name can be "Rajakaruna Mudiyanse", but the son can be given an honorary name as "Chandrasekara Mudiyanse". "Mudiyanse" (derived from Mudaliyar, a Dravidian word for a chieftain) was conferred on such persons as had secured the goodwill of the reigning prince by some service to the country, or who had displayed much value on the field of battle. Sinhalese kings generally selected Adigars, Disavas, and other chiefs from such families as had been thus ennobled. In tradition, the recipients of these official titles were prohibited from carrying loads, climbing trees, etc. He also received a royal grant of land for his maintenance and was allowed to wear on state occasions a cap and a frilled jacket. Similarly, "Appuhamy" is an officer who belonged to a family with proven loyalty and sacrificial devotion to the King. They commanded high respect and honour from the countrymen (Ekanayake, 1897).[210] This is the form in which Kandyan social hierarchy was formed and maintained.

The British ceased the Kandyan tradition of giving honorary names. Kandyans started using ancestral names (or "pelapath name") or most recent honorary name received by their parents or grandparents. So, ancestral name came first before the given name. For example, "Basnayake Mudiyanselage Punchi Banda". The last two names, "Punchi Banda" are the name to signify the person and the surname is the front part which is "Basnayake Mudiyanse" the

---

[210] Ekanâyaka, A. de Silva (1876). "On the Form of Government under the Native Sovereigns of Ceylon" (PDF). *The Journal of the Royal Asiatic Society of Great Britain and Ireland.* **8** (2): 297–304.

honorary name granted by the king or by an authorised person to the name the holder and the descendants. The affix "-ge" means "belong to" or "connected to". In this form, this person called Punchi Banda belongs to, or connected to, ancestral link with Basnayake Mudiyanse.

Confusion with Similar Names.

It can be observed that some given names are commonly and widely used by each family in Kandyan villages (refers to chapter 19 for examples). Therefore, there will be so many persons who carry the same name Basnayake Mudiyanselage Punchi Banda in a village. To reduce the confusion, in some cases, fathers' name is added infront of the son's name. For example, if the father's name is "Ranhamy", then in this tradition the child's name appears as "Basnayake Mudiyanselage Ranhamyge Punchi Banda". The part Ranhamyge stands for the father. The usage of this tradition helps to identify the person, reducing confusion. When the names are abbreviated the initials of such names are abbreviated as BM Punchi Banda or BMR Punchi Banda.

There are different variations of using the given name Banda or Bandara. In some cases, it tends to add on the expression of love or the position the child born to the family. For example, Heen Banda and Podi Banda mean small or junior son. Loku Banda means big or senior son. Madduma Banda means the son in the middle of the family. But this version is not always applicable for instance, in the names of Kalu and Ran Banda where "Kalu" stands for black and "Ran" stand for gold. Those names may express the affection and the admiration to the offspring.

Lots of female names[211] ended with "Menika", which means "jewel" or the "beloved lady." Ran Menika is golden jewel, Podi

---

[211] KD Paranawithana. website

Menika is small or junior jewel, Sudu Menika is white jewel and Tikiri Menika is small or beloved jewel etc. Further, Kumari or Kumara means princess and prince. Podi Kumari means junior princess. A number of female names ending with "-wathie", like Kusumawathie, Anulawathie, Chandrawathie and Karunawathie (literally watha means the face. Added adjectives to the front gives different literal colours).

Recent Name Changes.

In recent times, the second part of the surname (e.g., Mudiyanselage) have been dropped from the surnames to westernise names yet preserving the ancestry. For example, "Basnayake Mudiyanselage Punch Banda" has become Punchi Banda Basnayake or when abbreviated PB Basnayake. But this transformation was more popular in urban areas than in rural areas. EB Denham, in his Ceylon at the Census of 1911 (1912), noted the tendency of ge-names to be adopted as surnames after the European fashion by dropping the -ge at the end. He noted:

> "The tendency to-day in the towns is to drop the ge-name altogether and to adopt surnames after the English fashion. In the interior and in the villages the ge-name is scrupulously regarded."

Traditionally, Sinhalese women did not take their husband's surnames, but kept their family names. It was only because of British rule that local women gradually adopt their husband's surnames.

Name conventions have been further changed since the independence. Sri Lanka has introduced a law to enable people to adopt new surnames and to drop old surnames. Some names were obviously indicative of caste background which can be discriminative in modern economic society. People opted to remove such caste specific surnames and adopt modern names. According to this law, people must publicise both their old name and the new name in a daily newspaper to legitimise the change.

Nicknames and Meanings.

Before we go into genealogical records of the current generation of Kambuwatawana, I will touch on the sociological tradition of nicknames,[212] which generally adds colourful character to the people of Kambuwatawana. Almost every family in the village possesses a nickname, basically for the purpose of being an "easy and convenient" form of identification of them reducing any confusion of similar names etc. Nicknames, though generally originated focusing on one member of a family, has been later applied to the whole family. It served the purpose of a convenient way of communication and an easy way of identification.

Even though the nicknames could be given to express affection and respect, in this village, it was a form of amusement or insult. Many nicknames defamed the family character. An analysis of nicknames showed that they have originated from several ways to:

- ✧ label certain amusing behaviour characteristics of a person,
- ✧ identify ill personality type of a person,
- ✧ remind certain notable and amusing things the person has done in the history,
- ✧ refers to names based on the personal physical appearances, and
- ✧ to identify the villages where they have descended from.

Nicknames were mostly used by villagers behind their back or in their absence. They were instrumental for name calling and insulting. Villagers do not get angry or become violent when people use their nicknames. It was mostly accepted and tolerated. However, nicknames create some discomfort generally as they remind or focus

---

212 Known as "Anwarthanama" in Sinhalese.

on the shortcomings. The use of nicknames at face value was regarded as an insensitive practice. Further, when families leave the village and settle elsewhere, the nicknames were no longer relevant or valid in the new context. They became lesser in usage as the new groups do not adhere to the same effective meaning.

Kinship, Lineage, and Marriage Relationships

Traditionally, Kandyan law is applicable to Kurunegala District recognizes two types of marriages. One being *"Binna"* marriage – where the husband comes to the wife's village to live with the bride's family. The wife may inherit the property of her family in equal or higher fraction when the property is divided among the descendants. The husband cannot claim his wife's property, which will be transferred to the children. The husband, however, may administer the wife's holdings and has life interest on her property. Although in the Binna marriage, the wife dominates in the family, the offspring inherit the surnames of the father. So, the new surnames add into the village community with the Binna marriage type.

The other type of marriage is *"Diga"* marriage type – a marriage in which the bride is taken to the husband's family, usually into a house within another village, where the wife may only inherit a lesser or no share of her family property. Her dowry, if given, is incorporated into the husband's wealth. The Kandyan Marriage and the Divorce Act is the current legal framework applied. It recognizes both Binna and Diga marriages.

Split of Family Lineage.

Kambuwatawana village can be considered as single ethnical entity, and all the inhabitants were related to each other closely. If there had been any early historical natives before the Brāhmin migrant's domination, the original families had also potentially mixed up into the main fresh community. Minor splits of the family lineages could be identified within the village though they are not marked.

Some families claim that they are higher in the tribal terms than the other families. This term means that the families try to keep their marriage relationships within the same family roots of Govigama (farmer communities), *radala* (aristocrats) or from Brāhmin origins. The families which deviate from these norms of traditional marriage relationships are generally condemned and are barred from attending the weddings of the other recognised families. The families which had followed consistent wariga[213] lines in marriages are considered as superior and recognised.

Marriage Relationships.

Kambuwatawana people have traditionally established marriage relationships with the other villages who possess a clear wariga connections (e.g., origin of seven Brāhmin families, the caste, clan, and social status). Most of the marriages are arranged after finding suiters selected from the connected villages and matching horoscopes. This tradition can be seen as generally applied always. The families for suitable marriages are regarded as of a suitable bloodline, trustworthy and have a network of security. Traditionally, the prominent villages for building marriage relationships for Kambuwatawana are: Borawewa, Hathigamuwa, Herathgama, Nikawewa, Dembatogama, Eriyawa, Kandulawa, Rakwana, Nambadewa, Rambawa, Galgiriyawa, Doluwa, Karawilagale, Walaswewa, Girathalana, Giribawa, Makaduwawa, Wathuwaththegama, Rakogama, and Uduweriya.

In the recent times, marriage relationships and kinship patterns has changed rapidly. For example, the Kambuwatawana people have expanded their marriage relationships beyond the traditional

---

[213] Same family descent.

circles and has got expanded to the other families within the other districts of Kegalle, Kandy, Anuradhapura and Gampaha etc. Some marriages were outside of traditional wariga (ethnic) and clan boundaries. The main factors that influenced this change included:

- ✧ Love relationships for marriages rather than arranged or other types,
- ✧ demand for the economic potentialities and other social connections,
- ✧ expansion and availability of occupations in other parts of the country and exposure to the other families and networks, and
- ✧ explosion of new social relationships and connections.

In recent times, the traditional wariga and established relationships among the Brāhmins and Malala Bandaras have been gradually fading away, giving way to modern social and economic values in marriage relationships.

Chapter Nineteen

Kambuwatawana Current Genealogical Records

This chapter offers a comprehensive overview of all the families represented by the elders in the current generation of Kambuwatawana. It establishes their connections to the honorary names documented in palm-leaf manuscripts and explores their intricate kinship and marriage ties with a network of original Brāhmin villages and some Malala Bandara villages.

I have meticulously traced the ancestral origins of each family group in Kambuwatawana, spanning back to the late 1800s. The provided list encompasses the names of family elders, and alternative social brandings (nicknames) have been included to enhance clarity and minimize any potential confusion, thereby facilitating a better understanding of each elder and their respective nuclear family.

Family Groups with the Elder's Names.

1. Ekanayake Mudiyanselage Appuhamy, born in late 1800s.

The records of Appuhamy's sibling or parents are not available. He married Basnayake Mudiyanselage Tikiri Manika born late in 1800. Appuhamy and Tikirimanika both are natives of Kambuwatawana.

Tikiri Manika's two sisters married from Karawilagala and Uduweriya (to a Rathna Malala Bandara). Appuhamy and Tikiri Manika had seven children. EM Kuma, EM Ran Manika (she married Basnayake Mudiyanselage Dingiri Banda, a Kambuwatawana native, Pathira Senior, refers to the entry number 2 below), EM Manikhamy (she married from Madiyawa), EM Muthu Menika (she married from Datawa), EM Dingiri Amma (she married Basnayake Mudiyanselage Ukku Banda from Siyambalawa, refers to the entry number 3 below), EM Ukku Amma (she married from Giribawa), and EM Muthu Banda (he married from Doluwa, refers to entry 4 below).

2. **Basnayake Mudiyanselage Dingiri Banda** (also known as Pathira Dingiri Banda, born in mid-1910's.

His father was Basnayake Mudiyanselage Ranhamy. The details about Ranhamy's parents, wife or siblings are not available. Dingiri Banda had a brother, Basnayake Mudiyanselage Mudiyanse. Dingiri Banda married Ekanayake Mudiyanselage Ran Manika (from Appuhamy family above entry 1). Dingiri Banda and Ran Manika both are natives of Kambuwatawana.

Dingiri Banda and Ran Manika's children: BM Punchi Banda (married from Malagamuwa), BM Karunawathie (first marriage from Kandulawa and then Kambuwatawana), BM Kumarihamy (married from Borawewa), and BM (Bandara) Bandaranayake (married from Bogollagama).

3. **Basnayake Mudiyanselage Ukku Banda** (he is known by his village name - Siyambalawa), born in early 1900s.

Ukku Banda married Ekanayake Mudiyanselage Dingiri Amma (from Appuhamy family above entry 1) Ukku Banda and Dingiri Amma's children: BMU Mahindarathna, BMU Kusumawathie, BMU Tikiri Banda, BMUB Basnayake and BMU Sitha Kumari.

4. **Ekanayake Mudiyanselage Muthu Banda**, born in early 1900s.

EM Muthu Banda married Herath Mudiyanselage Pemawathie from Doluwa. Muthu Banda's and Pemawtahie's children: EM Dayawathie, EM Chandra Ekanayake, EM Ran Banda, EM Ariyawathie, EM Yamuna Ekanayake, EM Ariyapala Ekanayake, EM Amarasinghe, EM Aruna Shantha, EM Ramya Ekanayake, and EM Bandumathie.

5. **Basnayake Mudiyanselage Mudiyanse** (also known as Pathira Mudiyanse), born in mid-1910's.

His father was Bansyake Mudiyanselage Ranhamy. His brother was Basnayake Mudiyanselage Dingiri Banda. Mudiyanse had two daughters from a previous marriage, and they married from Makaduwawa and Hurigaswawa. Mudiyanse's second marriage was to Herath Mudiyanselage Muthu Manika from Makaduwawa.

Mudiyanse and Muthu Manika's children: BM Leelawathie (married from Wathuwaththegama), BM Kamalawathie (married from Balagolla), BM Thilakarathna (married from Ambagaswewa), BM Gunarathna (married from Mudiyannegama), and BM Bandara Manike (married from Mudiyannegama).

6. **Basnayake Mudiyanselage Udayarathna**, born in early 1900s.

Udayarathna's parents were Basnayake Punchirala and Basnayake Mudiyanselage Sittamma. Sttamma was a sister of BM Muthu Banda (the details of Muthu Banda's family in entry 13 below). Udayarathna had another brother Basnayake Mudiyanselage Piyathissa. Udayarathna married to Disanayake Mudiyanselage Ukku Amma from Kallanchiya. Udayarathna's children: BM Tikiri Banda, BM Punchi Banda, BM Disanayake, BM Ran Banda, BM Gunathilaka, BM Chandra Basnayake, and BM Basnayake.

7. Basnayake Mudiyanselage Piyathissa, born in early 1900s.

As stated in the previous entry his parents were Punchirala and Sittamma, and his brother was Udayarathna. Piyathissa married Ekanayake Mudiyanselage Bandara Manika from Hathigamuwa. Piyathissa's children: BM Anulawathie, BM Dingiri Banda, BM Wimaladharma, BM Muthu Manika, BM Karunawathie, BM Premawathie, BM Kapuru Banda, BM Kusumawathie, and BM Dhammika Basnayake.

8. Basnayake Mudiyanselage Kapuru Banda, born in late 1800s.

Kapuru Banda was an Arachchila (officially village chieftain, he was also known as Goje Rala). He married Herath Mudiyanselage Dingiri Amma from Herathgama, born late in 1800. They had two sons: Basnayake Mudiyanselage Kalu Banda Thilakarathna who married to BM Heen Amma Karunawathie from Borawewa. Basnayake Mudiyanselage Ran Banda Jayarathna, (a schoolteacher) married Tennakoon Mudiyanselage Karunawathie (a schoolteacher) from Pothuhera of Amunugama. They lived in Nikawewa and they had no children.

Kalu Banda Thilakarathna and Heen Amma's children: BM Mahinda Bandara, BM Surasena Bandara, BM Sumanawathie Kumarihamy, BM Padmawathie, BM Dayarathna, BM Chandra Kumari, and BM Kanthi Basnayake.

9. Basnayake Mudiyanselage Appuhamy (he is also known as Seeni Appuhamy), born in early 1900s.

Appuhamy married to Basnayake Mudiyanselage Makkamma who was a sister of BM Muthu Banda (entry 13 below). Appuhamy and Makkamma had nine children. The eldest daughter BM Muthu Manika married to HM Wijekoon Banda from Kandulawa. Appuhamy and Makkamma's children: BM Muthumanika, BM

Wijewardene, BM Ran Manika, BM Loku Bandara, BM Sumanawathie, BM Lilawathie, BM Podi Bandara, BM Tikiri Kamarihamy, and BM Bandara Manike.

10. **Basnayake Mudiyanselage Tikiri Banda**, born in early 1900s.

His parents were Basnayake Mudiyanselage Ukku Banda and Basnayake Mudiyanselage Muthu Menika from Nikawewa. Tikiri Banda had three siblings: Basnayake Mudiyanselage Ran Manika who married Basnayake Mudiyanselage Ran Banda (Ayurveda doctor). Basnayake Mudiyanselage Dingiri Amma, female, married from Hathigamuwa, and Basnayake Mudiyanselage Muthu Banda (entry 12 below).

Tikiri Banda married Ekanayake Mudiyanselage Kuma from Harthigamuwa. Their children: BM Wijerathna, BM Jayarathna, BM Anulawathie, BM Karunarathna, and BM Senarathna.

11. **Basnayake Mudiyanselage Ran Banda** (Ayurveda doctor), born in early 1900s.

Ran Banda married Basnayake Mudiyanselage Ran Manika. She was a sister of Tikiri Banda of the previous entry. Ran Banda had one child – BM Somawathie.

12. **Basnayake Mudiyanselage Muthu Banda** (He was known as Mudalali or shop owner), born in early 1900s.

Muthu Banda was a brother of Tikiri Banda and Ran Manika (of previous two entries). Muthu Bada married Wanninayake Mudiyanselage Heen Menike from Walassawa. Muthu Banda's children: BM Seetha Irangani, BM Karunarathna, and BM Chitra Basnayake.

13. Basnayake Mudiyanselage Muthu Banda, male, born in early 1900s.

BM Muthu Banda married to Ilangasingha Mudiyanselage Ukku Amma from Mankadawala. Muthu Banda had five siblings. The eldest sister BM Sittamma married BM Punchi Rala (her children BM Udayarathna and BM Piyathissa, as stated in previous entries). Another brother Basnayake Mudiyanselage Tikiri Banda, who married Ilangasinha Mudiyanselage Dingiri Amma from Mankadawala (the sister of his wife). This Tikiri Banda had three children, one daughter, BM Bandara Manika married STB Basnayake (entry 16 below), Mutu Banda's another sister was BM Makkamma who married BM Appuhamy (entry 9 above). Muthu Banda's youngest brother was Basnayake Mudiyanselage Bandaranayake (entry 14 below).

Muthu Banda and Ukku Amma's children: BM Dingiri Banda, BM Leela Kumarihamy, BM Ukku Banda, and BM Punchi Banda.

14. Basnayake Mudiyanselage Bandaranayake (also known as *anda* Bandaranayake because he was blind), born in early 1900s.

Bandaranayake was a brother of BM Muthu Banda (entry 13 above). Bandaranayake married to Rathnamalala Wanninayake Mudiyanselage Bandara Manika from Monnekulama. Bandaranayake and Bandara Manike's children: BM Wimalawathie, BM Chandrasena, BM Ukku Banda, BM Sumedhawathie, BM Kamalawathie, BM Sitha Kumarihamy, and BM Chandrasena.

15. Basnayake Mudiyanselage Loku Banda, born in late 1800s.

BM Loku Banda married to Rajakaruna Mudiyanselage Kiri Bandage Ran Menika from Nikawewa. Loku Banda had four children. BM STB Basnayake, School Principal, who married to BM Bandara Menika, a teacher. STB Basnayake's children: Tudor Basnayake, BM Priya Kalyani, and BM Madduma Banda. A daughter who married from Attahanapola, and another daughter married from Senapura, and the youngest was Basnayake Mudiyanselage Loku Banda Widanelage Herath Banda (Entry 16 below)

16. **Basnayake Mudiyanselage Loku Banda Widanelage Herath Banda** (also known as Pate Herath Banda), born in early 1900s.

Herath Banda married Wanninayake Mudiyanselage Ukku Bandage Leelamma from Eriyawa. Herath Banda's children: BM Jayasena, BM Karunarathna, BM Bandaranayake, BM Kusuma Kumari, BM Wimalawathie, BM Tikiri Banda, BM Jayasundara Basnayake, BM Dhanapala, BM Tikiri Kumarihamy, and BM Deepthi Kumari.

17. **Basnayake Mudiyanselage KD Banda,** a teacher, (he is known for his psychological disorder) born in early 1900s.

BM KD Banda's first marriage was to Basnayake Mudiyanselage Karunawathie who produced two children, BM Sumanawathie (married EJM Appuhamy from Girathalana), and BM Somapala (married EM Muthumenika from Doluwa).

BM Sumanawathie and Appuhamy's children: EJM Jayasinghe, EJM Lilawathie, EJM Karunarathna, EJM Thilakarathna, EJM Bandaranayake, EJM Jayasundara, EJM Amarasingha, and EJM Chandrika Jayasundara.

Somapala and Muthumenika's children: BM Jayawardena, BM Premarathna, BM Maithrirathna, BM Suraweera, BM Anulawathie Kumarihamy, and BM Nandawathie Kumarihamy.

KD Banda's second marriage was to BM Somawathie (Karunawathie's sister). This marriage produced two children, BM Ukku Banda also known as Punchi Mahaththaya (married to Ukku Amma from Nikaweratiya) and BM Kusumawathie married

Ekanayake Jayasundara Mudiyanselage Heen Banda from Thammitagama and live in Meegalewa.

Ukku Banda (Punchi Mahaththaya) and Ukku Amma's children: Udeni Malwila Basnayake and Kolitha Malwila Basnayake.

18. **Basnayake Mudiyanselage Kiri Banda,** (He is also known as Thapal Mahaththaya, or as KB Kambuwatawana), born in late 1800s.

K B Kambuwatawana's parents were BM Ukku Bandara, and Mother BM Ranmanika from Borawewa (Late 1800). KB Kambuwatawana married Ekanayaka Mudiyanselage Kawamma from Hathigamuwa. Kawamma's parents were EM Ukku Banda and mother was EM Manikhamy both from Hathigamuwa (Late 1800).

KB Kambuwatawana's siblings were BM KD Banda (as previously stated), Basnayake Mudiyanselage Amarasinghe, (Also known as Silva Mahaththaya); BM Dingirimanika married from Kirimatiyawa, and BM Bandara Manika married from Digana.

KB Kambuwatawana's children: BM Wimalawathie, BM Kusumawathie, BM Karunarathna, BM Bandaranayake, BM Arunawathie, BM Chandrasekara, BM Mallika Kumari, BM Swarna Basnayake, and BM Siripala Basnayake. The family has moved out of the village while the ancestral house is remaining.

BM Amarasinghe married WM Ranmanika Kumarihamy. Amarasinghe and Ranmanika's children: BM Bandula Basnayake, BM Lalithe Basnayake, BM Upali Basnayake, BM Meththa Basnayake, BM Ganga Basnayake. BM Kalyani Basnayake and BM Yamuna Basnayake.

19. **Basnayake Mudiyanselage Tikiri Banda** (he is also known as Namabara), born in early 1900s.

Basnayake Mudiyanselage Tikiri Banda had two marriages and had children from both marriages. His first marriage was to Ekanayake Mudiyanselage Muthu Manika (she is known for her psychological disorder) from Hathigamuwa. From this marriage, he had two children, BM Karunarathna, who did not marry, and BM Punchi Banda who married from Madiyawa. Tikiri Banda's second marriage was to Basnayake Mudiyanselage Kuma from Borawewa.

Kuma also had a previous marriage to Ekanayake Mudiyanselage Muthu Banda. From this marriage, Kuma had three children. Ekanayake Mudiyanselage Karunawathie who married to Herath Mudiyanselage Herath Banda from Kandulawa, (he is known as Podi Kandulawa); Ekanayake Mudiyanselage Kiri Banda who married to Herath Mudiyanselage Nandawathie from Henewa and EM Dindiri Amma, female, married Herath Mudiyanselage Punchi Banda from Kandulawa.

Karunawathie and Kandulawa Herath Banda's children: HM Tikiri Banda Herath, HM Muthu Banda, and HM Ukku Banda Herath. EM Kiri Banda and Nandawathie's children: EM Gamini Ekanayake, EM Mallika Ekanayake, EM Priyangika Ekanayake, EM Thilak Kumara Ekanayake, EM Chandrani Ekanayake.

Tikiri Banda and Kuma married (second marriage for both) again and produced three children. Tikir Banda and Kuma's children from second marriage: BM Ukku Amma, BM Bandara Manika, and BM Kapuru Banda.

20. **Basnayake Mudiyanselage Tikiri Banda** (also known as Ibbi Tikiri Banda) born in early 1900s.

BM Tikiri Banda married Basnayake Mudiyanselage Somawathie from Borawewa. Tikiri Banda and Somawathie had six children: BM

Karunawathie, BM Sirinayake, BM Piyadasa, BM Kusumawathie, BM Bandara Manika, and BM Anulawathie.

21. **Basnayake Mudiyanselage Dingiri Banda,** (he is also known as Kaande Dingiri Banda), born in early 1900s.

BM Dingiri Banda married Herath Mudiyanselage Ukku Amma from Borawewa. They had four children: BM Somapala, BM Ran Manike, BM Ukku Banda, and BM Punchi Banda.

22. **Basnayake Mudiyanselage Heen Banda** (he is also known as Kapi Heen Banda or Officer), born in early 1900s.

Heen Banda married to Wanninayake Mudiyanselage Bandara Manika from Eriyawa. He had a brother Basnayake Mudiyanselage Kiri Banda and a sister who married from Nikawewa. Heen Banda had seven children: BM Tikiri Banda, BM Punchi Banda, BM Pemawathie, BM Sumanawathie, BM Nandawathie, BM Dayani Mallika, and BM Ananda Dharmasiri.

23. **Basnayake Mudiyanselage Kiri Banda** (he is also known as Bari Kiri Banda), born in early 1900s.

BM Kiri Banda married Rajakaruna Mudiyanselage Ran Manika. Kiri Banda's brother was BM Heen Banda and he also had a sister who married from Nikawewa. Kiri Banda's children: BM Ran Banda, BM Dingiri Amma, and BM Muthu Banda.

24. **Basnayake Mudiyanselage Kiri Banda,** (he is also known as Thapal or Deyi Kiri Banda), born in early 1900s.

Basnayake Mudiyanselage Kiri Banda was a postman, and also had a devala where he practiced black magic. Therefore, he was also known as Deyiya or diety. He married to Herath Mudiyanselage Makamma from Makaduwawa. Kiri Banda and Makamma had the largest family in Kambuwatawana with twelve children.

Kiri Banda's children: BM Anulawathie Kumarihamy, BM Seelawathie Kumarihamy, BM Seetha Kumarihamy, BM Sirinama Bandara, BM Pathma Kumarihamy, BM Chandra Kumarihamy, BM

Ran Banda Basnayake, BM Indra Kumarihamy, BM Sandasili Kumarihamy, BM Kanthi Kumarihamy, BM Shakya Nanda Bandara, and BM Sujatha Basnayake.

25. **Basnayake Mudiyanselage Heen Banda,** (a teacher, he was also known as Dugi Heen Banda) born in early 1900s.

His father BM Appuhamy from Kambuwatawana and mother is from Herathgama. Heen Banda had one brother in Borawewa (BM Mudiyanse). Heen Banda married Ekanayake Mudiyanselage Muthumenika, from Hathigamuwa. Muthu Menika's father was EM Mudiyanse from Hathigamuwa, and mother was HM Punchi Menika from Henawa. Heen Banda and Muthumanika's children: BM Bandara Manika, BM Wijesinghe Basnayake, BM Ukku Amma, BM Sunil Basnayake, BM Mallika Basnayake, BM Padmasiri Basnayake, and BM Anura Basnayake.

26. **Basnayake Mudiyanselage Aberathna**, born in early 1900s.

Basnayake Mudiyanselage Aberathna married Ekanayake Mudiyanselage Manikhamy from Hathigamuwa. She was the sister of EM Muthumanika who married BM Heen Banda. Aberathna and Manikhamy's children: BM Sumanawathie, BM Amaratunga, BM Lalitha Basnayake, BM Swarna Basnayake, and BM Jayantha Ranjith Bandara.

27. **Ekanayake Mudiyanselage Ukku Banda Herathhamy** (he is also known as Nondi Herathhamy) born in early 1900s.

Herathhamy's father was EM Ukkurala. House No 399. Herathhamy married Wanninayake Mudiyanselage Dingiri Amma, from Giribawa. Herathhamy and Dingiri Amma's children: EM Ekanayake, EM Leelawathie, EM Wanninayake, EM Pemawathie, EM Sirinayake, EM Semasinghe Bandara, and EM Premarathna Bandara.

28. **Ekanayake Mudiyanselage Ran Banda** (also known as Walasse Ran Banda), born in early 1900s.

Ekanayake Mudiyanselage Ran Banda was from Walassewa village. Father EM Punchi Rala from Walassewa. Ran Banda married Ekanayake Mudiyanselage Menikhamy. Manikhamy's father was EM Punchirala from Kambuwatawana, mother was Kiri Menika from Moragaswewa. House No 400. Ran Banda and Manikhamy's children: EM Ukku Banda, EM Kusumawathie, EM Kiri Banda, EM Nandawathie, EM Wijesundara, EM Karunawathie, EM Sumanawathie, and EM Disanayake.

29. **Herath Mudiyanselage Ukku Banda** (he is also known as Hodi Banda), born in early 1900s.

Herath Mudiyanselage Ukku Banda married Herath Mudiyanselage Tikiri Menika from Borawewa. Ukku Banda's children: HM Dingiri Amma, HM Leelawathie, and HMUB Herath Banda.

30. **Herath Mudiyanselage Herathhamy** (he is also known as Hodi Herathhamy) born in early 1900s.

Herath Mudiyanselage Herathamy, married Wanninayake Mudiyanselage Ukku Amma from Eriyawa. Herathhamy's children: HM Herathhamy, HM Dingiri Amma, and HM Ran Banda.

31. **Herath Mudiyanselage Mudiyanse,** (also known as Rakwaana Mudiyanse), born in early 1900s.

Herath Mudiyanselage Mudiyanse (born in Rakwana), married Ekanayake Mudiyanselage Mak Amma, Kambuwatawana. Rakwana Mudiyanse's children: HM Muthumanika, HM Somawathie, HM Kamalawathie, HM Ekanayake, HM Karunarathna, HM Bandara Manika, and HM Anulawathie.

32. Ekanayaka Mudiyanselage Kiri Banda (he is also known as Lokada Banda) born in early 1900s.

His father EM Appuhamy and mother, EM Manikhamy from Kambuwatawana. Kiri Banda married Disanayake Mudiyanselage Ran Menika, from Maha Ambogama. Ran Manika's father DM Herathhamy from Maha Ambogama and mother was from Walaliya. Kiri Banda's brother EM Dingiri Banda lived in Siyambalangomuwa. Kiri Banda's children: EM Appuhamy, EM Ukku Banda Ekanayake, EM Dingiri Amma, EM Ran Banda, EM Kusumawathie, EM Jinadasa, EM Pemawathie, EM Sumanawathie, and EM Punchi Banda.

33. Ekanayake Mudiyanselage Kapuru Banda, born in early 1900s.

Ekanayaka Mudiyanselage Kapuru Banda's father was Ekanayake Mudiyanselage Tikiri Banda, from Kambuwatawana, Mother Rathnayake Mudiyanselage Bai Amma, from Kubukkadawala. Kapuru Banda had a brother, EM Ran Banda lived in Siyambalangomuwa, had married from Miyagalewa. Kapuru Banda married Kariyapperuma Mudiyanselage Dingiri Amma, from Rakogama. Her parents, KM Appuhamy and RM Muthumenika, both from Rekogama. Kapuru Banda and Dingiri Amma's children: EM Amara Kumarihamy, EM Kanthilatha, EM Bandula Ekanayake, EM Swarna Ekanayake, and EM Nimal Ekanayake.

34. Ekanayake Mudiyanselage Wijekoon Banda (he is also known as Hathigamuwe Wijekoon Banda as he was born in Hathigamuwa), born in early 1900s.

Ekanayake Mudiyanselage Wijekoon Banda and his wife Herath Mudiyanselage Bai Amma both lived in Borawewa. But Bai Amma inherited a land at Kambuwatawana. They built a house at Kambuwatawana and a couple of their offspring live in this house.

Wijekoon Banda's children: EM TB Ekanayake, EM Somarathna, another daughter, and EM Wijethissa.

35. **Basnayake Mudiyanselage Tikiri Banda** (he is also known as Bacha Karunarathna) born in mid-1900s.

Basnayake Mudiyanselage Tikiri Banda lived at Jayalathgama (a part of Kambuwatawana). His father BM Kapuru Banda from Kambuwatawana and mother Wanninayake Mudiyanselage Ran Menika from Eriyawa. Tikiri Banda is married to Rajakaruna Mudiyanselage Somawathie, female, from Wathuwaththegama. Tikiri Banda and Somawathie's children: BM Priyantha Basnayake, BM Chandana Saman Bandara, BM Sandya Kumudu Kumari, and BM Nisantha Basnayake.

36. **Ekanayake Mudiyanselage,** (known as Thaka family, parents born in late 1800s).

This family moved out of the village. This family had three sons and one daughter. HB Ekanayake, male, HM UB Ekanayake, male, HM Karunarathna, male, all three settled in Giribawa. The youngest daughter HM Kusumawathie married and live at Rakwana.

Summary

All the family units retain surnames such as Basnayake Mudiyanselage, Ekanayake Mudiyanselage, and Herath Mudiyanselage, consistent with the genealogical legacy outlined in N1. It is evident that these descendants have primarily upheld matrimonial connections with the original Brāhmin villages to safeguard their identity and lineage. Moreover, there have been instances of marriages with descendants of the Malala Bandara lineage, contributing to the continued existence of the South Indian elite legacy within Sath Korale. It is worth noting that further research, even in the coming decade or so, can shed light on evolving trends of family relationships in the modern era.

Chapter Twenty

Afterword

This book provided a historical and sociological exploration of a South Indian Brāhmin group that settled in Sath Korale during the 16th century. It endeavoured to trace their remarkable journey through history and revealed the process by which they integrated into Sri Lankan society.

The enduring legacy of this group was illuminated by exploring into the genealogical heritage of the villages where they established themselves, with a particular focus on the Brahmi village of Kambuwatawana.

Conditions that Facilitated the Brahmins Flight.

During the 15th and 16th centuries, the political landscape of South India was marked by instability, with the collapse of the Vijayanagar Empire and the dominance of the Muhammadians in North India, who frequently invaded the southern regions, causing turmoil and destruction. Additionally, internal disputes among smaller kingdoms in South India added to the chaos. The defeat of the

Malala Kings by the Maravar kings forced some Malala royals to seek refuge in Sri Lanka.

Simultaneously, Sri Lanka was experiencing its own political challenges. The island nation faced ongoing conflicts between regional kingdoms and a growing threat from European forces. Sri Lankan kings had historically enlisted mercenaries from South India during internal conflicts, and the arrival of new elite migrants presented an opportunity to bolster the population in sparsely inhabited rural areas.

Local rulers sought to address the thinning population in rural regions by welcoming new migrants who could not only settle in these areas but also contribute to agricultural development and enhance the rural economy and social infrastructure. The conditions were favourable for facilitating the integration of these newcomers into Sri Lankan society.

Facilitation of Brahmins Settlement.

This study sheds light on the relatively lesser-known regional kingdom of Sath Korale, specifically Mundukondapola, where the local rulers actively facilitated the influx of South Indian immigrants.

The rulers of this region had a well-thought-out strategy when it came to welcoming and integrating the new immigrants. The newcomers received a warm reception, complete with land grants and authoritative titles provided by the local regime. They were encouraged to adopt Sri Lankan names and were settled in areas predominantly inhabited by Sinhalese. Some of the prominent immigrants were even appointed to regional chieftain positions, which enhanced their security and stability and allowed them to exert control over individual villages or entire regions (known as Divisions or "rata"). However, it was expected that the newcomers would make an effort to learn the local languages and customs in order to effectively communicate with the indigenous population.

Many of the migrants, particularly the Malala Bandaras, who were battle-hardened warriors, readily enlisted in the King's Army. This support from the monarchy bolstered the newcomers' influence, ultimately leading to their dominance over the local population.

In addition to their strategic integration, there were other factors that contributed to the successful assimilation of the new migrants. These individuals were educated and skilled, with the Brāhmins, in particular, being intellectuals qualified to serve as advisors to the kings. They often claimed descent from certain royal dynasties or warna, which helped legitimize their eligibility for prominent positions. Furthermore, these newcomers brought wealth and a specialised skill set with them, and they demonstrated their commitment to the new community by making generous contributions, such as repairing shrines shortly after their arrival or enroute to the royal palace. Many Malala warriors, having been battle-hardened soldiers, were readily available to join the royal army, further solidifying their place in the local hierarchy.

The local cultural norms in the region seemed to be conducive to the integration of incoming migrants. Throughout history, the indigenous population had demonstrated a deep respect and appreciation for individuals possessing elevated qualities, including intelligence, education, and advanced expertise. As a result, the areas where these newcomers settled likely underwent a rejuvenation, benefiting from the infusion of fresh talent and knowledge.

Religious Integration

It is important to recognize that not all of the migrants discussed here were necessarily Buddhists; the majority might have practiced

Hinduism. Transitioning from Hinduism to Buddhism was not a challenging shift, as Buddhism can be followed without necessitating a conversion..

In the context of Hinduism, the Buddha was regarded as the seventh avatar of the god Vishnu. According to legend, the Buddha had sought the protection of Buddhism in Sri Lanka from the god Vishnu. Sri Lanka already had a deep-rooted foundation in Hindu mythology, encompassing Hindu beliefs, practices, and rituals over centuries. John Clifford Holt notes[214] that Hindu ideas and practices gained prominence from the twelfth to the sixteenth century in Sri Lanka. Elements of the extensive Hindu pantheon were integrated into common Buddhist practices. Similarly, the culture of migrating Hindus from South India became part of the broader Sri Lankan culture, giving rise to a new amalgamation.

The inclusion of Hindu elements into Buddhism and Sinhalese culture increased as a result of this emerging pattern of accommodation. Hindu deities started to appear more prominently in Buddhist temples. While previous generations of Sri Lankans traditionally worshipped Hindu gods, the new breed of Brahmins facilitated the methodical conduct of Hindu rituals such as yaga and homa, adding a distinct touch to these practices.

Furthermore, the new migrant Brahmins and Malala Bandaras emphasized their legitimacy by claiming descent from those who arrived with the Bodhi tree, suggesting a significant role in shaping the emerging heritage of the region. However, it's crucial to acknowledge that this ancestral claim lacks conclusive evidence (Obeyesekere, 2005). Ultimately, what appears evident is the

---

[214] John Clifford Holt, 2004, Unceasing Waves: Brahminical and Hindu Influences in Medieval Sinhala Buddhist Culture in Sri Lanka.

assimilation of a South Indian Hindu community, predominantly Dravidian speakers, into the local rural community.

Extent of Assimilation.

In ancient times, the indigenous populations[215] of South India and Sri Lanka underwent a process of Sanskritization due to the dominant influence of North Indian Prakrit-language speakers, who shaped these regions through long-distance trade and colonization (Indrapala, 2007). However, a somewhat reverse phenomenon occurred during medieval times when South Indian Brāhmins and Malala Bandaras migrated to Sri Lanka. In this new context, they underwent a process of "Sinhalisation[216]," adapting to the unique culture, civilization, stable monarchy, language, religion, and robust institutions that had evolved in Sri Lanka by that time.

The Brāhmin families seamlessly integrated into the Kandyan social structure, assuming the role of farmers within the esteemed Govigama sub-caste. Over time, their origins became inconspicuous, fading away within a few generations. Remarkably, after nearly five centuries, the descendants of this Brāhmin group had completely lost awareness of their ancestral roots[217], a phenomenon evident in the smooth assimilation process in Sath Korale.

This assimilation process can be understood as acculturation, where individuals willingly and naturally adopted the social, psychological, and cultural aspects, including memories, sentiments, and attitudes, of the host nation. Several factors contributed to this smooth acculturation process in Sath Korale, as well as other parts of Sri Lanka. One key factor was the absence of distinct "biological

---

[215] Adivasi or Mesolithic.

[216] Also the people who settled in the north underwent a process of Tamilisation.

[217] For example, the people at Kambuwatawana.

factors," such as physical appearance, that would differentiate the local Sinhalese from the foreign Brāhmins, making the blending of these two communities relatively seamless.

Moreover, "psychological factors" also played a significant role. Both groups found it easier to consider themselves part of a shared society and culture due to historical connections and the common values they shared. These ties minimised the perception of being distinct societies.

There were also crucial "structural elements" in place from the outset to integrate new migrants into the local society. This involved assigning new names, titles, and lands, as well as recruiting them into the local workforce, including the military and technical professions, and appointing them to local chieftain positions. This process was undoubtedly characterised by mutual exchange and cooperation.

The Buddhist society, in particular, willingly accommodated Brahminical or Hindu rituals, showcasing a spirit of openness and acceptance within the broader community.

As time passed, it became evident that the South Indian Brāhmin and Dravidian elements had completely faded away to the extent that the descendants of Kambuwatawana were no longer aware of their South Indian roots. They had transformed into sentimental nationalists and patriots, assuming the role of guardians of Buddhism within the Sinhalese community[218]. Their evolution mirrored that of other Sinhalese community groups, originating from either local or immigrant backgrounds and later undergoing acculturation.

Ultimately, the descendants of Kambuwatawana seemed to have reached a point where they could easily be motivated to stand

---

[218] Popular nationalistic Sinhalese slogan "The need to become protectors of Rata (country), Jathiya (Sinhala race), saha Agama (Buddhism)".

against "Indians" and "Tamils." It is worth exploring whether the hundreds of young men from Brāhmin villages (including Kambuwatawana) who joined the security forces during the Sri Lankan civil war from 1983 to 2009 were driven by a genuine motivation to combat terrorism, possessed strong nationalist sentiments against a "Tamil" force, or were compelled by economic hardships that left them with no other option.

Social Transformation

The Brāhmin legacy and the transformation of Kambuwatawana and its surrounding villages have deep historical roots. The people who settled in this village over time played a crucial role in shaping its unique identity. Prior to the influence of the Brāhmins and Malala Bandaras, the village primarily revolved around farming, elephant kraaling for local and international trade, and occasional service in the royal army when needed. Economically, it was not a powerful village, relying on subsistence activities. Life was peaceful but relatively stagnant.

However, the arrival of new migrants in the 16th century, with their Brāhmin heritage, injected vitality and inspiration into the locality. These newcomers enjoyed a higher level of social recognition, all bearing the esteemed Brāhmin marker and lineage. Their Brāhmin roots facilitated their integration into the power structure of the ruling class. While they may not have been economically affluent, their birthright made them eligible for prestigious royal and local chieftain positions. This power structure ("radalaperuwa") persisted beyond the Kandyan kingdom, extending into British rule[219]. Even during British colonialism, families of the same class were appointed to ceremonial positions[220],

---

[219] De Silva, 2005, pgs. 421-426.
[220] E.g., appointment of Kambuwatawana Disawa

preserving traditions alongside the modernization of civil administration and the economy.

It appeared that successive Brāhmin generations supported each other to ensure the uninterrupted transfer of power from one generation to the next. They maintained traditional positions within the clan, advised and influenced the royalty to endorse and sustain the system, and demonstrated a strong sense of camaraderie. They shared intelligence within family circles, safeguarded their influence, and stood together in unity. This behavior reflected altruistic traits, as explained by evolutionary psychologists[221], which are essential for the survival of human beings, including their family, kinship, and tribe. The 1818 Rebellion serves as a noteworthy example of their commitment to re-establishing family connections and standing united. Many descendants of Brāhmins, including those with the supreme leader Kappetipola[222], continued to fight even after his execution, emphasizing their unwavering dedication to their cause.

Restrictions and New Trends.

The Brāhmin families historically restricted their marriages to within their clans, predominantly relying on the "wariga" (a closely-knit tribal family group) or the same "wansa" (a larger elite community) for matrimonial relationships. The villages that Kambuwatawana people had established marriage connections with for centuries were primarily the same. Prominent among these were Borawewa, Hathigamuwa, Herathgama, Nikawewa, Dembatogama, Eriyawa, Kandulawa, Rakwana, Nambadewa, Rambawa, Galgiriyawa, Doluwa, Karawilagale, Rakogama, Walaswewa, Girathalana, Giribawa, Makaduwawa, and Uduweriya. These villages all had

---

[221] David Buss, 1998; Leda Cosmides and John Tooby, 2005; Hamilton, 1964.

[222] It could be debatable if the 1818 Rebellion was a national freedom struggle or power struggle of the Kandyan chiefs to maintain their power and privileges.

Brāhmin or, in some cases, Malala Bandara origins due to South Indian royal claims.

Traditionally, the Brāhmins held religious beliefs that they were born from the head of the creator or were the second-born. They refrained from maintaining marriage relationships with those outside their caste or warna. Although there were ideological conflicts with Kshatriya, in the Sri Lankan context, Kshatriyas were often regarded as either superior or equal in status to the Brāhmins. The Brāhmins were considered the eligible class to replace the kings in Sri Lanka (Obeyesekere, 2013).

Marriages within the clan in Brāhmin villages may have contributed to the weakening of their gene pool over time. Studies, such as one from 1994, have found that inbreeding among cousins can lead to excess mortality (Bittles, 2001). There is a historical example of genetic issues arising from incestuous marriages[223] within ruling families, such as the Pharaohs in Egypt, who are believed to have inflicted genetic diseases upon themselves, leading to their decline.

Intermarriage between ruling families from different countries has been practiced in the past as part of strategic diplomacy for national interest. While it was sometimes enforced by legal requirements for royalty, more often it was a matter of political policy or tradition in monarchies[224].

Recently, I have noticed that the Kambuwatawana community has expanded its marriage connections beyond their traditional boundaries. This shift is a response to the younger generation's acceptance of contemporary economic values and their

---

[223] Elshazly H. (2005). Hamilton J. (2010).
[224] Beeche, Arturo (2009, 2013).

understanding of the necessity to adjust to evolving circumstances for prosperity and well-being.

The social mobility of the Kambuwatawana people recently has been facilitated by educational qualifications and professional skills, rather than solely relying on privileges based on birth. However, traditional patronage elements may still persist through marriage relationships, clan connections, or political affiliations.

As traditional social status and power structures began to decline, the prominence of Brāhmin villages, including Kambuwatawana, also diminished. These villages reverted to the normal process of power struggles without divine Brāhmin assistance or privileges. New educational and commercial parameters became the means of socio-economic transformation and social mobility. Nonetheless, it's important to note that traditional social infrastructure and values have not fully disintegrated in these Brāhmin villages in Sath Korale.

Buddhist Institutional Leadership.

As previously mentioned, the descendants of South Indian Hindu Brāhmins integrated into the Buddhist Sinhalese society in Sath Korale and the Kandyan regions, eventually ascending to leadership positions within Buddhist hierarchy.

Within organized higher Buddhist Chapters, the operational principles are guided by the Vinaya, which encompasses all the rules and duties of the priesthood. However, the hierarchical structure often relies on tradition. The succession of leadership within leading Buddhist sects, such as the Siam Nikaya, and institutions like the Niyadawane temple, has been influenced by factors like birth, ancestry, and inclination since the establishment of the Siam Chapter. This tradition emerged primarily to safeguard the religion and the priesthood, which had faced challenges before the establishment of the Siam Chapter.

While this tradition contradicts Buddhist teachings, some argue that it has proven to be an effective model. Traditionalists contend that it has strengthened temple institutions and extended the longevity of "the Buddha Sasana" in Sri Lanka. This practice appears to have bolstered internal security, leadership, and succession planning, facilitated by clan relationships and networks. Senior monks can guide junior monks within this system, aligning with traditional values and norms. Clan relationships enhance this process by fostering shared family values. This paradoxical tradition provides certainty, predictability, and assurance in safeguarding Buddhist heritage, despite potential philosophical and ideological contradictions. Evaluating the efficacy of such a traditional value system that appears to be functional can be challenging.

Implications for the Ethnic Identity.

Throughout Sri Lanka's history, its strategic location in the Indian Ocean has attracted explorers, invaders, traders, and colonists. The ethnic makeup of modern Sri Lanka is the result of successive waves of immigrants and their integration into both the ruling class and local society, resulting in evolving identities. The north-western region, including Mannar, Anuradhapura, Vavuniya, Puththalama, Halawatha, and Kurunegala regions, served as a "frontier" where new Indian immigrants interacted with early Sri Lankan settlers. As customary, this cultural mix continuously transformed and influenced other parts of the country. However, being an island nation, Sri Lanka has also developed unique identities independent of Indian influence over time.

Numerous historians, sociologists, and anthropologists have observed the development of two ethnic communities in Sri Lanka:

the Sinhalese and Tamils. According to Obeyesekere (2013), the assimilation of Brāhmins into the Sinhalese community was precise. He identifies two groups of South Indian Brāhmins, purohits, and popular ritual specialists, who became "Sinhalised" and integrated into the prevailing caste system as govigama, the dominant farmer caste. This assimilation also applied to groups like the hettis and certain kshatriyas, such as the Malala princes, who eventually became Sinhalese govigama.

Obeyesekere (2016, 2013) emphasizes the significance of statements made by the Brāhmins who settled in Matale, as they align with historical knowledge. For example, Brāhmaṇa Ranmenika Ratvatte, the daughter of Kopuru Brāhmaṇa Rāla originally from Maddadesa (Madya Pradesh), resided in Kappetipola, home to the renowned 1818 Rebellion leader, Kappetipola of Monaravila. These Brāhmins appear to have abandoned their Brahminic names and become part of the radala or aristocratic segment of the govigama or farmer caste. Despite their high varna in the Indian caste system, the Brāhmins continued to exist as a sub-caste of govigama, which is also the sub-caste or varna of the Kandyan kings. The evidence presented in this book supports these assertions.

Sivaratnam (1960) presents a simple formula to explain the aspects of general migration of South Indian Tamils and their broader assimilation process in the new country:

"The Tamils came under two major categories (No 1) soldiers [and] (No 2) no soldiers. The soldiers were further sub-differentiated into (a) invaders and (b) mercenaries. The no soldiers comprised mainly of innocent immigrants, agriculturalists, merchantmen, and other such people who came not through war, settlers who migrated on summons from princes who themselves had arrived earlier and entrenched in this country. As examples, the Vanniyars came to Ceylon in the 5th century on an invitation from Prince

Kulakoddan and colonised Tambalakaman, because of the expertise in agriculture." (pg. 8)

Mudaliar P W Gunawardhana[225] tries to give an overarching theory of assimilation.

"Sinhalese are a composite race with these three elements in their composition, viz. the aboriginals (Yakkas and Nagas), a Pandyan contingent which was Tamil, and Vijaya's contingent (Aryans). However, in GC Mendis' view, "Vijaya's contingent was not Aryan in blood as they were totemistic, but Aryan in speech only".[226]

There have been diverse views about the factual assimilation process in Sri Lanka.

Similarly, Tennent (1859) explains a potential assimilation process of South Indians into the Sinhalese community from the medieval times:

"From the beginning of the thirteenth century to the extinction of Sinhalese dynasty in the 18th century, the island cannot be said to have been entirely free from the presence of Malabars. Even when temporarily subdued, they remained with false professions of royalty. Damila soldiers were taken into pay by the Sinhalese sovereign, the devales of Hindu worship were built in close proximity to the viharas of Buddhism and frequent intermarriages, the royal line was almost closely allied to the kings of Chola and Pandya as to the blood of the suluwansa." (Tennent, 1859 pg. 417)

Indrapala (2007) noted that the evolution of the two identities of Sinhalese and Tamils was by assimilating into many small cultural groups who had arrived in the completion of 1200 AD. Further assimilation and the development of changes continued in the

---

[225] Quoted in Sivarathnam (1968), pg. 5.
[226] Quoted in Sivarathnam (1968), pg. 5.

following centuries. However, a marked geographic division among the two communities is visible.

Mendis (1948, pg. 9) identifies the Dravidian as a stock of people who had helped to form the Sinhalese race. They exercised their cultural influence mainly through Hinduism which not only became firmly established in the eleventh century, but also influenced Buddhism to a considerable extent.

Rasanayagam (1926) states that after the 14th century, when South India was disintegrated, many respectable Vellalar families emigrated to Ceylon. Some of them settled in Jaffna and others sought refuge under the Sinhalese kings and accepted positions of honour and trust. They became the forebears of some of the most respectable Vellalar families of the South. There are hundreds of respectable Vellalar families in different parts of the Jaffna Peninsula, who trace their descent from one or other of these early colonialists.

Liyanagamage (1988), also states that the Alakeswaras and many others who came from south Indian territories settled in the northern parts of the island in increasing scales. Sinhalese in the north became a minority and absorbed into the dominant culture. They became Tamilised in the course of time. According to Liyanagamage, the reverse order took place in the south. Tamil minorities living among the Sinhalese were Sinhalised with the passage of time. Liyanagamage says that:

> "It is the irony of history that when the Sinhalese and the Tamils confronted each other in the battlefield, as indeed they did in the fourteenth century, the former would scarcely have known that they were not quit Sinhala as they thought they were, much as the latter would hardly have known that they were ultimately not quite so Damila either." (Liyanagamage, 1988, pg. 51)

Geiger[227] says, "[I]t is obvious that owing to the continuous influx of Damilas[228], both soldiers and non-soldiers, the Sinhalese must have been considerably influenced by the Dravidian race not only culturally but also physically and mentally. But complete amalgamation of the two races never took place in Ceylon. The two people are still conscious of their differences as they were in ancient times and during the medieval times" (Geiger, 1960, pg. 20). Apparently, Geiger does not recognise the assimilation of Sinhalese race to Tamils in the north and vice versa in the south (e.g., Sath Korale). Mendis (1948, pg. 20) stated that, "It is difficult to gauge the extent of Tamil blood among the Sinhalese, but there is no doubt that it is considerable."

These scholars basically validate that many Sinhalese in the north became Tamils and many Tamils (Dravidians) in the south became Sinhalese through a specific assimilation process over the passage of time.

This process was also applicable to people in Vanni regions and the southern Sinhalese communities like Karawa, Salagama, Durawa and Chetty. However, Indian Tamils in the Plantation sector remained unaffected by this assimilation process. They were geographically distanced from Sinhala or Sri Lankan Tamils, lived in their own isolated clusters, involved in routine occupation in a restricted geographic area without needing to go into, and interact with, different areas in the country, and therefore, they were prevented from being assimilated into the broader Sri Lankan communities.

A process of community assimilation unfolded over time in both India and Sri Lanka, amalgamating numerous waves of human

---

[227] Geiger, 1960, Culture of Ceylon in medieval times, pg. 20.
[228] Another name for Tamils.

migrations that penetrated the subcontinent. This assimilation gained momentum particularly in geographical frontier regions (like Sath Korale) where new and early immigrants interacted.

However, it is conceivable that this assimilation faced obstacles when individuals began organizing themselves within ideological frameworks such as race, varna, caste, or class. Additionally, from a social historical perspective, it is essential to acknowledge that advancements in warfare, social and economic advantages, as well as technological developments, were strategically employed by an elite class to establish dominance and integrate the subordinate communities.

Final Word.

This historical publication sheds light on the process by which South Indian Hindus and speakers of Dravidian languages transformed into Sinhalese in Sath Korale and the Kandyan regions of Sri Lanka. This transformation may offer insights into similar historical processes that occurred elsewhere in Sri Lanka, both in the north and the south. It is evident that the present-day ethnic divisions in Sri Lanka may be more rooted in ideological differences than in bloodlines.

I believe that I have unravelled a phenomenon of how South Indian Brāhmins integrated into the rural Sri Lankan community in the past and eventually acculturated into the Sinhalese Buddhist community. I have supplemented historical evidence with genealogical records. It is expected that future generations and researchers will build upon this work, identifying gaps, challenging findings, and exploring new research directions in history, sociology, or anthropology. The process of advancing knowledge often follows a thesis-antithesis-synthesis model.

The inclusion of palm-leaf manuscripts in this publication highlights their value in uncovering hidden historical events and facts. Developing concepts and hypotheses before examining the contents of palm-leaf manuscripts can be a beneficial approach.

I acknowledge that our forefathers who painstakingly prepared ola-leaves and meticulously wrote manuscripts to document historical events, territorial boundaries, and successive generations, including genealogical information, on this challenging medium is a testament to their foresight, scholarship, and civic responsibility.

I particularly acknowledge Dembatogama Rajakaruna Mohottala, the author of the manuscript "Nikawa Gampaha Korale Vitti saha Mayim Wattoru," which I had the privilege of reading and copying in the 1970s. This manuscript served as a primary source of information as well as inspiration for the publication. I appreciate his impartial approach to recording events, opting for factual accuracy over exaggeration or the propagation of myths. Whether driven by discipline, duty, or personal conviction, this Mohottala dedicated the time and effort to produce the manuscript independently and impartially to the best of his ability.

I see this publication as an extension of Dembatogama Rajakaruna Mohottala's enduring legacy, and I am confident that I have upheld his commitment, vision, and dedication, all with the aim of benefiting future generations.

It is my sincere wish that readers have found this research as captivating, intriguing, and enlightening as I, the author, did while undertaking its preparation.

Appendix One

The Dissawaship of Sath Korale

(This document contains details about Kambuwatawana Disawa and Hulugalle Disawa.)

Source: Tropical Agriculturalist: (1904) Edited by the Hon. John Ferguson, C.M.G, (page 135)

During the time of the Kandyan Kings, the Seven Korale had always a Disawa, having been one of eleven principal divisions or disawanies, into which the ancient Kingdom was divided. The first Disawa, after the British occupation, was Kambuwatawana, the elder. Both he and his brother were Ratemahatmayas. After their death, the name is extinct.

Kambuwatawana was, in addition to Disawa, the first Kandyan Justice of the Peace of the Seven Korale and the first President of the Village Tribunal, when Gansabhawas were introduced to the district. He was a fine old Kandyan gentleman, and when a youth of seventeen was in the Court of the last King of Kandy, Sri Wikrama Raja Sinha. He was a personal friend of the late Mr A M Ferguson, O.M.G, to whom he communicated the information in 1866, when both these veterans were present at the kraal at Nelugolla the former as one of the chief organisers, and the latter as reporter to the "Ceylon Observer," that the grand old Kandyan Chieftain had taken part in twenty-one kraals under the British Government, twenty successful and one blank.

Mr. Ferguson wrote:

"The Kandyan Monarch, greater than Mahomet (who went to the mountain, because the mountain would not come to him), did not take the trouble of going to the kraal, as the English Rajjuruwos do. The elephants were actually driven on the esplanade and captured under the eye of the Monarch, as he sat surrounded by his court in the octagon; and mine ancient friend (who insisted on pledging me in a glass of London bottled stout) states that the same custom was pursued in the time of Bishop Heber's schoolfellow, the semi-Buddhistical Sir John Doyly. The old Ratemahatmaya quite agreed with me that the presence of the Governor and his friends, however, pleasant and interesting to them, was an impediment to the kraaling of the elephants; and he added that Lord Torrington's kraal (the one described by Sir J E Tennent) did not succeed until his lordship's platform was removed."

The Disawa was in the Court of the Kandyan King at the period of Mr. Ferguson's birth.

After a long interregnum, Halps, during the closing years of his official career, was appointed Disawa, and he did not live very long to enjoy the honour and dignity of the much-coveted title.

Another panse ensued; then came the present appointment which is unique. After representing his brethren in the Legislative Council the rank has been conferred on him, and he has been appointed not Dissawa of the Seven Korale only, as his predecessors were, but Disawa of the North-Western Province. This may appear an anomaly, for the N.W. Province includes two divisions, Chilaw and Puttalam, which are not Kandyan, except a portion of the latter, namely Demalahatpattu, and in respect of these districts which are presided over by Mudaliyars and Muhandirams. Hulugalla Dissawa may strictly speaking, to adopt a Biblical phrase, be not known in his country! However, the honour seems to be greater than that enjoyed by his illustrious predecessors, in that the territorial limits of his disawanies is made to cover a whole province, which it never did before, and we congratulate him on his extended jurisdiction, and may he live long in health, happiness and prosperity to enjoy the well-merited rank. By a strange coincidence all the Dissawas of the Seven Korale were reputed "kraalers."

Hulugala's appointment was recommended by Mr Burrows, and the selection is not only a good one but one that would meet with universal favour in the eyes of all Kandyans outside the Province. It is said, perhaps facetiously, of Sir Harry Dias, that when Sir William Gregory saw him riding he was so struck with the splendid seat which the Sinhalese Knight kept, that he remarked " Well, if he could sit so well on horseback, I have no doubt he would be able to keep as excellent a seat on the bench of the Supreme Court," and the next Gazette saw the appointment of Barrister Dias as a Puisne Justice. Could the same sort of feeling have actuated Mr Burrows in his recommendation of his protege? Here's the Government Agent's description of the present Disawa in 1886, when he never expected to act in his present office, much less to be instrumental in securing the honour in question for Hulugala.

"We are not long in finding ourselves in the presence of the captain of the hunt. He is a fine brawny specimen of a Sinhalese gentleman, and on great occasions, when he is attending a government levee for instance or welcoming a new revenue officer, is a very smart bedizened personage indeed. At present his costume is rather adapted to circumstances than remarkable for abundance. A handkerchief round his head, the anspicions of a cloth round his loins, sandals on his feet, and the rest-as nature made it, with the exception of a huge meerschaum pipe, from which he is enjoying a few final puffs; while near him stands a trusty henchman with his Winchester repeater and his double-barrelled express."

Be it said to the credit of Hulugala, he wears his Kandyan dress at all times, and this brings me to the very apposite remarks made by Sir West Ridgeway on the necessity of the Kandyans adhering to their national costume. Aa pointed out by a local writer in a recent work:

"But it is really pitiful to behold a transformation scene which is of frequent occurrence in the Kandyan districts. At one moment there appears a highlander in all time panoply of Kandyan state; in the finest embroidered muslin swelled out by a number of tuppoti put on one over the other; his shoulders widened in appearance by a jacket stuffed and puffed out into gigot sleeves the whole surrounded by a large pin-cushion hat, which Tennent likens to a goffered Vandyke—the tout ensemble comprising a striking national costume.

"Five minutes elapse and in steps an apologetic looking individual in a doubtful array of miscellaneous European clothes, showing off his dignified muslin circumference, his pin cushion hat, his radiant jacket and his state jewels, his face hidden by the depressed ruin of an ancient Elwood, a veritable jackdaw without his plumes, in this case not borrowed!

"Some officials in our opinion very properly refuse to give audience to such ill-clad Kandyans, while others do not mind it, with the result that the bad example, set by those who ought to know better, is widely followed by all ranks of society and breeds slovenliness and an indifference for elegance of dress and the donning of the national costume on necessary occasions, a circumstance which is much to be regretted."

Appendix Two

The Sath Korale Brahmi and other Leaders in the 1818 Rebellion

"Sinhala and the Patriots 1815-1818" written by P E Pieris in 1950, Appendix Q, page 638 – 640.

Abstract report of the headmen of Seven Korale who have been in rebellion (Vol 543A)[229]:

Kandulawa Mohottala and his two junior brothers . . .This Mohottala whether considered as to rank, wealth, influence or talents, is the first in the Ihala Dolos Pattu. He joined early in the attempt to subvert the English Government established "in the Interior. He was one of the most active and formidable opposers we had. He more than once held the highest offices under the English and Kandyan Governments. He says it had been his intention to come in previous to -20th September, but extreme ill health prevented. His personal appearance gives a colouring of truth to this, looking most wretchedly ill. The vast stores of grain in his possession were appropriated to feed the insurgents, and he frequently commanded *in person* his followers. It is true no act of cruelty stained the. rebel career of this leader; he has received praise for his humane conduct to some w-ho fell into his hands. He had no appointments under the Pretender's party. This I consider by no means favourable, because it indicates that no necessity existed to bribe him to exertion. Almost the whole of his properly has fallen a sacrifice, viz. houses, grain and cattle. His lands remain and are very extensive. I am informed he can raise on his lands about 1,000

---

[229] Some of the place name and persons names were modified to give meaning.

amunas[230] of paddy annually including both seasons. Gardens and his most valuable effects remain, though many of the coconut trees have been cut down. The latter, viz. effects, he carried off into Vanni.

He has two brothers, the youngest was Korale of Poossalle at the commencement of the Rebellion and joined his efforts to those of his eldest brother, remaining with him until his surrender on the loth instant. The second brother was not in any office under the British Government. His efforts were also joined to those of his elder brother. They have all three suffered severely during the struggle by the Privations sustained in partaking, in common with the Brutes of the jungle.

Wallawa Loku Mohottala . . . next in importance, whether in regard to talents or influence, is this Chief. He held the office of Rate Lekam in 1816. He had considerable property much of which was destroyed, viz., Houses, and grain brought into our granaries. His property is not very considerable; he did not come in till alter 20th September. When the Adigar was in the Seven Korale about six months ago the Mohottala came in and was pardoned. He subsequently joined the rebels, and he alleges, by compulsion, having been made prisoner by them. It is true that he did not take a very active part against us. I never heard of his being personally engaged in hostility, like several of the others; on his surrender he used all his exertions to induce others to submit. The Kandulawa Chiefs were brought in by him.

Wallawa Kuda Mohottala, . . . this Mohottala though he has not the intelligence of the first, has been a more active and determined rebel— a restless disposition and holding at the commencement of the rebellion, Rate Lekam of the Ihala Dolos Pattu. Tie persisted in adhering to the rebel cause uniformly, and was a principal adviser with Pilimathalawe, whom he guided. Under the rebel Chiefs he held the appointment of Rate Lekam of the Ihala Dolos Pattu bestowed by Pilimathalawe, to encourage and reward him for his active exertions. He surrendered previous to the 20th September; necessity alone dictated his surrender. He soon saw the result of the divisions among

---

[230] Sinhalese measurement of paddy land.

the rebels, by the disputes of Pilimathalawe and Kappetipola, and resolved to relinquish a falling cause. His doing so very materially injured their measures; separation took place among all; and mutual distrust led to reflections that soon determined many others of a minor consideration also to secede from the cause of rebellion and come in. He was possessed of a large portion of the properly, and from being early prepared, secured, by carrying off all his personal effects.

Hunupola Mohottala …The Hunupola Mohottala is of a good family but inferior to the above. He took a very active part in the insurrection prosecuting his efforts with considerable perseverance and success even to the vicinity of the cantonments of Kurunegala. His exertions were used between this and Kandulawa. He had not held any office under the English Government. From the rebel Leaders he had that of Atapattu Lekam in consideration of his enterprising efforts. He did not surrender until the 26th October, though I had been in correspondence with him since August, nor was it till he was convinced of the in utility of resistance that he adopted the more prudent line of preferring " Life " as the *only condition* to the chance of being taken prisoner and *certainly hanged.*

Hewapolle, …this man has been a most determined rebel from the first. He has been more mischievous as his influence commanded a portion of the country on the communication to Kandy and the 4 Korles. Hewapolly, his property is situated near the Pattecodie Pass close to Pellassay, Pilimathalawe continued him as rebel Wallawa Lekam until the other day, which he had held under the English Government. He surrendered to the Detachment placed at the disposal of George Nadoris Mohotty Modeliar on the 25th October. He had much property but in an inferior degree. The houses have been destroyed, cattle and grain seized, lands considerable.

Arampolla Mohottale, …this Chief's case demands particular consideration, he is entitled to less favour than any other of the same class. His first efforts in the rebellion were of the most determined kind. Of an animated disposition, with considerable wealth and talents, all these were combined in the several attacks on the detachments of troops marching to and from the road to Kandy. On his first submission in May last he acknowledged to me that he not only committed (?) all adherents, but carried a firelock, and neither repeated use of it, firing at our men. As the Adigar had pardoned this daring villian, I ratified it on the conditions that he made atonement for the past by evincing his loyalty for the Government. He promised; a month after joined the rebels and became a terror of our friendly Kandyans. He commanded that portion of the country from Ilookwella Baddegama and towards the. . .having established his residence on the Boolwell Mountains overlooking the whole flat country between that and Kurunegala. He hesitated much and long before he surrendered to George Nadoris and I had specially excluded him from having even *life* promised, as I deemed him a proper subject for the gallows, by being taken prisoner. His voluntary surrender precludes this, but I recommend some extraordinary severity in his case. He has suffered in property like the others. Pilimathalawe appointed him Attapattu Lekam in rebellion. He was taken prisoner on the 19th instant as I find on a *more particular enquiry*. I have therefore recommended his being tried for his life by a Court Martial.

Oedoolopolla Mohottale. . .This headman took an active part against the Government at the commencement of the rebellion. He commanded the Hewawisse people and had directed the passes into Madura Korle by Hangorankatawah to be obstructed and built batteries. He appeared in May last with others and in consequence of his house being destroyed much of his grain and cattle taken he was pardoned. Again, he relapsed into rebellion and only submitted shortly after mv expedition with Lieutenant Colonel ... into the Madure Korle in August. He is rather weak in intellect, has been the tool of others, and far from being formidable, having but little influence in the country.

He gives a list of sixty-five names of those who had come in, indicating the relative importance of each as a rebel, In the first group in addition to those already mentioned are the Mohottalas, Oedanwettc, Malimwela, Kambuwatawana, Bamoenapota, Rangama, Delwitta Lekama, Delwita Dugganna Rala, Dodanwatewene Nilamay, Kallotuwagama Nilamay, Paragawewa Mohottale.

Of Delwita Lekama he said " who with talents and ambition has been very active in the hostile measures of the rebels and only submitted from conviction of our cause being irresistible. He advised the rebel Chief Mohottalas to Submit as the English troops were dispersed like so many mosquitoes over the whole country and not to be opposed."

Among those still resisting were the Mohottalas. . .Curundu Koombre and two brothers, Embiligodde, Meddegama, Hooloogalle, Diagama, Coobokewewa, Cokwewe, Kekoenewewe, Torawatura, Doluwa, Borellewa, Deeyawa, Oedewella, Arampolle junior and Kambuwatawana junior.

Hook to Lusignan, 10th November. "After these rebels have suffered the punishment due to their crimes, is it the intention of Government to render them ineligible to any office? It is unfortunate that almost all the chiefs of Talents or who had considerable knowledge of the country were among the rebels. I have received more information from them than from our friends."

Arampola Loko Mohottala. "Taken prisoner and hanged." Hook, 10th November.

Appendix Three

Kambuwatawana Generations in Other Parts of the Country

Molagoda Family of Harispaththuwa.

The Gazeteer of the Central Province (part 2, pg. 602) written by AC Lawrie, provides an account of Molagoda Walawwa.

"There are two, one Dunuwila Walawwa on the North, which now belongs to the wife of Rathwaththe Basnayaka Nilame; the other lies on the south of a range of fields which is crossed by a very ancient and curious raw of large stones across which plank could be laid as a temporary bridge. These large stones (tradition says) were brought from Danture in one night."

The first Walawwa is known as Ratwaththe Walawwa and the second one is known as Molagoda Walawwa. Kambuwatawana connection was with the Molagoda Walawwa.

Dingiri Banda Kambuwatawana who was potentially a son of a Kambuwatawana Mohottala who was involved in the 1818 Rebellion fled to Harispattuwa and married to this Molagoda family. His father-in-law was Molagoda Muthu Banda Disawa.[231] Because of this connection, Dingiri Banda continued to maintain Kambuwatawana surname. Thereafter, the original Molagoda surname became Chandrasekara Herath Nawarathna Atapatthu Wasala Mudiyanse Ralahamilage Kambuwatawana Molagoda.

---

[231] This explanation provided by Lal Molagoda, Molagoda Walawwa, Harispattuwa.

Dingiri Banda Kambuwatawana Molagoda had four children: Madduma Banda Kambuwatawana Molagoda, Loku Banda Kambuwatawana Molagoda, Tikiri Banda Kambuwatawana Molagoda, and Madduma Kumarihamy Kambuwatawana Molagoda.

Maduma Banda had five children, Hugh Molagoda (Commissioner General of Inland Revenue), Chitra Molagoda (married to Dr Wadanda), Chandra Molagoda (married to Dambawinna Walawwa), Hema Molagoda (married to Madugalle walawwa), and Lal Molagoda[232] (married to Rathwatte Walawa of Kalawewa).

I have not conducted extensive research about this generation but wanted to highlight some Kambuwatawana descendants expanded to other parts of Kandy and established a network through marriage.

Nawarathna family at Kirindigala (Balangoda)[233]

A Kambuwatawana descendant known as "Kambuwatawana Chandrasekara Herath Nawarathna Atapatthu Wasala Mudiyanse Ralahamilage Dingiri Banda" got married to "Kalupahana Abeysekara Thilakarathna Senanayaka Jayasingha Mudiyanselage Ukku Menike" of Kirindigala Walawwa at Kirindigala, Balangoda. This marriage potentially occurred in the mid-1800. He was known as "Kambuwatawana Bandara" at Kirindigala. Dingiri Banda's children and grandchildren use his illustrious surname to-date in their birth certificates but have shorten to "Nawarathna" for convenience.

Dingiri Banda and Ukku Manike had two children, Loku Bandara and Punchi Bandara. Loku Bandara Nawarathna married from Kandy and had two children, Indra Devi Nawarathna Kumarihamy and Lokananda Wimaladharma Nawarathna.

Punchi Bandara Nawarathna married from Hidellana (Rathnapura) and had nine children, Pushpa Badhrawathi Nawarathna Kumarihamy, Soma Damayanthi Nawarathna Kumarihamy, Sirinaga Wimaladharma Nawarathna, Daya Kumarasiri Nawarathna, Chandranatha Anura

---

[232] Lal Molagoda's name appears in his birth certificate as "Chandrasekara Herath Nawarathna Atapatthu Wasala Mudiyanse Ralahamilage Kambuwatawana Molagoda Walawwe Lakshmi Rawanya Molagoda".

[233] This information provided by Srinaga Wimaladharma Nawarathna.

Nawarathna Bandara, Nayana Chitra Nawarathna Kumarihamy, Uththiya Badhra Nawarathna, Indra Kumari Nawarathna Kumarihamy, and Hema Mala Nawarathna Kumarihamy.

Dingiri Banda's descendants live in various part of the country. His surname has similarities to the Molagoda family. At this stage I have not established Dingiri Banda's connection to the Molagoda family or to his native Kambuwatawana village. I gathered that Ukku Manike had a close family relationship to Demodara Mohottala who was a leader of the 1818 Rebellion from Belihuloya. It is possible that Kambuwatawana Mohottalas' children fled or travelled to various parts of the country and connected to an elite network that was developed following the 1818 Rebellion.

Delwita Family.

There was a Ratemahaththaya at Delvita with the name of Kambuwatawana Chandrasekara Ekanayake Basnayake Mudiyanselage Tikiri Banda. There are two Walawwas at Delwita connecting with Kambuwatawana, namely, Hapugama Walawwa and Ihala Walawwa, both Walawwas use Kambuwatawana name.

I came across a court case dated 19th November 1891 at Kurunegala high court, challenging the inheritance of the properties of the Rate Mahatthaya.[234] The court declared that the petitioner Kambuwatawana Chandrasekara Ekanayake Basnayake Mudiyanselage Tikiri Kumarihami of Delwita Walauwa is the sole heiress as the next of kin (wife) of Kambuwatawana Chandrasekara Ekanayake Basnayake Mudiyanselage Tikiri Banda Rate Mahatthaya.

Tikiri Kumarihamy's tomb states that she died on 1 May 1893 at the young age of 28 years. The cause of death is unknown.

Tikiri Kumarihamy was born and brought up at Kambuwatawana. Tikiri Kumarihamy's parents were from Kambuwatawana and other specific details about this family were not discovered at the time of this publication. It is highly likely Tikiri Kumarihamy was a daughter of the Kambuwatawana Disawa or Rate Mahathtaya, and that status could

---

[234] *Ceylon Government Gazette*, No 5102, Friday December 4th, 1891.

have been an attraction for this union. The marriage occurred during the time Kambuwatawana two chiefs holding Disawa or Rate Mahaththaya positions. Kambuwatawana chiefs and Delwita chiefs could have had connections before. Probably known within the circle of Rate Mahaththyas, and they also strongly associated at the1818 Rebellion.

There is another potential theory that possibly the Delwita Rate Mahathtaya took wife's surname which has been another tradition of Sinhala system of things. Delwita family had extensive land and properties and I gathered that there had been numerous disputes for inheritance of the properties among the family members.

Appendix Four

Eriyawa and Madagalla Sannasas

Eriyawa Sannasa

එරියාවේ රන්ගෙයි බණ්ඩාර සිංහ ප්‍රතාප මලල බණ්ඩාර වන්නිනායක මුදියන්සේ වෙත සවන භුවනෙකබාහු මහා රජු විසින් ලබාදුන් සන්නස පතයි (ක්‍රිඹ 1540)

ශ්‍රී, ශක වර්ෂ එක්ව දහස් පන්සීය හතලිහට පැමිණි මෙම වර්ෂයේදී වෙසක් මස පුර පස්වන තිථිය ලත් ගුරු දින මෙම දවසදී එරියාවේ රංගේ බණ්ඩාර සීතාවක වැලි මළුවේදී ඇතා ඔප්පු කර දෙමින් මුණ පාපු තැනේදී ශ්‍රී ලංකේශ්වර වූ දේව ස්වාමි දරුවන්ගේ කරුණ දිවස් එලියට ගෙනහැර දක්වා බොහෝසේ කරුණා සම්භාරවල් ලබමින් එරියාවට අතරගල්ල සතර කඩහින් නැගෙනහිර විගස වැවේ ගල හින්නෙන් දකුණු දිග ගල් ලිද කන්දෙන් මෙහායින් බස්නාහිර මී ඔයේ උතුරු දිග සියඹලා පොතානේ ගල්ටන් වලින් මෙහායින් එරියාවේ ගන්දොළහ ඇතුළ්ව තුම්පත්තුවේ වන්නි මුත්තිල කමට සතර කයින් නැගෙනහිර රැස්සේරු කන්දේ දිය වුනු තැනින් කලන්කුට්ටියේ ගල්ටන් වලින් මෙහා දකුණු දිග පන්ස ගුලුගල වැටියෙන් නාපාන ඇල්ලෙන් නියදවනේ කන්දෙන් මෙහාත් උතුරුදිග දිවුරුන් ගලෙන් අන්දර වැවේ වෙල පස ලගල් ටැම්බෙන් මොරගහ වැවේ ගල් හින්නෙන් මේගනවෙද මිට මැදිවූ මහනාගල්සෝලේ ඇතුළ දස කරකඩයින් උතුරින් කලා ඔයෙන් කලන්කුට්ටියේ ඇලෙන් නැගෙනහිරින් එම ඇල ඇතුළ්ව සමලදිගින් කළුවැල් පොතානේ ගල්ටැම්බෙන් මේ හත් ඔය හා ගිරි සියම්බලන්ගමු ඇලේ කලා ඔයද මෙකි කඩයිම් ඇතුළ්ව ද මහා ගල්ගමුව දස්කන් නිලය අමුණු තුනේ වපසරිය වැවේ අමුණු තුනේ වපසරිය ද ඇතුළ්ව එරියාවේ රංගේ බණ්ඩාර වන්නිනායක සිංහ ප්‍රතාප මුදලි පටබන්දවා කඩඑළු තිරප්පු තුවක්කු ඇත්දත් අලිදත් මිදි හුගන් පලිමරලා ජාම මුර නැති

හැටියට තව බඳු ඇතුළුව ලැබෙමින් ත්‍රී සිංහලඩීස්වර රාධිපති එක චිත්‍ර ශ්‍රී ලන්කේස්වරවූ භුවනෙකබාහු දේව ස්වාමිදරුවනන් වහන්සේගෙන් වන්නි මුත්තිල කොමට මේ ශ්‍රී සන්තනස දේවා වදාළ පණිවිඩ වූ පනතයි.

Abstract: This document represents the royal land deed bestowed upon "Range Bandara Sinha Prathapa Malala Bandara Wanninayake Mudiyanse" of Eriyawa by the illustrious King Buvanekabahu the Seventh during the Shaka Warsha of 1540. It serves as recognition for his exceptional skills in handling elephants at the Sithawaka royal court.

The grant encompasses the villages of Eriyawa and Atharagalla, with well-defined geographical boundaries extending in all directions: north, west, east, and south. Additionally, it bestows upon him the esteemed honorary title of "Range Bandara Wanninayake Sinha Prathapa of Eriyawe," along with royal gifts and the prestigious position of "Vanni Munnila" chieftain.

Madagalla Sannasa

Published on 26 February 2014, by Divayina Newspaper. A copy of the Madagalla Thalpotha (palm-leaf), No 2, 189.S.1566 (AC 1644).

ශක වර්ෂ එකවාදහස් පන්සිය හැටහයක් වූ මෙම වර්ෂයෙහි ඇසල මස අව තියවක සහ දෙනටෙ නැකැත් ලත් බ්‍රහස්පතින්දා මේ දවස රාජසිංහ මහාරාජෝත්තමයානන් වහන්සේ විසින් වදාළා වූ පනත නම් මදගල්ලේ මාරසිංහ මුදලියා රඟගවත්තේදි තරම කපා දැක්වාපු තැනේදි සත් කෝරලේ දිසාවේ නිකවාගම්පහ බඳ මදගල්ලේ මුල් බීපු දෙලොහොමුන වපසරිය හා ඊට කඩඉම නැගෙනහිර මහ ඇලෙන් මෙපිටද උතුරු දිග පිදවිල්ලේ ඇලෙන් මෙපිට බස්නාහිර වැකන්දෙන් මෙපිටත් මෙම බින්වාසිය මදගල්ලේ මාරසිංහ මුදලියාට ප්‍රවේනිව මොහුගේ දරු මුනුබුරු පරම්පරාවට බඳ වැඩිල්ල පිනිස අහස පොලොව ඉරසඳ රාජාඥාන පවතිනා තුරු බුක්ති විදිනා සැටියට ත්‍රී සිංහල ද්වීපයෙහි එකවත්‍රා තන්වා දිපච්චකුවර්ති ස්වාමි වූ රාජසිංහ නම් මහා රාජෝත්තමයානන් වහන්සේ විසින් දේවා වදාළ පනත මේ සන්නස පෑ තහතම් කරගෙන භුක්ති විදීමටත් ඒ පනතත් මෙසේම යෙදි පනිවිඩ පනතයි.

Abstract: This document represents the royal land deed granted to Marasinha Mudali of Madagalle in the year 1566 during the Shaka

Warsha. This grant is a recognition of his heroic acts, which included the slaying of Portuguese soldiers in battle and presenting their severed heads to King Sithawaka Rajasinghe, who was encamped at Raggwaththa.

The deed specifies the allocation of twelve ammunos of paddy land in Madagalle, which is to be enjoyed by Marasinghe Mudali and his successive generations. It provides clear and well-defined boundaries in all directions: north, south, east, and west. Importantly, the document declares that this land grant is valid for perpetuity, ensuring its enduring significance and value.

Appendix Five

Bibliography

Abewardana, H A P. (1998). Boundary Divisions of Medieval Sri Lanka, Academy of Sri Lankan Culture.

Alahakoon, C N K. (2006). *Identification of physical problems of major palm leaf manuscripts collections in Sri Lanka*. Journal of University Library Association Sri Lanka. (Vol. 10).

Alahakoon, Champa N K., (2012). *The Division of Labour in the Production of Sri Lankan Palm Leaf Manuscripts*, Journal of the Royal Asiatic Society of Sri Lanka. Vol. 57, pp. 215-228 https://www.jstor.org/stable/43855214

Alba, R. & Nee, Victor. (1997). Rethinking Assimilation Theory for a New Era of Immigration International Migration Review 31(4):826-874 DOI: 10.1177/019791839703100403

Amaramoli, Ven. Egodamulle. et. al. (ed) (1995). Sri Rathanapala Abhinandana.

Ariyapala, M B (1968), *Society of Medieval Ceylon*, PhD Thesis, University of London, Department of cultural Affairs, Colombo, Ceylon.

Arunachalam, P. & James Sutherland. (1910). *Kandyan Provinces*. The Journal of the Ceylon Branch of the Royal Asiatic Society of Great Britain & Ireland, Vol. 22, No. 63 (1910), pp. 103-123 https://www.jstor.org/stable/43483635.

Balachandran, P K. (2006). Tracing the Sri Lanka-Kerala link. Hindustan Times. Mar 23, 2006.

Bandarage, Asoka. (1983). Colonialism in Sri Lanka: The Political Economy of the Kandyan Highlands, 1833–1866. By. Berlin: Mouton.

Bandaranayake, Bandara. (2011). Gamratawa, Gogage Publishers.

Bandaranayake, Senake. The pre-modern city in Sri Lanka: the 'first' and 'second' urbanization.

Beeche, Arturo (2009). The Gotha: Still a Continental Royal Family, Vol. 1. Richmond, US: Kensington House Books. ISBN 9780977196173.

Beeche, Arturo (2013). The Coburgs of Europe. Richmond, US: Eurohistory. ISBN 9780985460334.

Bell, H C P. (1920). *Prince Taniyallabahu of Madampe.* The Journal of the Ceylon Branch of the Royal Asiatic Society of Great Britain & Ireland, Vol. 28, No. 73, pp. 36-53 https://www.jstor.org/stable/43483170.

Bittles, AH $ Neel LV (1994) *The costs of human inbreeding and their implications for validation of the DNA level.* Nature Genetics. 8 (2): 117-121.

Brito C. (1999). Yalpanavaipavamalai. Asian Educational Services,

Brow, James. (2011). *Reconstituting Village Communities: Sir William Gregory's Efforts to Renovate Village Agriculture in Ceylon's North Central Province*, Essays for Gananath Obeyesekere Book Editor(s): H. L. Seneviratne Published by: Anthem Press. (2011) https://www.jstor.org/stable/j.ctt1gxpffq.9.

Brown, S. K., & *Bean*, F. D. (*2006*). Assimilation Models, Old and New Explaining a Long-Term Process. Migration Information Source, 3-41.

Brown, Susan K., Frank D Bean. (2006). *Assimilation Models, Old and New: Explaining a Long-Term Process*, October 1, 2006, Migration policy institute.

Budhadhathta, Ven Polwaththe. (1964). Samipathayehi Boudacharyawarayo.

Buss, David. (1998). Evolutionary Psychology.

Census of Ceylon. 1911, Cotte Government printer Ceylon.

Ceylon Administrative Reports 1912 -13. (1914). Government Printers, Ceylon, 1914.

Ceylon Government Gazettes, No 6791, – Friday, April 28, 1916, Ceylon Government Press, Colombo

Ceylon Government Gazettes, No 8454 – Friday, May 26, 1939, Ceylon Government Press, Colombo.

Ceylon Government Gazettes, No 8454 – Friday, May 26, 1939, Ceylon Government Press, Colombo.

Chandra, Satish. (2007). *History of Medieval India* (800-1700), 2007 First published by Orient Blackswan Pvt. Ltd. 2007.

Chitty, Simon Casie. (1834). The Ceylon Gazetteer, Cotta Church Mission.

Codrington, H W (1929), *A Short History of Ceylon*, Macmillan, London

Coomaraswamy, Ananda K. (2011). Mediaeval Sinhalese Art.

Cosmides, Leda & John Tooby. (2005). *What is Evolutionary Psychology? Explaining the New Science of the Mind (Darwinism Today)* Hardcover – August 1, 2005.

Crul, Maurice. & Jens Schneider. (2010). Comparative integration context theory: participation and belonging in new diverse European Cities https://doi.org/10.1080/01419871003624068

Darmarakkitha, Ven. Walimitiyawe & Ven. Kakkapalliye Anuruddhha. (ed). (1975). Vidyalankara Pirivena Shathasanswathsaraya. Department of Cultural Affairs.

Darmarakkitha, Ven. Walimitiyawe & Ven. Kalkiriyagama Dharmakirthi. (ed. 1961). Sri Dharmarama Shahithyankaya. Kalaniya University Press.

Davy, John. (1821). An account of the Interior of Ceylon, and its inhabitants, with travel in that island. London. 1821.

De Silva, KM. (2005). A History of Sri Lanka, Vijitha Yapa Publications,

De Silva, W A (1927). *Sinhalese Vittipot (books of events) and Kadayimpot (books of division boundaries).* The Journal of the Ceylon Branch of the Royal Asiatic Society of Great Britain & Ireland, 1927, Vol. 30, No. 80, Parts I, II, III and IV. (1927), pp. 303-325 http://www.jstor.com/stable/43483797

Devaraja, L S. (1972), *The Kandyan Kingdom (1707-1760).* Lake House Investments

Devendra, DT (1951)., Guide to Yapahuwa, Colombo.

Dewaraja, Lorna. (1985). *The Kandyan Kingdom: The secret of its survival.* Journal of the Royal Asiatic Society Sri Lanka Branch, 1985/86, https://www.jstor.org/stable/23730765.

Dharmasena Bandara Y M. (2011) Mahasammatha Vitti Book, in Nikawa Gampaha Aththayen Bindak.

Dharmawardana, M C. (2010). 18 Parapura, Syrya Prakashakayo,

Diary of John D'oyly, 1917, Colombo Apothecaries, Printers.

Dikshitar, V R R. (1939). *The Sillapadikaram,* Oxford University Press.

Ekanayake, A. de Silva, (1876). *On the Form of Government under the Native Sovereigns of Ceylon,* The Journal of the Royal Asiatic Society of Great Britain and Ireland. Vol. 8, No. 2 (Aprox., 1876), pp. 297-304, https://www.jstor.org/stable/25207732.

Elshazly H. (2005). Familiarity breeds: incest and the Ptolemaic dynasty. Journal of Hellenic Studies.2005;125:1-34.

Ethnic and Racial Studies journal, New insights into assimilation and integration theory: Introduction to the special issue, Article in July 2010.

Ferguson, John. (1893). *Ceylon in 1893,* John Haddon and co, London.

Ferguson, John. (1904). *Tropical Agriculturalist,* 1904.

Fernando, A. Denis N. (1986). *Ancient Maps of Sri Lanka - as a Primary Source of Information for the Study of human settlements and political boundaries,* Journal of the Royal Asiatic Society Sri Lanka Branch, 1986/87, New Series, Vol. 31 (1986/87), pp. 82-114 https://www.jstor.org/stable/23731039.

Fernando, A., Denis N. (1987). *Peninsula Jaffna from Ancient to Medival Times: Its Significant Historical and Settlement Aspects.* Journal of the Royal Asiatic Society of Sri Lanka, 1987/88, New Series, Vol. 32. pp. 63-90.

Figueira, DM. (2002). *Aryans, Jews, Brāhmins: Theorizing Authority through Myths of Identity*, State University of New York Press.

Geiger, W. (1960). *Culture of Ceylon Medieval times*, Harrassowitz.

Geiger, Wilhelm. (1912). The Mahawansa or the Great Chronicle of Ceylon. Oxford University Press. Amen Corner, E C.

Godden, Lee and Niranjan Casinader. (2013). *The Kandyan Convention 1815: Consolidating the British Empire in Colonial Ceylon*, 1.2.179 (2013) 1(2) CLH 179–210, http://dx.doi.org/10.5235/2049677X .

Guilmoto, Christophe Z. (1993). *The Tamil Migration Cycle, 1830-1950*, Economic and Political Weekly, https://www.jstor.org/stable/4399307.

Hamilton J. (2010). Frail and sickly, King Tut suffered through life. NPR website. February 16.

Hamilton, I W D. (1964). The Genetical Evolution of Social Behaviour. The Galton Laboratory, University College, London.

Heesterman, J C. (1995). *Warrior, Peasant and Brāhmins Modern Asian Studies* / Volume 29 / Issue 03 / July 1995, pp 637 - 654

Henry, W. Cave, MA. (1904). *The Ruined Cities of Ceylon.* 3rd Edition. London

Hermann Kulke • K Kesavapany • Vijay Sakhuja, Ed. (2009). Nagapattam to Swarnadwipa, Reflections on the Chola Naval Expeditions to Southeast Asia.

Hettiarachchi, AS. (1968). *Kandyan Dynasty,* The Journal of the Ceylon Branch of the Royal Asiatic Society of Great Britain & Ireland, New Series, Vol. 12 (1968), pp. 123-129. https://www.jstor.org/stable/43483432.

Holt, John Clifford. (2004). *"Unceasing Waves": Brahmanical and Hindu Influences on Medieval Sinhala Buddhist Culture.* In the book, Sri Lanka Book, Title: The Buddhist Visnu Book Subtitle: Religious Transformation, Politics, and Culture. Columbia University Press. (2004): https://www.jstor.org/stable/10.7312/holt13322.6.

Holt, John Clifford. (2004). *The Buddhist Visnu. In Religious Transformation, Politics, and Culture.* Columbia University Press. (2004): https://www.jstor.org/stable/10.7312/holt13322.14.

Indrapala K. (1969). *Early Tamil Settlements in Ceylon.* The Journal of the Ceylon Branch of the Royal Asiatic Society of Great Britain & Ireland, 1969, New Series, Vol. 13 (1969), pp. 43-63.https://www.jstor.org/stable/43483465.

Indrapala, K. (1970). The origin of the Tamil Vanni chieftains of Ceylon. Journal of the Humanities, July 1970, Vol 1, No 2

Indrapala, K. (1971) *South Indian Mercantile Communities in Ceylon, circa 950-1250, in Social Studies,* Vol1, No 2, July-December 1971.

Indrapala, K. (2007). Evolution of an Ethnic Identity, Vijitha yapa Publications, Sri Lanka.

Jayaraman, R. (1967). *Indian Emigration to Ceylon: Some Aspects of the Historical and Social Background of the Emigrants.* First Published October 1, 1967. https://doi.org/10.1177/001946466700400402

Karunananda, U B. (2005). Nuwarakalawiya, 1815-1900, S Godage Brothers

Karunarathna, A M. (2020). Wideshiya Akramana ha Lankawe Wimukthi Satan, Madyathana Yugaya, Vol 2. Dayawansa Jayakody.

Karunarathna, Nihal (1986). Udawaththa Kale – The forbidden Forrest of the Kings of Kandy, National Archives, Sri Lanka.

Kulasekera, Kulasekera Mudiyanselage Padmasiri. (1984). *British Administration in the Kandyan Provinces of Sri Lanka, 1815-1833,*

With Special Reference to Social Change. PhD Thesis, University of London.

Lagamuwa, A. (2001). *Some Dialectic Elements Found in Palm-leaf Manuscripts*. Journal of the Royal Asiatic Society of Sri Lanka, New Series, Vol. 46 pp. 79-100

Lawrie, A C. (1986). A Gazetteer of the Central Province of Ceylon, (Excluding Walapane), Vol 1 & 2, Government Printer, Ceylon, 1896

Laxman, Shibi. K. (2016). *Aryans and Dravidian Metanarratives, Proceedings of the Indian History Congress*, Vol. 77 (2016), pp. 697-705 https://www.jstor.org/stable/10.2307/26552699

Lewis, J P and J M Senawirathna. Ed. (1926). *The Ceylon Antiquity and Literal Register*, Vol VI, 1920-1921, Colombo Ceylon.

Liyanagamage, A. (1988). *Keralas In Medival Sri Lankan History: A study of two contrasting roles*, Social Science review, No 4, January.

Liyanagamage, Amaradasa. (1963). *The decline of Polonnaruwa and the Rise of Dambadeniya (circa 1180 - 1270 A.D.)*, Thesis submitted for the Degree of Doctor of Philosophy, University of London, 1963.

Lockard, Craig A. (2007), *Societies, Networks, and Transitions*. Volume I: to 1500, Cengage Learning, ISBN 978-0618386123[7].

Ludde, David. (1999). *The New Cambridge History of India*. IV. 4, An Agrarian History of South Asia, Cambridge University press, 1999.

Malalgoda, Kitsiri. (2011) *Mandārampura Puvata: Essays for Gananath Obeyesekere* Book Editor(s): H. L. Seneviratne Published by: Anthem Press. (2011) Stable URL: https://www.jstor.org/stable/j.ctt1gxpffq.18.

Malekandathil, Pius. (2007). *Winds of Change and Links of Continuity: A Study on the Merchant Groups of Kerala and the Channels of Their Trade*, 1000-1800, Journal of the Economic and Social History of the Orient, 2007, Vol. 50, No. 2/3, https://www.jstor.org/stable/25165196.

Maloney, Clarence. (1970). *The Beginnings of Civilization in South India.* The Journal of Asian Studies. https://www.jstor.org/stable/2943246

Manatunga, Anura. (2011). 1818 Prathama Nidahas Satane Purogamiyo (Pioneers of 1818 Freedom Struggle), Colombo: Ministry of Culture and the Arts

Manawadu, Samitha. (2017). Resurrecting the Capital City of Mundukondapola. A Medieval Regional Capital in Sri Lanka, Conference Paper. July 2017

Manual of the Administration of the Madras Presidency, Records of Government & the Yearly Administration reports. Printed by E Keys, at the Government Press, Madras, 1886.

Marshall, Henry. (1846). Ceylon: A general Description of the Island and Its Inhabitants. London.

Medananda Ellawala, (2005). The Sinhala Buddhist Heritage in the East and the North of Sri Lanka, Dayawansa Jayakody, Colombo.

Mendis, G C. (1948). *Early History of Ceylon,* 1948 Asian Educational Services

Mendis, G C. (1952). Ceylon Under the British, Colombo Apothecaries Company, 1952.

Mendis, G C. (1956). *The Colebrook-Cameron Papers, Documents on British Colonbial Policy in Ceylon 1796-1833,* Oxford University Press.

Mendis, G C. (1967). *The Evolution of a Ceylonese Nation,* The Journal of the Ceylon Branch of the Royal Asiatic Society of Great Britain & Ireland, New Series, Vol. 11 (1967), pp. 1-22, https://www.jstor.org/stable/43483835.

Menon, Sreedhara. (2007*). A Survey of Kerala History,* D C Books.

Modder, F (1893), *Kurunegala Wistharaya with Notes on Kurunegala ancient and Modern,* No. 44 Journal of Royal Asiatic Society (Ceylon) Vol XIII.

Moorjani et al., (2013). *Genetic Evidence for Recent Population Mixture in India*, The American Journal of Human Genetics, http://dx.doi.org/10.1016/j.ajhg.2013.07.006.

Nigosian, A. (1994). *World Faiths.* Second edition. Victoria College, University of Toronto, Palgrave Macmillan, 1994.

Nikawewa Kadayim Sannasa (A copy from RM Karunarathne).

Nilakanta Sastri, KA. 1967, Cultural Contacts between Aryans and Dravidians, Mankatas, Bombay.

Obeyesekere, Gananath (2016). Caste Conflicts and Discourses during the Kandyan Kingdom: evidence from the Matale District. Keynote Speech 19 November 2016. International Centre for Ethnic Studies.

Obeyesekere, Gananath (ed. 2005) Vanni Upatha, Vanni Vitti and Vanni Kadayim potha, S Godage & Brothers.

Obeyesekere, Gananath (ed. 2005). Bandarawali and Kadayim Poth, S Godage & Brothers.

Obeyesekere, Gananath (ed. 2005). Malala Viththiya, Malala Kathawa saha Rajasinghe Rajuge Pruthigisi Satan Pilibandawa sandahan Vitti book, S Godage & Brothers

Obeyesekere, Gananath (ed. 2005). Vanni Rajawaliya, S Godage & Brothers.

Obeyesekere, Gananath. (2004). *The Matrilineal East Coast Circa 1968: Nostalgia and Post Nostalgia in Our Troubled Time.* Speech on 2004 July

Obeyesekere, Gananath. (2013). The Coming of Brāhmins Migrants: The Śudra Fate of an Indian Elite in Sri Lanka. Faculty of Social Sciences at South Asian University, New Delhi Presents Contributions to Contemporary Knowledge Lecture Series – 2013.

Obeyesekere, Gananath. (2017). Between Portuguese and the Nayakas: the many faces of the Kandyan Kingdom, 1591-1765, Sr Lanka at the Crossroads of History, Z Biedermann and A Strathern (ed. 1917).

Obeyesekere, Gananath. (2017). *The Doomed King,* Sailfish Colombo, 2017.

Obeyesekere, Gananath. (2019). *On Mundukondapola: Resurrecting the History of a Defunct Kingdom.* Sri Lanka Journal of Sociology Vol-01 – 2019.

Obeyesekere, M. (2016). *Kanda Udarata Samaja sanwidanaya saha Prabhuwaru,* 2016, Samanthi Prakashakayo, Jaela.

Panikkar, K M. (1960). *A Survey of Indian History,* Asia Publishing House,

Panikkar, T K Gopal. (1900). *Malabar and its folk, Christian College.* G A Natbshan & Co.

Paranawithana, K D. Personal names of Ancient Sinhalese. http://www.worldgenweb.org/lkawgw/sinhalanames.htm.

Paranawithana, S. (1967). Sinhalayo. A Visidunu Publications.

Park, Robert, E. & Burgess, EW. (1969). Introduction to the science of sociology, New York, Greenwood Press

Parker, H. (1909). Ancient Ceylon, London 1909.

Perera, B J, (2009). *The "Ge" names of the Sinhalese: Journal of the Royal Asiatic Society of Sri Lanka,* 2009, https://www.jstor.org/stable/23731092.

Peris R, (2016). Sinhala Samaja sanwidanaya: mahanuwara Yugaya, Sisidunu Prakashana.

Philippe, Beaujard. (2019). *The Worlds of the Indian Ocean: A global History. Volume 1. From the Fourth Millennium BCE to the Sixth Century CE.* Cambridge University Press.

Philippe, Beaujard. (2019). *The Worlds of the Indian Ocean: A global History. Volume 2. From seventh century to fifteenth century.* Cambridge University.

Pieris, PE (1920). Ceylon and the Portuguese. 1505 – 1658. American Ceylon Mission Press. Ceylon. 1920.

Pieris, PE (1950). Sinhala and Patriots 1815-1818. Colombo Apothecaries.

Polwathathe Buddhadaththa (1950), Samipathithayehi Boudhacharyayo, Pujawaliya. Kirielle Gnanawimala.

Raghavan, MD (1964). India in Ceylonese History, Society and Culture. Indian Council for Cultural Relations Mew Delhi* 1964.

Raghavan, MD (1964a). Tamil culture in Ceylon: A general Introduction, Indian Council for Cultural Relations Mew Delhi* 1964.

Raghavan, MD. (1961). Karawa of Ceylon: Society and Culture, KVG De Silva & Sons, Colombo. 1961.

Rakogama, K M S. (2019). Anabhibhawaniya Ithihasayak Urumakotagath Wyamba. Thammanna Asiriya: Sarasangrahaya.

Ramesh Somasundaram, British Infiltration of Ceylon, A study of the D'oyly papers between 1805 and 1818. University of Western Australia, 2008.

Ranasinghe, D D (1917) Dambadeni Ashna. Published by DA Amarasinghe Siriwardena Appuhamy.

Ranasinghe, Ravindra, Oruwala Sannasa and Ranasinghe Liniage https://www.academia.edu/7970281.

Rasanayagam, C. (1920). Ancient Jaffna: History of Jaffna.

Reimers, E (1930*). Some Sinhalese Names and Surnames. The Journal of the Ceylon Branch of the Royal Asiatic Society of Great Britain & Ireland,* 1930, Vol. 31, pp. 437-452 https://www.jstor.org/stable/43483363.

Rohanadeera, Mendis. (1998). Asgiriyen Udarata Ithihasaya, Ashoka Circle, Batththramulla,1998.

Sagayadoss A. (2015). *South Indian Black's Culture and Religion Academia and Society* Volume 2 Number 2 ISSN: 2393-9419 ISSN: 2393-8919

Sannasgala, Punchibandara. (1964). Sinhala Sahithya Wansaya. Lakehouse.

Sarao, K T S (2012). *The Decline of Buddhism in India, A Fresh Perspective,* Munshiram Manoharlal Publishers Pvt. Ltd. 2012.

Schreuder, Johann, et. Al. (1946). *Memoir of Jan Schreuder, Governor of Ceylon, Delivered to His Successor Lubbert Jan Baron van Eck on March 17, 1762.*

Senaveratne John M. H. W. (1914). *The Date of Buddhas Death and Ceylon Chronology.* Journal of the Ceylon Branch of the Royal Asiatic Society of Great Britain & Ireland, 1914, Vol. 23, No. 67 (1914). https://www.jstor.org/stable/43483670.

Senevirathna, A. (2004). Anusmruthi, Vol 1 and 2, Godage Publications.

Senevitathna, A. (1983). Kandy. Central Cultural Fund, Sri Lanka.

Senewipala, Nimesha Thiwankara. (2019). Kurunegala Wistharaya, Samanthi Poth Prakashakayo, Jaela.

Sewwandi A K C (2018). *A study of the Demographical Structure of Pre-modern Times Sri Lanka.* http://journal.unnes.ac.id/nju/index.php/paramita.

Shirras, G Findley. (1931). Indian Migration.

Shulman, David Dean. (1985). The king and the Crown in the South Indian Myth and Poetry.

Silva, K. M. De (1995). The "traditional Homelands" of the Tamils: Separatist Ideology in Sri Lanka: a Historical Appraisal. International Centre for Ethnic Studies. p. 40. ISBN 9789555800044.

Siriweera, WI. (1971). *History of Sri Lanka*, Dayawansa Jayakody, 1971.

Sivarathnam, C. (1968). Tamils in Early Ceylon, Colombo.

Sivasundaram, Sujit (2007) *Tales of the Land: British Geography and Kandyan Resistance in Sri Lanka* c. 1803-1850, Modern Asian Studies, Sep. 2007, Vol. 41, No. 5 (Sep. 2007), pp. 925-965: https://www.jstor.org/stable/4499807.

Sivasundaram, Sujith. (2007). Land: British Geography and Kandyan Resistance in Sri Lanka. Modern Asian Studies 41, 5 (2007) pp. 925–965. C 2007 Cambridge University Press.

Stoudt, Howard W. (1961). Physical Anthropology of Ceylon, National Museum.

Sudharma, Ven. Rawaele. (2019). Niyadawane ha Bandunu Pethiyagala Sanga Parapura.

Sweet, J D. (2014). *Colonial museology and the Buddhist chronicles of Sri Lanka: agency and negotiation in the development of the palm-leaf manuscript collection at the Colombo Museum, Museum & Society,* vol. 12, no. 3, pp. 225-246.

Tambipillai, V J (1908). *THE ORIGIN OF THE TAMIL VELALAS,* The Journal of the Ceylon Branch of the Royal Asiatic Society of Great Britain & Ireland, 1908, Vol. 21, No. 61 (1908), pp. 1-38, https://www.jstor.org/stable/43482996.

Tennent, J E, (1859). Ceylon: An account of the Island, Longman, London,

The Ceylon blue book. (1877), Department of the Registrar-General; Ceylon. Department of Statistics and Office Systems; Ceylon. https://www.jstor.org/stable/10.2307/saoa.crl.26228391.

The Ceylon Government Gazette. (1893). No 5200, Friday Jan 27, 1893

The Ceylon Handbook and Directory, Edition of 1898-99 (edited by J Ferguson).

The Rajawaliya, edited by B Gunasekara, Colombo 1900.

Tieken, Erman. (2010). Blaming the Brāhmins: Texts Lost and Found in Tamil Literary History, Studies in History 26(2) 227– 243 © 2010 Jawaharlal Nehru University, SAGE Publications.

Transactions of the Royal Asiatic Society of Great Britain and Ireland, Vol 111, London, 1835.

Tripathy, Vikal; Nirmala, A.; Reddy, B. Mohan (4 September 2017). *"Trends in Molecular Anthropological Studies in India"*. International Journal of Human Genetics.

Vaidyanathan, K R. (2016). Temples and Legends of Kerala. Vidya Bhavan.

Vijayalakshmi, M. (1995). *Kerala in the Indian Ocean Trade Network CIRCA 800-1500.* Proceedings of the Indian History Congress,

1995, Vol. 56 (1995), pp. 418-424
https://www.jstor.org/stable/44158644.

Vimaladharma, Kapila Pathirana. (2000). *Family Genealogies in the Study of Pre-colonial Kandyan Society and Polity.* Journal of the Royal Asiatic Society of Sri Lanka, Vol. 45, (2000), https://www.jstor.org/stable/23732462.

Vimalananda, T. (1970). Great Rebellion 1818, Vol 1, 2 and 3. M D Gunasena,

Wickramasinghe, Ananda. (2005). *British Capital, Ceylonese Land, Indian labour: the imperialism and colonialism of evolution of tea plantations in Sri Lanka.*
https://www.researchgate.net/publication/242263010.

Wijayanayake, P. B. Jagath. (1976). Kurunegala, Journal of the Sri Lanka Branch of the Royal Asiatic Society, 1976, New Series, Vol. 20 (1976), pp. 42-46, https://www.jstor.org/stable/23728449.

Wikipedia, Cultural assimilation. 2021.

Witzel, Michael. (1993). *Toward a History of the Brāhmins, Journal of the American Oriental Society*, Vol. 113, No. 2 (Apr. - Jun. 1993), pp. 264-268 http://www.jstor.org/stable/603031.

Yinger, J. Milton. (2010). Toward a theory of assimilation and dissimilation. Ethnic and Racial Studies 13 Sep 2010.

Zimmer, Heinrich (1952), Joseph Campbell (ed.), Philosophies of India, London, E.C. 4: Routledge & Kegan Paul Ltd, ISBN 978-81-208-0739-6.

About the Author

Bandara Bandaranayake Completed his B.Ed. (Honors) Degree and MPhil Degree from University of Colombo. He completed his PhD at Monash University on a Monash Graduate Scholarship.

After his first degree, he joined the Ministry of Education in Sri Lanka and held several teaching and senior administrative positions. After completing his PhD, and after a short-term tenure at Monash University, he joined the public service. He held several senior positions at the Department of Internal Affairs (New Zealand), the Department of Innovation, Industry and Regional Development (Australia), and the Department of Education and Training (Australia) for nearly three decades.

His research interests are in educational governance, ethics and integrity, public sector reforms, public policy, cultural anthropology, and evolutionary psychology. He has published several books and number of journal articles.

Currently, he engages in independent research and counselling.

He can be contacted on bandaranayakeb@gmail.com.

www.ingramcontent.com/pod-product-compliance
Lightning Source LLC
Chambersburg PA
CBHW060029030426
42334CB00019B/2248

* 9 7 8 0 6 4 5 2 1 3 3 0 0 *